Strength Training *for* Speed

Scientific Principles and Practical Application

Second Edition

JAMES WILD

lotus
publishing

Chichester, England

First published in 2014. This second edition published in 2022 by
Lotus Publishing
Apple Tree Cottage, Inlands Road, Nutbourne, Chichester, PO18 8RJ

Illustrations Amanda Williams and Matt Lambert
Cover Design Chris Fulcher
Cover Image Courtesy of Shutterstock, Inc.
Text Design Medlar Publishing Solutions Pvt Ltd., India
Printed and Bound in Turkey by Kultur Sanat Printing House

British Library Cataloguing-in-Publication Data
A CIP record for this book is available from the British Library
ISBN 978 1 913088 34 7

Dedication

To Leanne, Rocco, Milo, Orla and the rest of the Wild family

Contents

Introduction

An estimated 95 million television viewers tuned in to watch Usain Bolt race in the men's 100 metres (m) final at the World Athletics Championships in Berlin in 2009. He did not disappoint. Bolt eclipsed his own world record set the previous year, finishing the race in 9.58 seconds (s). Putting this into context, only three sporting events received higher viewing figures in the same year. Usain Bolt's mere presence attracted six and 46 million more television viewers worldwide than the men's tennis singles final at Wimbledon and the final day of the US Golf Masters respectively.

Bolt's ability to attract a considerable global audience reflects the desire of every recreational and elite level athlete: ultimately, everyone wants to be faster. In the sporting world, where one hundredth of a second can mean the difference between winning and losing, sprinting speed strikes fear into opponents and captures the imagination of nations around the world.

As a result of this fascination, many turn to the latest 'speed training' gimmicks which lack scientific grounding or logic, and all too often these extravagant training modalities do not live up to their promise.

Consequently, it is commonplace for athletes to blame their lack of progress on a genetic makeup incongruous with proficient sprint performance. There is little doubt that genetics play a significant role in determining how fast someone will be, but anyone can become faster with the correct type of training. If genetics were the only important factor to running speed, what need would there be for world class sprinters to spend endless hours throughout their training year performing sprint training or lifting weights?

To better inform the training methods adopted by an athlete looking to increase their speed, it is important to understand the underlying causes of motion. Essentially, the pushing and pulling influences of force are what gets things moving and determine the changes in motion of a body once it is moving.

To understand how forces affect a body's ability to move quickly, Sir Isaac Newton's second law of motion provided valuable insight:

Force = Mass × Acceleration

Upon first reading, this equation doesn't seem to mean much and can appear quite confusing. However, it soon becomes clear how Sir Isaac Newton laid the groundwork for sports scientists and coaches the world over. Mass can be explained by how much something weighs without gravity. Since gravity (the force which pulls us toward the earth) is ever present and always constant on earth, mass within this context equals what the body weighs. Acceleration is defined as the rate at which velocity changes with time. Velocity in simple terms means speed in a given direction.

Taking these factors into account and assuming a body is only travelling in one direction (i.e. linear sprinting), Newton's equation can be simplified to read as follows:

Force = Bodyweight × Change in speed per unit of time

Assuming the time over which force is being produced remains the same, working backward through this calculation, it is then possible to work out what the equation is for change in speed:

Change in speed = Force ÷ Bodyweight

With this rearrangement, we can see that the speed of a body can be increased by one of two ways:

1) a reduction of its weight while the force applied to it is maintained (or increased). *For example, if 120 newton (the unit used to measure force) is applied to a body that weighs 100 kilograms, then its change in speed can be calculated as follows:*

120 ÷ 100 = 1.2 metres per second (m/s)

If the force applied to the object remains constant (120 newton), but its weight has decreased to 80 kilograms then it will be accelerated to a greater extent:

120 ÷ 80 = 1.5 m/s

2) speed of a body can also be increased through an increase in the force applied to it while its weight is maintained (or reduced).

For example, following on from the above calculation if the force applied to the body increases to 200 newton while its weight remains constant (80 kilograms), then it will be accelerated to an even greater extent:

200 ÷ 80 = 2.5 m/s

Considering an athlete's bodyweight is likely to remain relatively unchanged (although not in all cases) throughout their competitive days, we can begin to see how increasing the amount of force applied to the athlete influences their speed of movement. But how does an athlete apply a force to their own body? This can be answered by Newton's third law of motion which states that:

For every action, there is an equal and opposite reaction.

This law of motion is, perhaps, easier to understand in a practical situation:

Stand with your feet together and your arms outstretched in front of you (at chest height) with your palms flat against a wall. Now bend your elbows, moving your chest closer to the wall as if you were performing the lowering phase of a press up. Now push against the wall without moving your feet.

What you should have noticed is that you moved in the opposite direction to which you applied force, returning to the start position. For the wall to fall over, a force far greater than what you are capable of producing would be needed and, as a result, the reaction force of the wall (the equal and opposite reaction) pushed you in the opposite direction. By applying more force to the wall (pushing harder), you should also notice that you move away from the wall more quickly and that the amount of force you apply directly influences the speed you move in the opposite direction.

The same principle applies to sprinting when your foot strikes the ground. Because it is impossible to move the ground away from you when your foot makes contact with it, an equal and opposite ground reaction force is applied to your body propelling you through the air and into your next step. The greater the external force being applied to the ground, the greater the ground reaction forces are and the greater the speed of movement will be in the opposite direction to which your foot strikes (assuming your bodyweight remains constant).

Since it is impossible to apply force to the earth's surface in between steps (i.e. in 'flight'), strategies to increase the amount of force that can be produced into the ground form the cornerstone of an effective training program

for the development of sprinting speed. This is why sprinters spend countless hours refining their technique on the track so as to apply the right levels of force at the right time and in the right direction. This also explains one of the reasons why strength training is an essential component of any athlete's speed program; to increase the ground reaction forces that they are capable of generating.

However, there are many different methods of strength training and it can be difficult to know where to start and what to do because ground force magnitude alone is not the sole factor in deciding how quick someone is. Moreover, the type of strength program carried out by one person to improve their running speed may not be appropriate or productive for someone else.

The intention of this book is to provide coaches, athletes, students and anyone with an interest in designing strength programs for speed the knowledge of how to construct a logical and progressive program underpinned by scientific research and practical experience.

Overview

Section 1, 'Strength Training Terminology and Adaptations', is concerned with the terminology associated with strength training and the adaptations it elicits, for it is these adaptations which drive the process of strength training program design. The human body has an ability to respond to a stimulus (i.e. a strength training session) by changing its structure and function, following a period of recovery, to perform this activity better in the future. In order for this to happen, the body needs to be placed under stress and then it needs time to recover and adapt. The correct balance of stress and recovery is key to the adaptation process.

Section 2, 'Sprinting Biomechanics', discusses another key consideration when constructing a strength training program. From understanding how an athlete sprints and what causes them to move in a certain way, it is possible to identify the limitations of an individual in reaching their speed potential. What limits an individual during the acceleration phase of a sprint may actually enhance their maximum velocity sprint performance and vice versa. This knowledge can help better inform the strength programming decisions made by coaches and athletes and maximise the transfer of strength training to sprint performance in different strength phases.

Section 3, 'Associations of Strength Qualities with Speed', provides an overview of the strength of relationships between different strength qualities and performance over different sprint phases. Knowledge of this area can help inform coaches of the strength capacities of athletes which, if enhanced, may help them to improve phase specific speed of athletes. This section also discusses how changing strength qualities may influence the techniques adopted by athletes. This understanding is useful for coaches looking to create 'permanent changes to the movement strategies of athletes during sprinting'.

Section 4, 'Designing Individual Training Sessions', is concerned with the actual construction of individual strength training programs. The numerous different training variables are covered in detail with program design guidelines given for athletes of all levels and at whatever stage of training they are in. This section concludes with a number of sample training sessions designed to enhance the different strength qualities of beginner, intermediate and advanced level athletes in their quest to maximize speed.

Section 5, 'Periodisation', brings together the information from the previous sections and tackles the subject of planning training for a full year/season. Short-term planning through individual training sessions is ineffective unless the individual sessions are factored into training weeks, months and years. Long-term planning is the key to realizing one's speed potential and without a well-structured long-term plan, this potential will never be attained.

Section 6, 'Exercise Library', provides a visual library of all strength training exercises mentioned in the book. Each exercise is accompanied by a number of key teaching points and is the final piece in the jigsaw, essentially providing a large exercise inventory from which an athlete or coach can design their strength training programs. Each exercise is categorized into the type of strength quality it is most suited to developing and according to its mechanical specificity to the sprinting action.

The Second Edition

In this second edition of *Strength Training for Speed: Scientific Principles and Practical Application*, substantial changes to the book have been made. I decided to remove the opening section from the first edition. Whilst

I felt it was a good book section, the content (anatomy and physiology) is now readily available at our fingertips online. I felt like the core contents of the book could be digested without an in-depth knowledge of anatomy and kinesiology. Whilst a number of updates have been made to each chapter, the most noticeable changes to the book include the following:

1. The '*Sprinting Biomechanics*' section has been completely overhauled and contains an up-to-date discussion on the mechanical determinants of sprint performance, technical models and more

2. A completely new section ('*Associations of Strength Qualities with Speed*') has been written. This section discusses the muscular contributions to sprinting and the relationships between different strength-related qualities and phase specific sprint performance. This section provides readers with a more detailed understanding on the importance of 'strength' for speed

3. *The exercise library is now a video library. This is an excellent resource for coaches and athletes. Each exercise can be watched by scanning a QR code and alongside demonstrations, each video includes important information on aspects of technique and a range of coaching cues and analogies to help maximise the training effect of these exercises*

Strength training only fulfills one part of the training puzzle in improving speed, but it is an important one. While technical training and sprinting as an activity by itself is by far the best approach to improve one's sprinting speed, strength training can accelerate this development. Furthermore, it has the ability to improve technique when technique training alone is not enough.

Ultimately, physical and speed potential cannot be reached without progressive, well-structured and targeted strength training, yet its incorporation into an athlete's overall program is frequently performed through guesswork and its role often misunderstood.

I hope that this book will enable you to share some of my passion developed over years of research and coaching in this area.

James Wild
May 2022

Strength Training Terminology and Adaptations

It is well documented that strength training can increase a person's ability to produce force (strength). Regardless of the amount of strength training carried out by an athlete, there are limitations to strength development which are genetically determined. However, it requires many years of consistent and dedicated training to reach such limits, and it is possible to increase strength levels by several 100% over an athlete's career. Such increases can have a significant impact not only on speed development, but can also play a role in helping to prevent future injury.

For the purposes of this book, strength training is defined as the use of specific exercise modalities to provide resistance to muscular force and stress to the neuromuscular system. Strength can be categorised into a number of different types according to varying capabilities of the neuromuscular system and differing time frames of force expression. The type of training employed and strength quality targeted will dictate the neuromuscular adaptation(s) elicited and the overall training effect. An understanding of this is critical in the effective design of a strength program.

Fundamental Training Principles

The Adaptation Process, Overload and Specificity

The human body has the ability to respond to a stimulus such as strength training by changing its structure and function following a period of recovery to perform this activity better in the future (Figure 1.1). This process of adaptation forms the basis of strength training, where the type of adaptation(s) that takes place is dependent on the type of strength training employed by an athlete.

A training adaptation occurs only in response to an 'overload'; a situation where the body is required to perform an activity beyond which it is used to. Within the realms of strength training, this relates to the neuromuscular system exerting forces greater than it is accustomed to (i.e. lifting a heavier weight than usual).

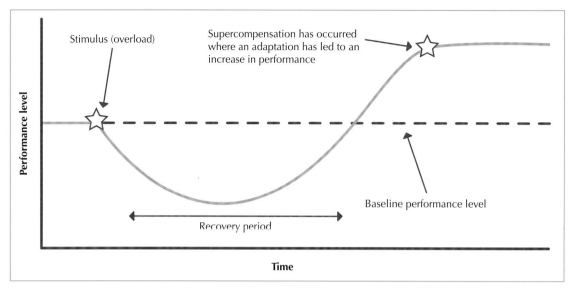

Figure 1.1. The stimulus, fatigue and adaptation model.

Overload doesn't have to take place through the use of external loads (i.e. weights). The use of bodyweight to provide overload can be a useful modality for evoking training responses. For example, the average and peak ground reaction forces generated by the leg extensor muscles during hopping have been shown to be 82 and 63% greater, respectively, than the forces produced by the leg extensors during a sprint (Weyand, Sandell, Prime, & Bundle, 2010).

Generally, the greater the overload, the larger and more rapid the adaptation is. However, it should be noted that this is a somewhat simplistic way of viewing the adaptation process and there are many other factors to consider in regard to how well an individual will respond to training (e.g. genetics, nutrition, sleep/recovery, stress).

Additionally, there appears to be a minimum load in strength training, below which no training adaptation will take place. However, overload should be applied progressively

and gradually in relatively small increments, in order to continue adapting. Simply lifting the same weight repeatedly over time will result only in adaptations to this load, and so strength gains will plateau. It is equally important to vary the type of stress being applied to the body with planned phases of reduced intensity and rest, so as to avoid inhibiting adaptations and to reduce the risk of injury.

As already mentioned, the training response and improvements in performance to the type of overload applied are specific to the type of strength training executed. In order for exercises to have a positive transfer of training effect to sprinting performance, it has been suggested that they should conform to the principles of 'dynamic correspondence' (Siff, 2003; Verkhoshansky, 2006) and be mechanically specific to the sprinting action.

It is important to remember however, that other than practicing sprinting itself, no other form of training activity will have

100% carryover, and more general training means can have also an effective transfer to performance. These principles are discussed in Section 4 (Designing Individual Training Sessions) of this book.

Program Design Variables

Repetitions, Sets and Intensity

A repetition or *rep* is one complete movement of an exercise. A series of reps performed in one go is known as a *set*. Generally, the heavier the weight (load) lifted during a set of a specific exercise or the faster the load is moved, the greater the stress imposed on the nervous system and the more intense therefore that set will be.

Intensity during strength training should not be confused with the amount of general fatigue encountered or how hard a training session feels (known as relative intensity). For example, performing ten sets of ten reps of an exercise will feel tougher overall than performing four sets of three reps of the same exercise, assuming the load used in each case permits the completion of no more than the intended number of reps in each set (i.e. a maximum of ten and three reps respectively). However, the load lifted when performing sets of three reps will be greater—as will the stress to the nervous system—and so the training intensity is deemed higher (according to the accepted definition of strength training intensity), even though the stress to the muscular system is likely to be higher completing ten sets of ten.

As a general rule of thumb, lower repetitions elicit neural adaptations and higher repetitions emphasise ones of a muscular nature (Figure 1.2).

The term repetition maximum or *RM* can be used to define the intensity of an exercise. For example, the maximum load that can be lifted (with correct technique) just once during a back squat would be known as the 1RM for

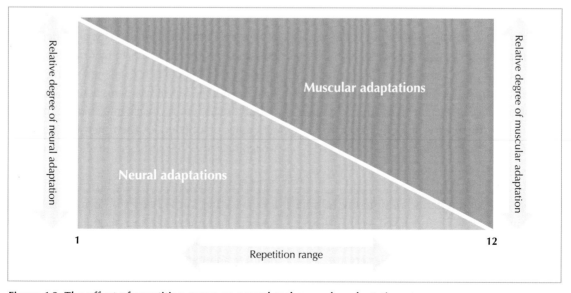

Figure 1.2. The effect of repetition range on neural and muscular adaptations.

that exercise. The maximum weight that can be lifted three times only during a deadlift, for example, would be the 3RM for that exercise, and so on.

Intensity can also be expressed as a percentage of 1RM—the load lifted as a percentage of the maximum that can only be lifted once. For example, lifting a load at 85% of an athlete's 1RM during an exercise is more intense than lifting a load at 70% 1RM. Regardless of the way in which intensity is described, the type of adaptation elicited will change depending on the level of intensity at which an athlete trains.

Volume, Rest Periods and Frequency

Strength training volume gives an indication of the total amount of work completed, and is typically calculated by multiplying the total number of repetitions (sets x reps) by the load lifted (volume load). Volume load within a session can be increased by increasing the number of reps and/or sets performed. Volume over a time period (e.g. week, month) can also be raised by increasing the frequency of training sessions (the number of training sessions performed each week).

Typically, completing multiple sets of an exercise produces superior strength and power gains than performing a single set (Galvão & Taaffe, 2004; McDonagh & Davies, 1984). One to two sets may be enough as a training stimulus for an athlete new to strength training—but after a period of time the volume of training needs to be increased—otherwise a strength plateau will be reached. Once initial strength gains are made, multiple sets are recommended—typically in the range of three

to six—although up to ten or more sets can be employed in very experienced athletes.

The number of sets performed can depend on multiple factors and is mainly influenced by the number of reps completed. As a general rule of thumb, the fewer the number of reps an athlete performs per set, the more sets need to be completed in order to achieve the appropriate training response at relatively low rep ranges (i.e. neural adaptations). Conversely, sets with a relatively high rep range require the completion of fewer sets per exercise in order to elicit intended training responses (i.e. muscular adaptations). While a greater number of sets may be superior to strength gains than employing a single set approach, there seems to be an optimal number of sets where the completion of any more sets will result in diminishing strength response returns.

Rest periods are employed between sets, exercises and training sessions. The lengths of these rest periods are dependent on the goal of the training session. Longer rest intervals are required between sets when a smaller number of reps are completed, and smaller rest periods between sets are necessary to provoke the training responses desired when carrying out sets of a higher rep range. Steps should be taken to build sufficient recovery into the weekly schedules of athletes, i.e. the timeframe between workouts should be sufficient to allow recovery.

As already discussed, in the short-term fitness levels decline immediately following a strength session, and managing the frequency of training sessions is important to bring about positive adaptations. The stimulus (training session) induces fatigue in an athlete while simultaneously initiating a series of underlying physiological mechanisms (e.g. biochemical, hormonal, neural).

During the subsequent recovery period, these physiological mechanisms must be adequate to promote adaptations that allow an athlete to perform at a higher level. If the recovery and adaptation processes are not permitted to occur on a session-to-session basis, then a lack of long-term progress will prevail. The inability to recover from an exercise stimulus could be due to excessive frequency, volume and intensity. A prolonged attempt by an athlete to push themselves without varying stress and sufficient recovery will inevitably increase the risk of overtraining (see Section 5: Periodisation).

Strength Qualities

A more detailed investigation of the appropriate program design variables takes place in Section 4, 'Designing Individual Training Sessions'. A brief look at the development of specific strength qualities however, is necessary to lay some foundational knowledge prior to this discussion.

Maximum Strength

Maximum strength can be described as the peak force that the neuromuscular system is able to produce during a single maximal voluntary muscle contraction, irrespective of time of force development.

Maximum strength can generally be expressed during concentric, eccentric and isometric

muscle contractions and can be subdivided into two further strength qualities: absolute and relative strength. *Absolute strength* is the maximum force an athlete can produce irrespective of their bodyweight and time. *Relative strength*, however, is concerned with the amount of force that can be generated per unit of bodyweight irrespective of time.

For example, athlete 'A' who has a body mass of 100kg and athlete 'B' who has a body mass of 70kg both have a 1RM of 100kg in the back-squat exercise. While they both have the same absolute strength, athlete 'B' has greater relative strength in this exercise, as they are able to lift more weight per unit of bodyweight. The load lifted should be divided by the athlete's bodyweight to find their relative strength in a given exercise.

In the example given, athlete 'A' can lift equivalent to their bodyweight (100 ÷ 100 = 1) whereas athlete 'B' can lift 1.4 times their bodyweight (100 ÷ 70 = 1.4). Relative strength is more important than absolute strength to sprinting performance, since moving bodyweight quickly is critical.

The exercises that tend to have the greatest strength developing effects are those that stress multiple joints and the biggest muscle groups (i.e. upper legs, gluteals and back). These multi-joint lifts are known as *compound exercises*, an example of which includes the back squat. Single joint or isolation exercises, such as the biceps curl do not typically play a significant role where maximum strength gains are of concern (Figure 1.3).

In maximum strength exercises, the movement will often be slow, but the intent of the lifter

Figure 1.3. Compound isolation exercises.

should be to move the weight during the concentric phase of the lift explosively. Typically, maximum strength is developed using loads that allow an athlete to complete just 1–5 reps at approximately 85–100% 1RM. This intensity, combined with long rest periods and relatively low volumes, results in neural adaptations and minimal gains in muscle mass compared to training with loads of a lower intensity. While maximum strength gains can be made using loads equivalent to 70–84% 1RM (approximately 6–12 reps), this intensity range combined with larger volumes of training and reduced rest periods results in muscular adaptations and in particular muscle hypertrophy. Less experienced athletes should begin strength training at this intensity range or lower.

Speed Strength

Speed strength can be described as the ability of the neuromuscular system to produce the greatest possible force within the shortest possible timeframe. Speed strength within a sporting context—where expressing force quickly is deemed important—is also commonly termed 'power', which can be calculated as follows:

$$Power = Work \div Time$$

Work is the product of force and the distance moved and time represents how long it takes to perform the given movement. Since the distance through which the limbs move will remain relatively constant during a sports movement, power can be increased by applying a greater amount of force in a given time or by reducing the amount of time the force is produced over (i.e. increasing velocity of movement).

Power can be 'positive' such as during a concentric contraction, which is also described as 'power generating', or 'negative' (power dissipating) such as during an eccentric contraction. Within the context of sprinting, the greatest instantaneous power during a single movement performed with the intention to produce maximum velocity at take-off (maximal power) is more important than the measure simply of power itself. For these reasons, the rate at which force can be generated is an important factor in sprinting.

Rate of force development (RFD) is critical in most sports, especially sprinting. For instance, the ground contact times of elite sprinters are approximately 0.09 s during the maximum velocity phase of a sprint, yet the time course of the development and transmission of muscular force in the human knee and ankle extensors far exceed this time frame (Harridge, et al., 1996). In fact, it takes longer than 0.3 s for human skeletal muscle to reach maximum force (Aagaard, Simonsen, Anderson, Magnusson, & Dhyre-Poulsen, 2002; Thorstensson, Karlsson, Viitasalo, Luhtanen, & Komi, 1976). Speed strength is therefore more important than maximum strength during a sprint.

For example, in Figure 1.4 athlete 'B' is able to produce more force in a shorter time than athlete 'A', despite athlete 'A' possessing greater maximum strength.

Speed strength can be split into two main strength qualities—*explosive* and *reactive strength*.

Explosive strength is defined by the time it takes to reach maximum force and can be further subdivided into *starting strength*, which is the ability to generate force quickly at the start of a movement (muscle contraction) when there is little force developed in the muscle; and, *acceleration strength*, which is the ability to generate force quickly later in a movement when there is already some degree of tension within the muscle.

Reactive strength is the ability to change quickly from an eccentric to a concentric contraction, whilst using the stretch-shortening cycle (SSC). The SSC is a naturally occurring function where a rapid, active 'stretch' of the muscle-tendon unit during an eccentric action is immediately followed by a shortening of the muscle-tendon unit and a concentric muscle contraction. The resulting concentric muscle contraction is more powerful than if the same muscle was to contract only concentrically (i.e. without the pre-stretch first).

Although the mechanisms responsible for improved performance during SSC movements are not entirely clear, this enhanced force production of the muscle is commonly said to be due to the storage and re-utilisation of elastic energy. This suggests that energy is absorbed by the muscle and tendon during the eccentric portion of the action as the pre-stretch takes place, which is then released during the ensuing concentric contraction.

Reactive strength during a sprint is, in part, thought to be linked to 'leg stiffness'—the ability to resist the applied stretch placed on it during the ground contact phase of running—since the greater the leg stiffness of an athlete, the shorter the delay between the eccentric and concentric contraction when the SSC is employed.

Where favourable changes to an athlete's power and RFD are concerned, the intent

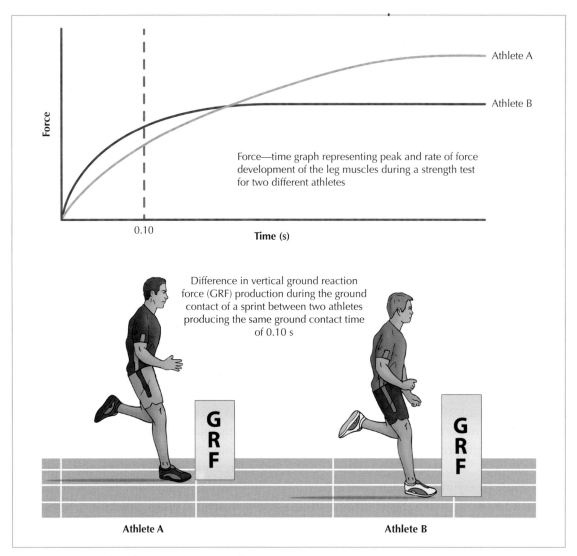

Figure 1.4. RFD during the ground contact phase of a sprint.

to move the resistance being applied during an exercise as fast as possible is important. It has been shown that when an athlete aims to achieve this, the greatest changes to their RFD will be stimulated (Holtermann, Roeleveld, Vereijken, & Ettema, 2007; Sahaly, Vandewalle, Driss, & Monod, 2001). The number of repetitions, sets and the intensity as a percentage of an athlete's 1RM in an exercise used to develop power will vary—0 to > 85

1RM—depending on the nature of the power required (Section 4: Designing Individual Training Sessions).

The type of exercises used to develop speed strength also vary according to the strength quality and adaptation required.

Classically in the development of explosive strength, the exercises used include those that enable their completion to be accomplished rapidly, such as in Olympic Weightlifting, medicine ball throws or squat jumps (Section 6: Exercise Library). There is a 'release' phase in explosive strength exercises where the load lifted is thrown or a jump is involved.

If the resistance being used is not released or there isn't a 'jumping' action to the movement, then the primary focus becomes one of deceleration toward the end of the movement, and so power adaptations will not occur in the range of movement required. This type of training will help train the antagonist muscles to delay the rate at which they also decelerate the concentric movement of the action. For these reasons, the types of exercises employed during maximum strength training are not typically used for speed strength training.

Plyometric exercises—specifically used to develop reactive strength—are characterised by movements involving an eccentric loading of a muscle group preparatory to a rapid change to a concentric contraction of the same muscle group through utilisation of the SSC. Due to the nature of plyometric exercises, the load used should remain relatively low. Bodyweight or light medicine balls should be favoured over heavy weights, because increased loads would slow the movements down, negating the potential benefits of the exercises.

Strength Endurance

Strength endurance is the capacity of a muscle to maintain consistent force output with repeated contractions over time. In its typical form, strength endurance and the training methods used to enhance this strength quality are not applicable to the development of sprint performance over small distances. While a degree of strength endurance is needed in order to maintain force output over the course of a short sprint, this type of capacity may be developed through increasing the volume of training during maximum strength and speed strength training.

Furthermore, maximum strength and power gains may be advantageous where strength endurance is required. For example, as each motor unit and muscle fibre is able to produce greater force output, fewer motor units will be used for a given force output of lower intensities, creating a motor unit reserve available for additional work. Training with high repetitions and low loads used during strength endurance training is generally not conducive to enhancing sprint performance.

Power Endurance

Power endurance—also known as *repeat power ability*—is the ability to repeatedly produce maximal or near maximal efforts (Natera, Cardinale, & Keogh, 2020). It is intuitive to see why this strength quality is likely to be more advantageous to sprinting performance than strength endurance. It would be of particular use during the latter stages of a 100m sprint, for example, where fatigue has set in, but there is a high requirement to continue to produce high intensity muscle contractions. This strength quality is also important in sports where intermittent power actions are required at multiple time points during competition, such as in team or racket sports.

There are a range of modalities which can be used to develop repeat power ability, but explosive strength or ballistic exercises are commonly used and have been shown to result in increases in repeat power ability (Natera et al., 2020). The intensities used during repeat power training are low in comparison to maximum strength training in regard to the loads being lifted—anywhere between 0 and 75% 1RM has typically been reported—but this type of training is still considered high in intensity due to the explosive intent required during each repetition.

Session training volumes are also high. Two common protocols are adopted for repeat power training—*low set/high rep* and *high set/low rep*. For example, a low set/high rep protocol previously reported consisted of 4 sets of 4–12 reps where this sequence is repeated up to 4 times in total (Schuster et al., 2018). An example of a high set/low rep protocol includes the use of up to 10 sets of 3–5 reps (Bosco, Cotelli, Bonomi, Mognoni, & Roi, 1994).

Due to the high intensities and high volumes undertaken, repeat power training can be very fatiguing and adequate rest and recovery is required to maximise the adaptations possible to this type of training.

Neuromuscular Adaptations to Strength Training

Muscle Fibre Type

A period of high intensity—maximum strength training—has been shown to decrease the number of type IIX muscle fibres and increase the number of type IIA fibres within human skeletal muscle (Adams, Hather, Baldwin, & Dudley, 1993; Andersen & Aagaard, 2000). This would seem detrimental to performance, since type IIX fibres contract at the highest velocity and with the greatest force relative to other fibre types. However, this shift in type II fibre subtype is compensated for within the muscle as a whole by preferential hypertrophy of type II fibres (discussed later in this section) and an overall increase in contractile strength, power and RFD of the muscle(s) being trained (Aagaard, 2004).

Currently it is unclear whether speed strength training causes any shift in fibre type, although plyometric training evokes increases in maximal contraction velocity in all fibre types (Malisoux, Francaux, Nielens, & Theisen, 2006), and a decrease in muscle contraction time of the trained muscle (Kubo, et al., 2007).

Hypertrophy

Generally, the maximum force produced by a single muscle fibre is proportional to its cross-sectional area (CSA). Most forms of strength training performed with a sizeable load will lead to some amount of muscle hypertrophy in untrained or moderately trained muscle. The degree of hypertrophy which takes place, however, will vary according to the type of training taking place, the manipulation of program design variables—e.g. reps, sets, intensity, and rest—and the athlete performing the training.

Typically, maximum strength training at submaximal loads (i.e. 70 to 85% 1RM;

12 to 6 reps) with high volume is used for the specific purpose of increasing the trained muscle's CSA. This specific intensity range along with the appropriate volume and rest is typically termed 'hypertrophy training' rather than 'maximum strength' training. For the purpose of this book, this intensity range will be classed as maximum strength training at submaximal loads. Increases in fibre CSA take place with heavier loads (i.e. > 85% 1RM) and less volume, although not to the same extent as training with more submaximal loads.

While hypertrophic adaptations take place across all fibre types, lifting at higher intensities results in a preferential hypertrophy of fast twitch fibres compared to training at submaximal loads (Fry, 2004), and is therefore more beneficial where maximum force and contraction velocity are concerned. Progressive maximum strength training across a range of loads (3 to 12RM) has also been shown to increase the pennation angle (PA)—the angle between the line connecting the tendinous insertion and the end points of the fibre—of the trained muscle(s) (Aagaard, et al., 2001, Sopher et al., 2017) thus increasing its CSA.

The relatively lighter loads often used in speed strength training and the reduction in time the muscle is placed under tension results in little hypertrophy (Wernbom, Augustsson, & Thomee, 2007). This is equally true for strength endurance training where the loads used are relatively low. Additionally, it is not currently clear whether speed strength training elicits changes in pennation angle.

Motor Unit Recruitment

The overall force produced by a muscle is related to both the number and type of motor units recruited in an action. As already discussed, the recruitment of motor units follows the size principle (Henneman, Clamann, Gillies, & Skinner, 1974)—i.e. the order in which the motor units are activated is dictated by the motor unit size, proceeding from smallest (type I) to largest (type II) as muscle contraction increases (Figure 1.5). This principle relates to a slow muscle contraction of graded force, isometric contractions and ones of a more explosive nature. However, the ceiling of motor unit recruitment is generally lower during fast movements due to the rapid increase in force to high levels in a short period of time.

A novice athlete with little experience of strength training will only be able to recruit a certain number of motor units. This is to protect the muscle from developing too much force and damaging the muscle and connective tissues. With training, they are gradually able to recruit more motor units and produce more force. However, the force capable of being produced also depends on the type of motor units recruited. Where maximal power production is required, recruitment of the higher order (fast twitch) motor units is favourable, since they innervate the muscle fibres which produce higher forces and RFD (Enoka & Fuglevand, 2001).

A preferential recruitment of these motor units can occur in exercises that require near maximal force output, such as when performing heavy loads during maximum and

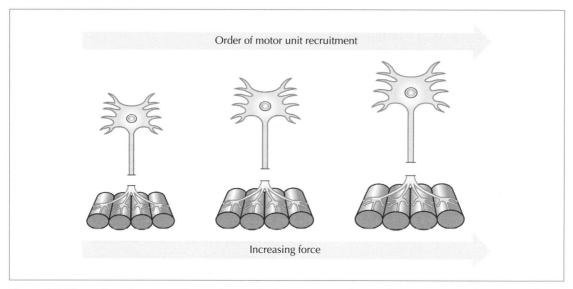

Figure 1.5. The order of motor unit recruitment during a concentric muscle contraction of increasing force.

explosive strength training (i.e. ≥ 85% 1RM). Moreover, a period of explosive strength training with lighter loads elicits an earlier activation of the higher motor units during ballistic muscle contractions (Van Cutsem, Duchateau, & Hainaut, 1998).

Rate Coding

The rate at which neural impulses are transmitted to the muscle fibres will affect the ability of a muscle fibre to generate force. An increase in motor unit firing frequency will augment the magnitude of the force generated by a muscle and its RFD without any increases in motor unit recruitment. If the frequency of nerve impulses is high enough, a fused tetanic contraction—where a motor unit has been maximally stimulated by its motor nerve cell—occurs.

Generally, the motor unit firing rate of each motor unit increases with increasing

muscular effort (known as rate coding) until a maximum rate is reached. During rapid muscular contractions, motor units fire at very high frequencies, increasing a muscle's RFD (Zehr & Sale, 1994). Rate coding can be enhanced through high-intensity maximal strength training and explosive strength training.

Rate of Force Development (RFD)

As already identified, the rate that force can be developed is generally more important during rapid actions than the maximum force that can be produced irrespective of time. RFD can be improved through maximum strength training (Aagaard, Simonsen, Anderson, Magnusson, & Dhyre-Poulsen, 2002) and explosive strength training (Van Cutsem, Duchateau, & Hainaut, 1998).

A number of adaptations cause increases in RFD, such as an increase in motor unit firing frequency and muscle-tendon hypertrophy and stiffness (Arampatzis, Karamanidis, & Albracht, 2007). However, regardless of the type of training adopted, to elicit such adaptations the intention to move the load as explosively as possible is important to evoke positive changes in RFD. These improvements are said to be driven by high rates of neural activation associated with the intention to move a load rapidly and with as much force as possible, regardless of the actual velocity of movement (Behm & Sale, 1993).

Intermuscular Coordination

Intermuscular coordination refers to the ability of agonists, synergists, antagonists and stabilisers to work together in the execution of movements. This includes both the appropriate magnitude and timing of force generation of the muscles. While force generation from the agonists is important to produce high levels of external force, support from the synergistic muscle(s) and a decrease in contraction of the antagonist muscle(s) results in a more forceful, effective and efficient movement.

For example, during the sprinting action, an athlete demonstrates a 'triple extension' pattern of the lower limbs (i.e. ankle plantar flexion, knee and hip extension) to produce force into the ground and propel themselves into the next step. To ensure maximal force production in the short period of time during ground contact, precise levels of timing and levels of activation and relaxation are required by the agonists, synergists, antagonists and stabilisers.

While a degree of activation of the antagonists is important to help protect a joint(s) from injury and coordinate movement, too much co-contraction around a joint will result in decreased activation of the agonist muscle(s) (Milner, Cloutier, Leger, & Franklin, 1995) and reduce force output. Speed strength exercises are of benefit over traditional maximum strength training exercises in this regard, since they require the acceleration of the load lifted through the entire range of motion to the point of release (e.g. a throw) or take-off (e.g. a jump). A decrease in co-contraction of the antagonist muscle(s) is deemed to be one of the adaptations to speed strength training, and is theorised to enhance performance (Folland & Williams, 2007).

Stretch-Shortening Cycle (SSC)

SSC muscle function has been categorised according to contraction times during activities. The SSC can be classified as 'fast' if the contraction times are < 0.25 s and small angular displacements of the hips, knees and ankles take place—a depth jump (Section 6: Exercise Library) would be a typical example in that the ground contact time in this exercise is typically less than 0.25 s.

A slow SSC is one considered to pertain to longer contraction times with larger angular displacements—e.g. a box jump (Section 6: Exercise Library)—thus training with slow SSC exercises may not be suited to activities that involve a fast SSC, because different mechanisms are likely to contribute to fast and slow SSC muscle function (Bobbert, Huijing, & Van Ingen Schenau, 1987). The ability of a muscle to change rapidly from

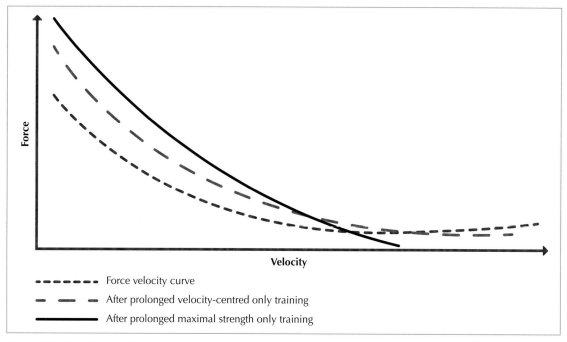

Figure 1.6. The force-velocity curve.

an eccentric to a concentric contraction in this fashion is an adaptation to reactive strength training (and some exercises used in explosive strength training) by the use of plyometric exercises (Markovic & Mikulic, 2010).

Force-Velocity Specific Adaptations

While the various adaptations mentioned so far are deemed to enhance performance, they will have their greatest impact at the velocities and loads used during training, culminating in force-velocity specific adaptations (Kaneko, Fuchimoto, Toji, & Suei, 1983). The force-velocity relationship implies that maximal force production can only occur at very low or zero velocities, whereas the greatest velocities are attained with zero or low loads.

Accordingly, there is an inverse relationship between force and velocity.

The force-velocity curve (Figure 1.6) can be used to show the different effects of *velocity-centred* and *force-centred* training. Maximum strength only training will rotate the curve clockwise, while high velocity only training will, over time, rotate the curve anti-clockwise. This would indicate that prolonged high-intensity maximum strength training may hinder RFD (when force production is relatively low), and sustained low-load high-velocity training may restrict maximal strength development.

However, it is somewhat misleading in certain circumstances to state that large forces cannot be produced at larger velocities, as this is possible in certain activities, e.g. weightlifting.

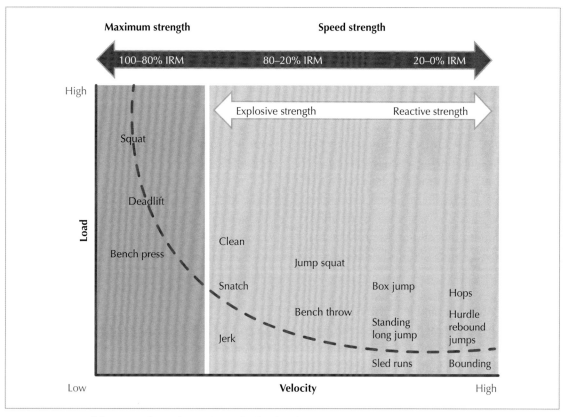

Figure 1.7. Trainable strength qualities along the load-velocity curve.

Equally, it can be misleading to state that large forces cannot be produced at higher velocities, as this is possible in certain activities, e.g. sprinting or plyometrics where ground reaction forces produced can be several times someone's bodyweight.

For these reasons, it can be more helpful to re-conceptualise the force-velocity curve as the 'load-velocity' curve when it comes to strength training, where load refers to the external load imposed on the athlete. Figure 1.7 illustrates trainable strength qualities and their position along the load-velocity curve, with example exercises and types of loads that can be used to develop different strength qualities.

Conclusion

The human body has the ability to respond to a stimulus such as strength training by changing its structure and function following a period of recovery to perform this activity better in the future. A training adaptation occurs only in response to an 'overload' which applies stress to the body. It is equally important to vary the type of stress being applied to the body with planned phases of reduced intensity and rest, so as to avoid inhibiting adaptations and to reduce the risk of injury. This can be achieved through the careful manipulation of program design variables, such as the number of repetitions and sets and the length of rest periods.

Effective program design can be used to augment the development of different strength qualities, namely maximum strength and speed strength. Maximum strength is concerned with the peak force that the neuromuscular system is able to produce during a single maximal voluntary muscle contraction, irrespective of time of force development. Speed strength on the other hand can be described as the ability of the neuromuscular system to produce the greatest possible force within the shortest possible time frame.

Both strength types can be further subdivided into a number of strength qualities, through which their developments elicit a number of advantageous adaptations, including a preferential hypertrophy of type II skeletal muscle fibres, increased motor unit recruitment and rate coding, improved intermuscular coordination and SSC muscle function. While the various adaptations mentioned so far are deemed to enhance performance, they will have their greatest impact at the velocities and loads used during training, culminating in force-velocity specific adaptations.

Such considerations require a long-term approach to strength training in order to induce the most advantageous adaptations for sprint performance. A detailed look at the mechanics of sprinting is important prior to examining the program design process, since this will heavily inform the type of training selected and the necessary adaptations to improve performance.

References

Aagaard, P., Andersen, J., Dyhre-Poulsen, P., Leffers, A., Wagner, A., Magnusson, P., Simonsen, E. (2001). A mechanism for increased contractile strength of human pennate muscle in response to strength training: changes in muscle architecture. *Journal of Physiology, 534,* 613–623.

Aagaard, P., Simonsen, E., Anderson, J., Magnusson, P., & Dyhre-Poulsen, P. (2002). Increased rate of force development and neural drive of human skeletal muscle following resistance training. *Journal of Applied Physiology, 93,* 1318–1326.

Aagaard, P. (2004). Making muscles stronger. *Journal of Musculoskeletal and Neuronal Interaction, 4,* 165–174.

Adams, G., Hather, B., Baldwin, K., & Dudley, G. (1993). Skeletal muscle myosin heavy chain composition and resistance training. *Journal of Applied Physiology, 74,* 911–915.

Andersen, J., & Aagaard, P. (2000). Myosin heavy chain IIX overshooting in human skeletal muscle. *Muscle and Nerve, 23,* 1095–1104.

Arampatzis, A., Karamanidis, K., & Albracht, K. (2007). Adaptational responses of the human Achilles tendon by modulation of the applied cyclic strain magnitude. *Journal of Experimental Biology, 210,* 2743–2753.

Behm, D., & Sale, D. (1993). Intended rather than actual movement velocity determines velocity-specific training response. *Journal of Applied Physiology, 74,* 359–368.

Bobbert, M., Huijing, P. A., & Van Ingen Schenau, G. (1987). Drop jumping I. The influence of jumping technique on the biomechanics of jumping. *Medicine & Science in Sports & Exercise, 19*, 332–338.

Bosco, C., Cotelli, F., Bonomi, R., Mognoni, P., & Roi, G. (1994). Seasonal fluctuations of selected physiological characteristics of elite alpine skiers. *European Journal of Applied Physiology and Occupational Physiology, 69*(1), 71–74.

Enoka, R., & Fuglevand, A. (2001). Motor unit physiology: some unresolved issues. *Muscle and Nerve, 21*, 4–17.

Folland, J., & Williams, A. (2007). The adaptations to strength training: morphological and neurological contributions to increased strength. *Sports Medicine, 37*, 145–168.

Fry, A. (2004). The role of resistance intensity on muscle fibre adaptations. *Sports Medicine, 34*, 663–679.

Galvão, D., & Taaffe, D. (2004). Single- vs. multiple-set resistance training: recent developments in the controversy. *Journal of Strength and Conditioning Research, 18*, 660–667.

Harridge, S., Bottinelli, R., Canepari, M., Pellegrino, M., Reggiani, C., Esbjornsson, M., & Saltin, B. (1996). Whole-muscle and single-fibre contractile properties and myosin heavy chain isoforms in humans. *European Journal of Physiology, 432*, 913–920.

Henneman, E., Clamann, P., Gillies, J., & Skinner, R. (1974). Rank order of motoneurons within a pool: law of combination. *Journal of Neurophysiology, 37*, 1338–1349.

Holtermann, A., Roeleveld, K., Vereijken, B., & Ettema, G. (2007). The effect of rate of force development on maximal force production: acute and training-related aspects. *European Journal of Applied Physiology, 99*, 605–613.

Kaneko, M., Fuchimoto, T., Toji, H., & Suei, K. (1983). Training effect of different loads on the force-velocity relationship and mechanical power output in human muscle. *Scandinavian Journal of Sports Sciences, 5*, 50–55.

Kubo, K., Morimoto, M., Komuro, T., Yata, H., Tsunoda, N., Kanehisa, H., & Fukunaga, T. (2007). Effects of plyometric and weight training on muscle-tendon complex and jump performance. *Medicine and Science in Sports and Exercise, 39*, 1801–1810.

Malisoux, L., Francaux, M., Nielens, H., & Theisen, D. (2006). Stretch-shortening cycle exercises: an effective training paradigm to enhance power output of human single muscle fibers. *Journal of Applied Physiology, 100*, 771–779.

Markovic, G., & Mikulic, P. (2010). Neuro-musculoskeletal and performance adaptations to lower-extremity plyometric training. *Sports Medicine, 40*, 859–895.

McDonagh, M., & Davies, C. (1984). Adaptive response of mammalian skeletal muscle to exercise with high loads. *European Journal of Applied Physiology and Occupational Physiology, 52*, 139–155.

Milner, T., Cloutier, C., Leger, A., & Franklin, D. (1995). Inability to activate muscles maximally during co-contraction and the effect on joint stiffness. *Experimental Brain Research, 107*, 293–305.

Natera, A., Cardinale, M., & Keogh, J. (2020). The effect of high volume power training on repeated high-intensity performance and the assessment of repeat power ability: A systematic review. *Sports Medicine (Auckland), 50*(7), 1317–1339.

Sahaly, R., Vandewalle, H., Driss, T., & Monod, H. (2001). Maximal voluntary force and rate of force development in humans—importance of instruction. *European Journal of Applied Physiology, 85*, 345–350.

Schuster, J., Howells, D., Robineau, J., Couderac, A., Natera, A., Lumley, N., & Winkelman, N. (2018). Physical-preparation recommendations for elite rugby sevens performance. *International Journal of Sports Physiology and Performance, 13*, 255–267.

Siff, M. (2003). *Supertraining.* Denver: Supertraining Institute.

Sopher, R., Amis, A., Davies, D., & Jeffers, J. (2017). The influence of muscle pennation angle and cross-sectional area on contact forces in the ankle joint. *Journal of Strain Analysis for Engineering Design, 52(1)*, 12–23.

Thorstensson, A., Karlsson, J., Viitasalo, J., Luhtanen, P., & Komi, P. (1976). Effect of strength training on EMG of human skeletal muscle. *Acta Physiologica Scandinavica, 98*, 232–236.

Van Cutsem, M., Duchateau, J., & Hainaut, K. (1998). Changes in single motor unit behaviour contribute to the increase in contraction speed after dynamic training in humans. *Journal of Physiology, 15*, 295–305.

Verkhoshansky, Y. (2006). *Special Strength Training.* Michigan: Ultimate Athlete Concepts.

Wernbom, M., Augustsson, J., & Thomee, R. (2007). The influence of frequency, intensity, volume and mode of strength training on whole muscle cross-sectional area in humans. *Sports Medicine, 37*, 225–264.

Weyand, P., Sandell, R., Prime, D., & Bundle, M. (2010). The biological limits to running speed are imposed from the ground up. *Journal of Applied Physiology, 108*, 950–961.

Zehr, E., & Sale, D. (1994). Ballistic movement: motor control and muscle activation. *Canadian Journal of Applied Physiology, 19*, 363–378.

Sprinting Biomechanics

n simple terms, biomechanics is concerned with the way the human body moves and why it moves in that way. Within the context of sprinting, an appreciation of the mechanics of human motion is important in order to identify technical features and strength-related qualities which limit an athlete's ability to run faster. In turn, more effective strength programming decisions to enhance sprinting performance can be made. With this in mind, it is first necessary to establish biomechanical factors pertinent to sprinting performance, before considering the subject of strength training program design.

For the first 25 to 80 m (approximately) of a sprint, an athlete will be accelerating (getting faster), until they reach their maximum sprinting velocity where it is no longer possible to continue accelerating. The point at which an athlete reaches their maximum velocity peak will vary according to a number of factors (Figure 2.1). However, this is largely determined by the magnitude of the maximum velocity athletes are capable of reaching, where those who achieve higher maximum velocities will typically reach them later within a sprint.

Aside from the odd exception, the 100-m performance of a sprinter is largely determined by their ability to achieve the highest maximum velocity relative to other competitors in a 100-m race. Proficient acceleration is clearly still of importance to sprinters since an athlete's accelerative abilities across the full acceleration phase culminates in reaching their respective maximum velocities.

Once an athlete reaches the maximum velocity phase, maintaining this velocity for as long as possible and limiting the amount of deceleration for the remainder of the race is important to sprint performance. During the latter stages of a sprint, a degree of deceleration takes place as a result of central nervous system fatigue and the accumulation of metabolic waste products (Hirvonen, Nummela, Rusko, Rehunen, & Härkönen, 1992; Ross, Leveritt, & Riek, 2001). Elite sprinters typically decelerate for the final 20 m of a 100-m sprint.

The mechanical demands imposed on athletes change across the different phases of a sprint (Figure 2.2), thus each phase has a broad mechanical objective that the athlete is trying to achieve across these phases. We will discuss

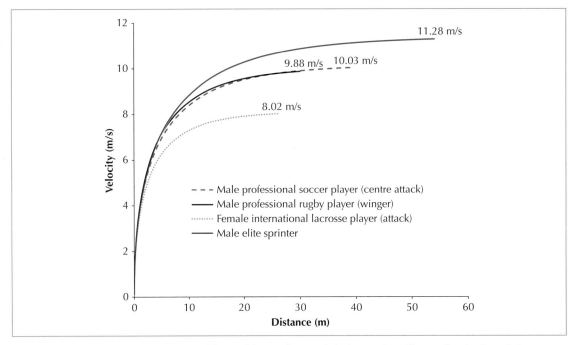

Figure 2.1. Distance-velocity curves of four athletes obtained during sprint efforts of a single training session.

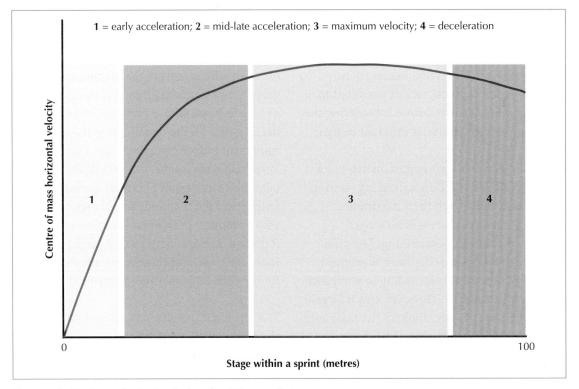

Figure 2.2. Horizontal velocity during the 100-m sprint.

these mechanical objectives now to help provide greater context for the more in-depth look at the biomechanical differences between phases and the underlying determinants of these sprint phases which will follow.

While the upper limbs play a part in sprint running performance (Hinrichs, 1987; Hinrichs, Cavanagh, & Williams, 1987), their contribution is largely a response to that of the lower limbs (Bhowmick & Battacharyya, 1988; Mann, 1981) and will not be focussed on in this section.

Mechanical Objectives

Ground Reaction Force Characteristics

The step cycle (Figure 2.3) starts when the foot makes initial contact with the ground (touchdown). This also signifies the beginning of the ground contact or 'stance' phase which ends at the instant the same foot is no longer in contact with the sprinting surface (toe-off).

At the point of touchdown, a sprinter loses momentum (and slows down) due to the braking effect caused by a negative anteroposterior force. Anteroposterior forces refer to the horizontal ground reaction forces during the stance phase. Negative horizontal force values represent the braking force at the start of ground contact, and positive horizontal force values represent propulsive force which takes place after the braking force has occurred (Figure 2.4).

As stated during the introduction, the amount of force produced into the ground during the stance phase is important to sprinting performance. However, the motion of an

| Touchdown | Toe-off | Flight | Touchdown |

Figure 2.3. The step cycle.

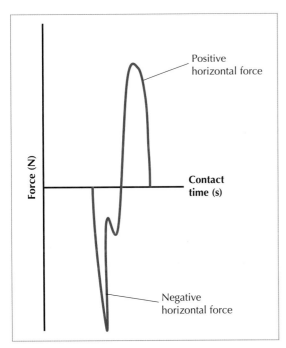

Figure 2.4. Anteroposterior (horizontal) ground reaction forces during a step of a sprint in the maximum velocity phase.

athlete resulting from the production of force into the ground is dependent not only on the size of the force applied, but also on how long that force is applied for.

The product of force and time (i.e. force × time) is known as *impulse*. Braking impulse is evident during ground contact when negative horizontal force is being produced, whereas propulsive impulse is apparent while positive horizontal force is being applied. Net propulsive impulse, established by subtracting the braking impulse from the propulsive impulse, directly determines an athlete's change in velocity. If the net horizontal propulsive impulse is positive during the stance phase, the athlete will have accelerated in the forward direction during that step—and if it is negative—they have decelerated.

Graphically, impulse is represented by the area under a force-time curve (Figure 2.5). For example, in Figure 2.5 during the second step of a sprint, net propulsive impulse is positive since the braking impulse is less than the propulsive impulse, and so the athlete is accelerating. During the step at the 40m mark—in this example—the net horizontal propulsive impulse is zero, since the braking and propulsive are the same as if the athlete has reached their maximum velocity and can no longer accelerate.

Therefore—during the acceleration phase—the principle mechanical objective for an athlete is to accrue net propulsive impulse rapidly, since this impulse will be directly proportional to the change in horizontal velocity and therefore represents the primary outcome objective of acceleration.

That said, it is important to respect the time over which this impulse is being developed—hence the word 'rapidly' in this context is important. This is because it is possible to have a high impulse—by spending a longer time in contact with the ground—but low acceleration if the magnitude of the impulse is achieved primarily through spending a longer time generating ground reaction forces rather than by generating greater ground reaction force magnitudes.

However, there is also a need for an athlete to overcome gravity and maintain balance. Therefore, an amount of vertical force is necessary during a step to produce the vertical impulse to address this requirement (Figure 2.6).

As the acceleration phase progresses, the mechanical constraints imposed on the athlete

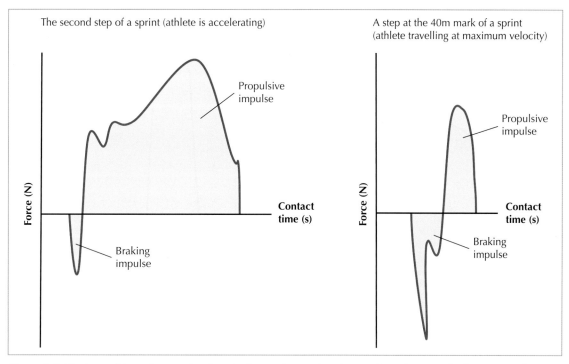

Figure 2.5. Horizontal impulse production during early acceleration and maximum velocity stance phases of an athlete during a sprint.

change somewhat. As the horizontal velocity of the athlete increases with each step, the ground passes from underneath them at a faster rate and the time to produce ground reaction force reduces. These constraints mean the athlete must manage diminishing ground contact times whilst still achieving the required vertical impulse to rebound into the air for the next flight phase and whilst still retaining sufficient net propulsive horizontal impulse to continue to accelerate. The athlete will then reach their limit to be able to cope with this challenge where it is no longer possible to keep accelerating and they will reach their maximum velocity, during which the main mechanical objective is to meet the vertical impulse requirements to overcome gravity and support bodyweight. This can only be achieved by an increase in the step averaged

vertical ground reaction forces—compared with the acceleration phase—but in a shorter contact time.

These mechanical demands are reflected in the pattern changes evident in the ground reaction force and impulse magnitudes and their directions during the different sprint phases (Figure 2.7). Braking forces are at their smallest at the start and increase with each step until they stabilise at their highest when maximum velocity is reached.

The opposite is observed with horizontal propulsive forces. They start at their highest and decrease with each step until they stabilise at their smallest when maximum velocity is reached. The decrease in net horizontal propulsive impulse is evident as

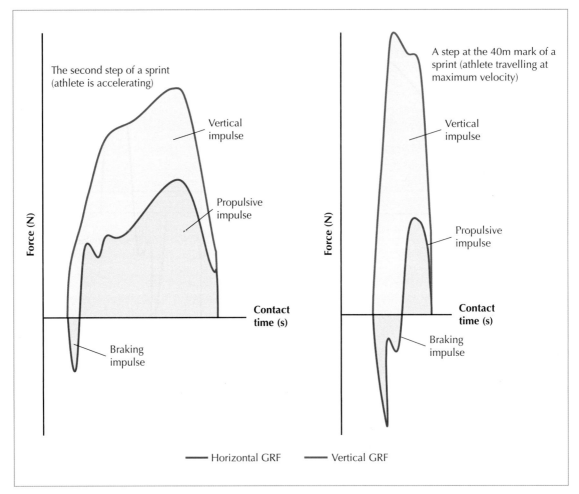

Figure 2.6. Ground reaction force and impulse production during early acceleration and maximum velocity stance phases of an athlete during a sprint.

the acceleration phase progresses, resulting in a gradual reduction in an athlete's change in velocity. At some point the net horizontal propulsive impulse equals the negative braking ground impulse, and the athlete will be travelling at constant (i.e. maximum) velocity.

Regarding vertical forces produced, they are at their lowest at the start and gradually increase with each step until maximum velocity is reached, where they are at their highest. Provided the vertical impulse produced is

enough to overcome the effects of gravity, a positive vertical impulse has been produced which is necessary to maintain balance and for upward acceleration to create a flight time in which an athlete can reposition their limbs in preparation for the next stance phase. These progresses change as a sprint progresses and are a function of increasing velocity and decreasing contact times.

Now that we understand these ground reaction force and impulse pattern changes, we will

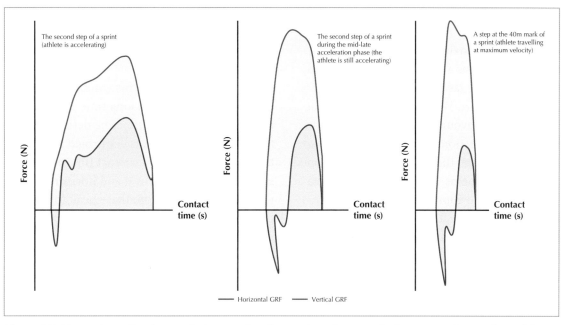

Figure 2.7. Ground reaction forces during acceleration and maximum velocity stance phases of an athlete during a sprint.

continue to explore which of their features are associated with the different phases of a sprint.

Kinetic Determinants of Sprinting Performance

The Start

For sprinters—having reacted to the starter's pistol—the main mechanical objective in the blocks is to maximise horizontal velocity in as little time as possible. Additionally, the athlete needs to produce sufficient vertical impulse to overcome gravity to maintain balance, and a gradual rise in the athlete's centre of mass.

Research has shown that sprinters with better 100-m personal bests and higher sprinting velocities at 2.5 m tend to generate larger relative horizontal block impulses than slower sprinters (Baumann, 1976; Mero et al., 1983). These higher impulses are due to increased average horizontal force production. That is, higher impulses are achieved by better performing starters in the same or shorter push durations, with higher rates of force development being the most likely explanation for this (Slawinski et al., 2010).

In sports other than track and field, different initial starting positions are used to optimise the start phase and sprint performance, although—from a stationary start—standing two-point split stance or parallel stance positions are most commonly adopted. Their starting position and how they initiate the sprint will obviously vary, depending on the context of the specific situation they are in.

For example, when there is some degree of uncertainty as to the direction in which someone needs to sprint, a parallel start in a more classic 'ready position'—where feet are parallel and approximately shoulder-width apart, and the hips are lowered somewhat—is likely to be more favourable than a crouched 2- or 3-point start. Whilst the athlete may not be in the most favourable position to sprint in the forward direction compared to a crouched 2- or 3-point start, they are far better positioned to manoeuvre themselves more quickly into a more optimal position to sprint in any other direction. Therefore, the trade-off between being potentially slightly slower sprinting forward is offset against being faster to get into position to sprint in any other direction.

A number of studies have investigated the differences in performance between starting conditions. Most commonly, these have involved comparing performance in a standing split stance 2-point position with false step and parallel step starting conditions. The false step and parallel sprint starts involve the athlete being positioned in a parallel stance (i.e. feet are parallel). However, the false step involves initiating the sprint with a backward step before moving forward, whereas the parallel step start involves initiating the sprint with a forward step.

The findings are typically consistent and the standing split stance and false step starting conditions are found to be faster than the parallel step start and have been associated with shorter times to 2.5m (Cronin et al., 2007; Frost & Cronin, 2011). Interestingly though— whilst the mean and peak horizontal forces produced are comparable—the horizontal impulses appear significantly lower in the split stance and false step start conditions compared with the parallel step start.

The average vertical forces are also greater in the split and false step starts. As discussed later, this is typically not what we are led to believe as being favourable for acceleration performance. However, this emphasises that— at the start—spending a long time generating high impulse can sometimes be detrimental to performance. This was confirmed in the same studies where contact time at the start, time to peak vertical and horizontal forces and the time from these peak forces to take-off were all less in the false step and split stance start conditions compared with the parallel step start (Cronin et al., 2007; Frost & Cronin, 2011).

As already mentioned, different starting conditions will apply to athletes according to the context within their sport and so the information presented here should not be taken as a guide or prompt to advocate which starting condition is better than another. Whilst generating large impulses is clearly important, it should be evident that—at the very start—the ability to produce force quickly is key. As such, producing higher ground reaction force impulses during the push off by spending a longer time pushing—rather than producing higher forces—is not always advantageous. However, this will also depend on what performance actually is during the sprinting taking place too.

For example, in a sport such as bobsleigh— during the push start—the time it takes to travel over the first few metres—or more specifically to try and cover the first few metres in as small a time as possible—is not necessarily the goal. Achieving the highest velocity at the point the timer starts further down the track is, and this may have different kinetic associations with the start. Moreover, within team sports, accelerating with maximum intent will often take place from a rolling start and how the kinetic determinants differ in this context compared to a standing start have not been investigated extensively.

To get a better understanding, however, of the external kinetic determinants from a rolling start, we can look simply at what is going on from step one onward following a standing start. For instance, by the time an athlete arrives at the first step following a standing start, they will be travelling at around 3–4 m/s, which is not an uncommon velocity for a team sport athlete to be running at before accelerating with maximum intent.

Acceleration—Ground Reaction Forces Characteristics

After the first flight phase following the push-off at the start—be that from a standing or block start—the first stance phase contains the greatest velocity increase during any stance within a maximal effort sprint. Even from this very first step, there is a braking phase.

Whilst the initial braking phase is short as a percentage of total stance time and peak braking forces are low, there is no evidence to suggest that no phase of braking exists during the first stance phase in sprinters of any level, despite this often being highlighted by coaches as an objective during the initial steps of a sprint. The advice to minimise braking would seem logical in the early steps—because theoretically reducing braking impulse would result in a greater net horizontal impulse—and therefore a greater positive change velocity,

assuming the propulsive impulse does not also decrease substantially.

Whilst reducing braking forces and impulses may seem advantageous to sprint performance, the evidence doesn't current support that lower braking forces and impulses are associated with better performance in the initial steps of a sprint. Braking forces and impulse do not appear to affect sprinting performance in this phase. This doesn't mean they aren't important to consider, but the research doesn't currently support that they are an issue during the initial steps.

For instance, Kawamori and colleagues (2013) found that the relative braking impulse of a range of team sport athletes at the first ground contact and at the 8-m mark were not related to time to 10 m in a sprint.

As another example, Morin et al., 2015 found no meaningful differences in the braking force and impulse produced between world class and high-level sprinters during the first 6 to 7 steps. In fact, they even found that there was no association between average braking impulses produced across each step over 40m and mean velocity over this distance.

Whilst logically it would make sense to try and reduce braking during the early stance phase during the initial steps, the research doesn't currently support this as being important to performance in acceleration. As already mentioned, reducing braking impulse whilst maintaining or increasing propulsive impulse would likely lead to better sprint performance due to the production of a higher net horizontal impulse, but we don't know how feasible this is. Braking and propulsive phases are still part of the same step—two sides of the same coin. Therefore, they are part of a complex system and attempting to adjust one is likely to cause an impact elsewhere.

For example, we can't rule out at this stage that there are potential beneficial effects of braking during the initial steps. There may be a potentiation effect that braking induces on the subsequent propulsive phase. Or maybe a degree of braking is necessary to attain high active state of muscles at the onset of propulsion. Or it may be that braking forces are just too small in early acceleration to make much of a difference.

Whilst the effects of braking in the initial steps is currently unclear, what does seem to be consistent in the literature is that the fastest athletes produce higher mean horizontal forces and mean horizontal propulsive forces. This was shown in the work of Morin et al. (2015) where—during the first few steps—what separated faster from slower sprinters was the propulsive ground reaction force values, rather than the negative ones.

This association was not just limited to the initial steps either. In the same study, higher mean horizontal ground reaction forces across the steps of sprinters were related to the whole acceleration phase, where positive and significant associations of mean horizontal and mean propulsive forces and average 40-m velocity were evident.

This is not the only research to show these findings. There is a strong body of evidence which shows that better sprint acceleration performance is strongly correlated with high mean horizontal forces (Colyer, Nagahara, Takai, & Salo, 2018; Colyer, Nagahara, & Salo, 2018; Hunter, Marshall, & McNair, 2005; Kugler & Janshen, 2010; Morin et al., 2012; Rabita et al., 2015).

A more detailed look at the waveforms of the ground reaction forces—which represent the instantaneous acceleration of an athlete's centre of mass during a step—it is possible to identify how the ground reaction forces produced at different time points during stance related to sprinting performance.

In 2018 Colyer et al. found horizontal propulsive forces to relate to sprinting performance throughout the acceleration phase. This was obviously consistent with previous research. However, they also identified the specific time points, when these propulsive forces were most related to performance. For example, during early acceleration, the production of greater propulsive forces during mid- and late stance is particularly important, and that typically with each step the importance of producing larger propulsive forces shifts to earlier in the stance phase.

As can be seen in Figure 2.8, the portion of the stance phase most related to performance shifts earlier as a sprint progresses as ground contact times shorten. Then, as the athlete reaches the later stages of acceleration—e.g. Figure 2.6, step 17—not only does the ability to produce large propulsive forces even earlier in the stance phase become important, but so too does the ability to attenuate horizontal braking forces. Lower magnitudes of braking appear to be a more important factor for sprinting performance during the late

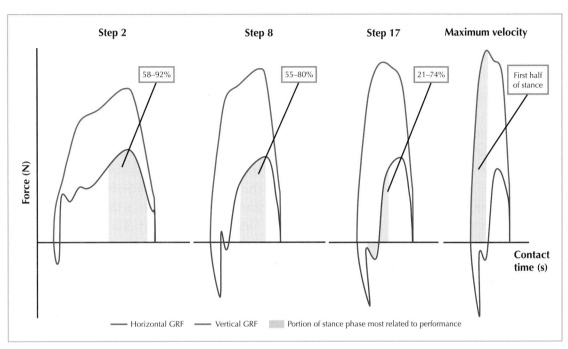

Figure 2.8. The portions of the ground contact phase where ground reaction forces are most related to performance during acceleration and maximum velocity (based on the work of Colyer et al. 2018 [acceleration] and Clark & Weyand, 2014 [maximum velocity]).

acceleration phase, compared with the earlier stages in acceleration (Colyer et al., 2018).

This finding is supported elsewhere, where Nagahara et al. (2018) found that braking impulse was significantly related to acceleration of male athletes at 85 and 95% of their maximal running speed.

During acceleration, whilst the magnitude of the average net horizontal force produced is key—as alluded to already—the duration this force is applied for is also important.

For example, in a study by von Lieres Und Wilkau and colleagues (2020), the relative importance of both duration and magnitude of force application to sprint performance during initial and transitional acceleration as

well as maximum velocity was investigated. During the acceleration phase, the highest relationships were found between sprint acceleration performance and average propulsive force at steps 3 and 9.

However, relationships between phase durations and sprint performance were also related to performance. Within their multiple regression analysis, it was observed—in step 3—that average propulsive force uniquely contributed 28% of the variance in sprint performance, but average propulsive force and propulsive time (duration propulsive force was applied for) when combined, contributed 61% of the variance. In step 9, the combination of average propulsive force and propulsive time, contributed to 30% of the variation in performance.

Acceleration—Vector Orientation

Considering vertical and horizontal ground reaction forces individually clearly aids our understanding of sprinting. However, it is important not to lose sight of the fact that when an individual's foot is in contact with the ground, they are actually only applying one force at any point in time and that vertical and horizontal ground reaction forces cannot be independently altered. They are part of the same force vector and are both important.

Beyond the relative magnitudes of vertical and horizontal forces, we need to consider the average force vector (resultant force vector) during the stance phase (Figure 2.9) and its orientation, because the direction of the force application is an important determinant of sprint acceleration performance.

Figure 2.9. The stance averaged force vector (resultant force vector) during an acceleration step.

By analysing ground reaction force data, it has been found that an athlete's 'technical ability' to direct the ground reaction force vector more horizontally is an important feature of their performance during acceleration (Morin, Edouard, & Samozino, 2011; Rabita et al., 2015). The direction of this ground reaction force vector has been termed the *ratio of force* since it is calculated as the ratio of horizontal to resultant or total forces (resultant or total forces calculated as the sum of the stance averaged horizontal and stance averaged vertical ground reaction forces). What the research typically shows is that a higher ratio of force toward the start of a sprint is related to early acceleration performance (Morin et al., 2011; Rabita et al., 2015).

Sometimes, ratio of force and its implications are misunderstood. Firstly, it's important to understand that there is a certain requirement to direct an amount of force vertically to provide some vertical impulse to counter the downward acceleration of gravity. Therefore, it is not possible to simply rotate the force vector so that it is directed more horizontally—with the same total force magnitude—as this would result in a drop in vertical ground reaction force below that required to overcome gravity. This means that the total ground reaction force must be increased, leading to both increased horizontal force and a changed angle.

Therefore, the limit angle of an athlete's resultant force vector applied through stance is determined by their ability to express more total force under the specified constraints to increase their ratio of force. The constraints in this context relate to the ability to apply force unilaterally in short time periods with moderate to fast muscle contraction velocities. Therefore, developing power-based qualities through strength training can logically help with this.

Ratio of force is often quantified across a whole acceleration phase. Ratio of force is then plotted with respect to horizontal velocity and a trend line is applied, with the slope of this trend line considered as an indication of an athlete's force application technique (Samozino et al., 2016). As a sprint progresses throughout acceleration, the ratio of force decreases gradually as the force vector gradually changes from being more horizontal to more vertical. The rate at which the ratio of force decreases is known as the *index of force application* and the ability to attenuate this decrease as a sprint progresses is related to late acceleration and maximum velocity performance (Morin et al., 2011; Rabita et al., 2015; Samozino et al., 2016). This may feasibly relate to the ability to attenuate the magnitude of braking forces in the early stance phase during later stages of acceleration.

As contact times reduce during the later stages of acceleration and ground contact times shorten, stance force production becomes more challenging, and—as contact time falls—the need for higher average vertical ground reaction forces increases to maintain the required vertical impulse. Eventually this results in the athlete 'using up' all their leg extension force capabilities to meet these vertical impulse demands. However, those athletes who can quickly generate sufficient force magnitudes to reach the required vertical impulse, but with enough 'strength reserves' left over, which can be applied to achieve this with a more forward oriented resultant vector, thus enabling a degree of continued acceleration will achieve the highest maximum velocities.

Before the kinetic determinants of maximum velocity are discussed further, it is worth noting that much of the research to date has been conducted on track and field athletes and some of the research conducted on team sport athletes doesn't necessarily match what has been found with sprint athletes. For example, when investigating the ground reaction forces of soccer players during the first step, peak vertical ground reaction force relative to body mass was significantly correlated to 5–10 m and 15–20 m sprint times (Wdowski & Gittoes, 2020).

Peak propulsive and mean propulsive ground reaction forces relative to bodyweight were also significantly related to 5–10, 10–15, 15–20 and 0–20 m split times. Whilst this would generally support what has been discussed so far regarding the kinetic determinants of acceleration performance, no relationships were found between sprint time over the first 5 m and any of the force or impulse measures in the study.

In another study which this time looked at the ground reaction force characteristics during the first, second and last step of 10-m sprints of a range of team sport athletes, only peak vertical force during the last step over 10 m was found to relate to 5–10 m split time (Lockie, Murphy, Schultz, Jeffriess, & Callaghan, 2013). No other horizontal or vertical force measures or ratio of force (discussed later in this section) in these steps were related to any split times.

So, do things differ in team sport athletes? In the aforementioned study by Lockie and colleagues (2013), they suggested that since field sport performers are conditioned for multiple short sprint runs during competition, most participants may have developed an impulse appropriate for effective 10-m sprint runs and that other factors would therefore determine their performance. However, the authors did not look at average forces, which may have been related to the short sprint performance given the findings of other studies. Nonetheless it seems surprising that the ratio of force measures and force vector angles were not associated with the performance of the athletes.

This is just a hint that things may differ at times with team sport athletes—perhaps the different starting conditions involved such as block vs standing starts or the use of spikes may contribute to this—or, it could be due to methodological differences in these studies.

For example, although the sprint distance performance was assessed over distances included up to the 20-m mark in Wdowski et al. (2020)—only the ground reaction force characteristics from the first step were obtained—meaning that the ground reaction forces of several other steps were not factored into the analysis, which would clearly influence performance over these distances.

More research is possibly needed with team sport athletes to gain an even more complete understanding on the external kinetic determinants of acceleration performance for team sport athletes. That said, the large body of evidence on the external kinetic associations with sprint acceleration performance in the scientific literature are otherwise logical when considering the basic physics involved during this sprint phase and form the basis of our understanding on this area.

Maximum Velocity

As already mentioned, the vertical forces produced are at their highest during the maximum velocity phase. This is necessary since contact times are at their shortest during this phase and an increase in vertical force is necessary to produce the vertical impulse sufficient to overcome gravity and to meet the athlete's bodyweight. The braking and propulsive impulses are equal in magnitude (Figure 2.7); thus, an athlete will be sprinting at or near a constant velocity. Collectively these characteristics result in a force vector more vertically oriented compared with the acceleration phase.

Although horizontal forces are important during maximum velocity, they do not tend to relate to sprint performance in this phase, with perhaps the exception being the ability to attenuate the rate of decline in ratio of force and braking forces. However, the vertical force component is of more interest to maximum velocity sprint performance.

The research clearly shows that higher vertical force relative to bodyweight and shorter contact times are related to maximum velocity performance. This was perhaps first brought to our attention over 20 years ago by Weyand and colleagues (2000), who found that human runners reach faster top speeds not by repositioning their legs more rapidly in the air, but by applying greater vertical forces to the ground. Essentially, the rate at which those higher vertical forces can be produced, the shorter the ground contact times can be. Returning to the air quickly is of benefit to an athlete during this phase because they have less potential to accrue net horizontal impulse to accelerate. Therefore, being airborne covering the ground is more valuable than being on the ground trying to accelerate.

In 2010, Weyand et al. demonstrated that producing higher vertical forces in shorter contact times was related to horizontal velocity, irrespective of the locomotive mode. Regardless of whether subjects ran forward, hopped on one leg, or ran backward, they attained faster speeds by applying greater vertical forces—relative to body mass—to the running surface during shorter ground contacts as velocity increased.

The ground reaction force mechanics or sprinters and non-sprint athletes (mainly team sport athletes) were investigated by Clark and Weyand in 2014. They found that elite sprinters applied significantly higher mass specific vertical forces during the first half of the contact phase compared with slower, subelite sprinters.

In turn, the same was found when comparing the vertical forces produced by the subelite sprinters compared with non-sprint athletes. This can be visualized in contact phase during maximum velocity in Figure 2.8. Interestingly, approximately the same vertical forces were applied to the ground during the second half of the stance phase across all groups and that the vertical forces produced during the portion of the stance phase were not related to maximum velocity performance.

Although consideration of vertical and horizontal force production (relative to the earth's surface) is important—and appears

attractive in terms of strength exercise selection—it is important to note that the function of skeletal muscle does not change, regardless of the direction the body is oriented relative to the earth's surface. All muscles are concerned with is the force they are being asked to apply to the bones at their ends, and it is the lower limb joint angles and trunk orientations at touchdown which will determine the direction the force is applied in with respect to the ground.

For instance, whether an athlete's trunk and lower limbs are positioned to apply force horizontally during acceleration or vertically during maximum velocity, the muscles of the calf will apply force to the bones at its ends in an attempt to plantar flex the ankle joint. Trying to mimic the forward lean of the trunk evident during acceleration when performing strength exercises to develop this sprint phase may not, therefore, be appropriate, especially at the expense of overload.

The changes in horizontal to vertical force production during ground contact is still of consequence, since differences in body configuration affect joint range of movement, joint velocities and joint power patterns. These factors affect the relative muscle contribution of the lower limbs to express the forces required during the stance phase. These differences change the demands placed on the athlete's neuromuscular system, which should then be taken into account when designing strength programs to target the development of different strength phases or individual weaknesses. Understanding joint kinetic and kinematic patterns can help inform some of these decisions.

Joint Kinetics

Regardless of the sprint phase, the hip joint has typically been shown to extend for the duration of the stance phase (Bezodis, Kerwin, & Salo, 2008; Hunter, Marshall, & McNair, 2004; Jacobs & van Ingen Schenau, 1992; Johnson & Buckley, 2001; Mann & Sprague, 1980).

At the beginning of stance, the muscles surrounding this joint are acting to extend the hip, and the magnitude of this net extensor moment and thus concentric power is important to sprint performance (Mann & Sprague, 1980). The hip extensors muscles—in particular the gluteal muscles—have been identified as likely contributors to horizontal ground reaction force and sprint acceleration performance during early acceleration (first 10 steps) performance (Morin et al., 2015).

Furthermore—during the first step—the hip has been shown to generate 54% and 35% of the maximal power exhibited from a block start during the first (Debaere, Delecluse, Aerenhouts, Hagman, & Jonkers, 2013) and second stance phase (Jacobs & van Ingen Schenau, 1992), respectively. The impulses produced by the hip extensors during acceleration have also been shown to explain a large amount (45%) of the forward acceleration magnitude during sprint acceleration (Schache, Lai, Brown, Crossley, & Pandy, 2019). Producing large hip extensor moments, therefore, appears to be important to sprint performance.

Although the hip joint contributes a meaningful amount to an athlete's centre of mass acceleration early in the stance phase, it appears that this is predominantly during the early stance phase and the extent to which it contributes to this acceleration is partly dependent on what happens at the ankle joint (Veloso, Joao, Valamatos, Cabral, & Moniz-Pereira, 2015).

For instance, Veloso et al. (2015) observed that the hip extensor moments produced during the first quarter of the stance phase of an elite sprinter exhibited the greatest contribution to horizontal and vertical acceleration—compared with knee and ankle joint moments—resulting from considerable force produced by the hip extensors. However, this contribution is only realised with an effectively functioning ankle joint, whereby the plantar flexor moments counteract those produced by the hip extensors, thus providing a stable position with regards to the foot to ground interface, so that the hip extensors can generate horizontal acceleration of the centre of mass (Veloso et al., 2015).

The synergistic interplay between the hip and ankle joint during the stance phase of sprinting has also been highlighted previously at higher running velocities (Dorn, Schache, & Pandy, 2012).

This has specific relevance to strength training for speed. For example, an athlete may possess large amounts of hip extensor strength and power qualities, but this may not be that beneficial if they do not possess the stiffness qualities (discussed later in this section and in Section 4) of their ankle.

By toe-off, the moment has changed to a flexor dominance in order to decelerate the rate of hip extension—hip flexors working eccentrically—so as to prepare for the subsequent recovery of the leg before the next step. However, the point at which the dominance switches from extensor to flexor seems to differ across individuals and is not dependent on the sprint phase (Bezodis, Kerwin, & Salo, 2008; Hunter, Marshall, & McNair, 2004; Jacobs & van Ingen Schenau, 1992; Johnson & Buckley, 2001).

So, while the hip joint may be extending throughout stance, the muscles surrounding it—at some point during stance—will actually be exhibiting a power dissipating (net eccentric) power pattern to decelerate the limb. The stage at which this 'switch' takes place may differ between individuals due to differing strength levels. For example, athletes capable of producing more powerful hip extensor muscle contractions may require an earlier switch to flexor dominance, in order to prevent the duration of the stance phase increasing.

During acceleration, the knee typically extends from touchdown onward (Jacobs & van Ingen Schenau, 1992; Johnson & Buckley, 2001), although this rate of extension is slowed by the horizontal braking forces early in stance. The muscles around the knee joint create a net flexor moment during the first few m/s of the stance phase, after which they act to extend the knee (net extensor moment) for the remainder of the stance phase (Jacobs & van Ingen Schenau, 1992), where the dominant muscle action of the knee extensors is concentric.

During maximum velocity the knee joint flexes for the first 60% of the stance phase (Bezodis, Kerwin, & Salo, 2008). There is typically a knee flexor moment of greater magnitude,

when compared to acceleration, resulting in an eccentric action by the knee extensors, likely due to the increasing influence of the braking forces as a sprint progresses. Shortly after touchdown, knee extensor dominance is achieved to terminate the negative velocity of the body, and for the production of positive velocity in a concentric action during the latter stages of the stance phase (Mann, 1981).

Due to these sprint phase differences, the knee joint appears to be considerably more involved in net concentric activity during the earlier stages of acceleration, whereas as a sprint progresses the knee musculature has been suggested to adopt a more compensatory role (Bezodis, Kerwin, & Salo, 2008).

In all stages of a sprint, the muscles surrounding the knee joint appear to switch to flexor dominance prior to toe-off, in an attempt to terminate ground contact. Although the knee clearly plays an important role during sprinting, its joint kinetics are not typically related to performance to the same extent as those at the hip and ankle.

The moments produced at the ankle have been shown to contribute the most to sprinting performance, especially during the acceleration phase. For example, Schache et al. (2019) found the impulse from the plantar flexor moment was larger than that at the hip and knee during acceleration and its magnitude was linearly related to centre of mass horizontal velocity, explaining 47% of the variation in sprinting performance.

Regardless of the sprint phase, the ankle initially dorsiflexes after touchdown, before plantar flexing for the remainder of the stance phase (Bezodis, Kerwin, & Salo, 2008; Jacobs & van Ingen Schenau, 1992; Johnson & Buckley, 2001). However, this transition from dorsiflexion to plantar flexion occurs at different stages of the stance phase—approximately 30% of stance in the first step of a sprint (Jacobs & van Ingen Schenau, 1992), around 50% of stance phase at mid-acceleration (Johnson & Buckley, 2001), and 60% during maximum velocity (Bezodis, Kerwin, & Salo, 2008).

As the ankle initially dorsiflexes during the stance phase, the plantar flexor muscles are helping to decelerate the downward velocity of the body through power dissipation (net eccentric contraction) (Bezodis, Kerwin, & Salo, 2008; Jacobs & van Ingen Schenau, 1992; Johnson & Buckley, 2001). Once the dorsiflexion has ceased, these muscles then generate power (net concentric contraction) to extend the ankle joint and help propel the body into the subsequent flight phase (Bezodis, Kerwin, & Salo, 2008; Jacobs & van Ingen Schenau, 1992; Johnson & Buckley, 2001).

It would appear, therefore, that the total work due to power dissipation at the ankle joint during early acceleration is less than the power generated (i.e. the plantar flexor muscles are doing more net concentric work than net eccentric work). By the time an athlete reaches the mid-acceleration phase, power dissipation and generation at the ankle joint are roughly equal. During maximum velocity, the amount of power dissipation exceeds power generation (i.e. the plantar flexors are doing more net eccentric work than net concentric work).

There is therefore clearly a larger power generating (net concentric) emphasis at the

ankle joint during early acceleration compared to maximum velocity. This information can help guide the type of strength training which can be used to optimise the force production capabilities of athletes during the different sprint phases.

Kinematic Determinants of Sprinting Performance

Linear Kinematics

Linear kinematics—in the context of this chapter—refers primarily to the horizontal locality of the stance foot relative to the athlete's centre of mass at touchdown and toe-off, and the horizontal translation of the centre of mass during the contact and flight phases. These features combine to influence some of the higher order spatiotemporal variables (step length, step frequency, contact time and flight time) discussed later in this chapter. At touchdown, the horizontal distance between the centre of mass and stance foot of the athlete (touchdown distance) is often deemed by coaches to be an important technical feature to consider.

Foot placement further in front of the body is related to higher braking impulses (Fenn, 1930; Hunter et al., 2005), and so it is commonly thought that touching down close to an athlete's centre of mass is desirable, so as to reduce the amount of deceleration at the beginning of the stance phase (Mann & Herman, 1985; Mero & Komi, 1992; Wood, 1987).

The differences in touchdown distance as a sprint progresses are evident in Figures 2.10

Figure 2.10. The first four steps of a sprint (the yellow circle is an approximation of the athlete's centre of mass).

and 2.11 where the point of contact of the foot moves progressively further forward relative to the centre of mass with each step during acceleration and reaches its peak during maximum velocity (Alexander, 1989; Hunter, Marshall, & McNair, 2004; Mero Luhtanen, & Komi, 1983).

The magnitude of braking during early stance is thought to be a function of touchdown distance and foot horizontal touchdown velocity (horizontal velocity of the foot just prior to touchdown). As touchdown distance and foot horizontal touchdown velocity increase with each step in a sprint, so to do the braking impulses produced (Figure 2.7).

These increasing braking forces amplify the reactive strength demands during a sprint. It is clear to see, therefore, that strength requirements differ dependent on the sprint phase, which should be taken into account when designing strength programs.

However, whilst touchdown distance and foot touchdown velocity may explain some of the variation in braking force magnitudes, they are not the sole causes since braking forces are still observed even when touchdown distances are negative (when the foot touches down in acceleration behind the centre of mass) and when the foot is moving slightly backward relative to the ground at touchdown. Therefore, regardless of these technical features

Touchdown

Mid-stance

Toe-off

Mid-flight

Touchdown

Figure 2.11. A step during the maximum velocity phase of a sprint (the yellow circle is an approximation of the athlete's centre of mass).

of an elite sprinter (Bezodis, Trewartha, & Salo, 2015) and physical education students (Kugler & Janshen, 2010), and therefore may be of interest to coaches.

Upon touchdown in the initial steps, athletes generally have to 'wait' for the centre of mass to rotate forward of the point of contact prior to extending the contact leg (Jacobs & van Ingen Schenau, 1992). Foot placement closer to or behind the centre of mass then, upon touchdown seems appealing since it would likely reduce the amount of time the athlete waits before producing leg extension, resulting in decreased contact time. It may also facilitate a more forward oriented shank angle (proximal end of the shank more rotated toward direction of travel) during the initial acceleration phase which, in tandem with a similar trunk angle is a technique deemed desirable by coaches (Goodwin, Tawiah-Dodoo, Waghorn, & Wild, 2018). Producing this technique will enable an athlete to direct their leg extension force more horizontally (relative to the earth's surface).

This suggestion is supported by the observations of Kugler and Janshen (2010) who noted that the higher propulsive impulses and greater centre of mass angles produced later in the stance phase by faster runners were facilitated by a greater centre of mass angle at touchdown (i.e. the foot was placed further back in relation to the centre of mass).

and others associated with them, braking, it seems, will always be present even from the very first step.

Touchdown distance has also previously been linked to the orientation of the ground reaction force vector during the first step

Despite touchdown distance appearing to be of significance to sprint performance, it is not currently clear whether it is an important feature. For example, in the early steps of acceleration, touchdown distance was found to separate sprinters and rugby players

(Wild, Bezodis, North, & Bezodis, 2018). That is, sprinters touched down with their foot more posterior relative to their centre of mass compared with rugby backs, who in turn produced a more posterior foot position compared with (slower) rugby backs. However, touchdown distance was not meaningfully related to initial acceleration performance of professional rugby players and sprinters (Wild, Bezodis, North, & Bezodis, 2018). This may be explained by an optimal touchdown distance that may apply to each individual.

For example, although placing the foot further back in relation to an athlete's centre of mass may reduce braking impulses, placement of the foot too far behind the centre of mass during acceleration may position the leg in a less favourable position for producing force (Bezodis, Salo, & Trewartha, 2009).

In addition, it may not necessarily be favourable for the foot to make contact immediately underneath the centre of mass during maximum velocity, since some of the world's top sprinters who consistently run the 100 m in less than 10 s demonstrate touchdown distances of 0.31 m (Ito, Fukuda, & Kijima, 2008), which is comparable to touchdown distances of other sprinters at maximum velocity sprint running who run the 100 m in 11 s (Fuduka & Ito, 2004).

Therefore, bringing the foot back in relation to the CM during maximum velocity may be beneficial up to a certain point, and placing the foot any further back may be detrimental to sprint performance. Nonetheless, striking the foot too far in front of the centre of mass at the instant of touchdown is unfavourable, and research on elite sprinters has shown that

better sprinters tend to limit this touchdown distance (Alexander, 1989b; Deshon & Nelson, 1963; Mann & Herman, 1985; Mann, Kotmel, Herman, Johnson, & Schultz, 1984), advocating a foot-strike close to the centre of mass to reduce the decelerating effects during early stance.

Whilst this may not directly affect performance in the initial steps, it may be necessary in the later stages of acceleration where attenuating braking force has been shown to relate to better sprinting performance (Colyer et al., 2018). Since contact times are related to higher maximum velocities (Weyand, Sternlight, Bellizzi, & Wright, 2000; Weyand, Sandell, Prime, & Bundle, 2010), touching down with the foot close to the centre of mass during this phase may be of benefit since it will likely reduce the distance the centre of mass passes beyond the point of contact.

At toe-off, the horizontal distance between the centre of mass and the stance foot has also been deemed important to acceleration performance previously, and results in the forward lean which characterises the acceleration phase (Figure 2.10). Having the stance toe further behind the centre of mass at toe-off was associated with increased horizontal power in professional rugby backs and forward, as well as sprint athletes (Wild et al. (2018). Therefore, this technical feature appeared to be reflective of an effective push-off.

A centre of mass further forward relative to the point of contact at toe-off during the first step has previously been associated with higher propulsive impulse (Kugler & Janshen,

2010). In the Wild et al. (2018) study, sprinters produced longer contact times relative to rugby backs and may have used this to achieve a greater toe-off distance as a result. A similar finding was observed in Kugler & Janshen (2010) with physical education students in the first step.

Start position (crouched in blocks vs standing) and footwear (spikes vs trainers) may play roles in the ability to achieve such a forward lean position; performer constraints may also be an important consideration.

For example, Lee and Piazza (2009) demonstrated that the longer toes of sprinters—compared with non-sprinters—prolonged the time of contact during a 'push-off', giving greater time for forward acceleration by producing greater propulsive forces. Whilst toe-off distance hasn't been investigated to the same extent as in acceleration, a large toe off distance (i.e. foot far behind the centre of mass at toe-off) is not thought to be a desirable technique since it will likely increase contact time and facilitate a cyclical leg action more posterior relative to the centre of mass during the swing phase.

Together, touchdown and toe-off distance combine to produce a given contact length (horizontal distance the centre of mass travels during the stance phase). Whilst the literature to date has not shown in isolation whether contact length is important for sprinting performance, there is likely to be a trade-off between achieving enough contact length during acceleration so that time can be spent accruing horizontal impulse, yet not so much that the contact time becomes so long that it negatively affects acceleration performance.

During maximum velocity sprinting, speed will be closely approximated to the distance the centre of mass covers during ground contact and the time of the contact phase (i.e. distance divided by time = velocity). However, given the advantage of being airborne rather than on the ground during this phase due to the lack of opportunity to accelerate, a contact length which is too long will increase contact time to a point that is detrimental for performance.

Touchdown Velocity and Angular Kinematics

Touchdown

The use of a highly 'active' touchdown by minimising the forward horizontal velocity of the foot immediately before contact (foot touchdown velocity; Hay, 1994; Mann & Sprague, 1983) has previously been purported to be a factor which affects braking force magnitude (Mann, R. & Sprague, 1983; Mann, Ralph & Herman, 1985; Putnam & Kozey, 1989). However, few researchers have explored this variable during the initial steps of acceleration.

During the first post-block step, Bezodis, Salo and Trewartha (2014) observed foot touchdown velocity to increase concurrently with maximum braking force magnitude in the three athletes in their study. In another study aiming to quantify the magnitude of braking impulse of ten male sprinters produced by accelerations at the foot-floor interface, showed foot touchdown velocity at the third step of maximal sprinting to be

0.57 ± 0.91 m/s, generating 143 ± 72% of the total relative braking impulse (von Lieres und Wilkau, H, Irwin, Bezodis, Simpson, & Bezodis, 2017).

Whilst foot touchdown velocity may be related to braking horizontal ground reaction force, its correlation to the net horizontal ground reaction force is not clear.

For example, Morin and colleagues (2015) found backward horizontal velocity (5.27 ± 0.77 m/s) of the foot just before foot-ground initial contact relative to the ipsilateral greater trochanter was not related to the net horizontal ground reaction forces of 14 males familiar with sprint running during 6-s sprints on an instrumented motorised treadmill. They suggested that the efficacy of a common desired technical outcome to 'paw back' the foot just prior to ground contact with the aim of generating a greater backward pushing action—i.e. a higher horizontal ground reaction forces—during ground contact, is therefore in question.

Moreover, in Wild et al. (2021), the horizontal foot touchdown velocities were not meaningfully related to the sprinting performance of professional rugby players during the initial steps.

Although the research doesn't seem to support attenuating horizontal foot touchdown velocity as being important during acceleration, there does appear to be substantial support for increasing the vertical foot touchdown velocity (i.e. maximising the downward velocity of the foot into the ground) during the maximum velocity phase (Clark, K., Ryan, & Weyand, 2017).

As discussed earlier in this chapter, faster athletes have been observed to achieve higher vertical ground reaction forces relative to their body mass earlier in the stance phase. The sharp rise in vertical force upon ground impact has been associated with faster vertical velocities of the lower limb at touchdown in combination with a rapid deceleration of the lower limb during initial ground contact (Clark, K., Meng, & Stearne, 2020; Clark, Kenneth P. & Weyand, 2014).

At touchdown, the orientation of segments has received some interest within research (e.g. Wild et al. 2011; 2018; 2021) and the wider literature (e.g. Goodwin et al., 2018; Mann & Murphy, 2015). Generally speaking, during acceleration, the foot, shank, thigh and trunk segments that are more oriented to the direction of travel (i.e. their distal ends are rotated more forward) are thought to be beneficial, since they prime an athlete at the beginning of the stance phase in a position to 'push' forward.

Note in Figure 2.10 how the lower limb and trunk segments are oriented in the direction of travel. A smooth and efficient acceleration phase is thought to be demonstrated, in part, by shank and trunk angles becoming progressively more vertical with each step. However, when the associations of these angular measurements with acceleration performance are determined, no meaningful relationships are often found (e.g. Wild et al. 2021).

During the maximum velocity phase, a vertical shin upon touchdown is thought to be a sign of effectively directing force vertically at the onset of the stance phase, although, again, it is not currently clear whether meaningful relationships exist during different athlete groups.

Toe-off

Efficient leg recovery is typically characterised by rapid knee and hip flexion into a 'high knee' position (of the same leg) before the subsequent downward movement of the leg into the next foot contact. In acceleration, to achieve large toe-off distances and produce large propulsive forces, athletes will typically achieve large amounts of leg extension at toe-off.

In the most proficient sprinters, the termination of ground contact takes place prior to the leg reaching full extension, where the knee joint is slightly flexed just prior to toe-off as shown during the toe-off positions in Figures 2.10 and 2.11 (Jacobs & Ingen Schenau, 1992; Johnson & Buckley, 2001; Mann, Kotmel, Herman, Johnson, & Schultz, 1984; Mann & Herman, 1985). This action aids the recovery of the leg immediately following toe-off, helping to make the recovery as efficient as possible by contributing to the speed at which the knee of the recovery leg is brought forward.

Thigh Angular Motion

Large angular velocities of the thigh have been shown to be important for maximum velocity performance, particularly as the thighs cross each other during the step cycle.

For instance, Clark et al. (2020) observed thigh angular velocity to be related to greater lower limb vertical velocity at touchdown which, as discussed earlier, is deemed an important factor for generating large vertical forces required during maximum velocity. Clark et al. (2020) obtained linear and angular kinematic data between 31 m and 39 m and found—among the athlete participants—that measures of thigh angular velocity demonstrated a strong positive linear correlation to running speed and also lower limb vertical velocity at touchdown.

Knee Flexion Angles During Swing

Coaches often advise that the heel of the toe-off leg should be 'recovered' up toward the gluteal musculature as the hip of the same leg flexes (Bosch & Klomp, 2005; Deshon & Nelson, 1963; Fenn, 1930), and that a smaller peak knee flexion angle may be related to faster sprint velocity (Ito, Fukuda, & Kijima, 2008) by reducing moments of inertia about the hip joint, thus allowing a faster rotation of the thigh segment. This does appear to be beneficial during maximal velocity sprinting, where athletes have been shown to achieve a peak knee flexion angle of approximately 40° (Mann & Herman, 1985; Ito, Fukuda, & Kijima, 2008).

In Figure 2.11b—during maximum velocity—the athlete achieves a small knee flexion angle of the recovery leg. If the recovery leg is slow to swing forward, then effectively the leading leg must 'wait' for this trailing leg to catch up, likely resulting in a greater anterior hip angle of the recovery leg when the knee reaches peak flexion.

However, during the early stages of acceleration, it is often deemed by coaches as necessary to keep the heel of the recovery leg low to the ground and in a more direct and forward motion in the early stages of acceleration; a more 'piston' like action, as opposed to a cyclical action more akin to the maximum velocity phase.

This can be seen in Figure 2.10b where at the point of ankle cross—where the ankle of the swing leg crosses the stance leg—the recovery foot starts lower compared with the maximum velocity phase and gradually increases in height with each step. This may also provide a strategy for athletes to spend more time producing horizontal forces in the stance phase and maximize horizontal velocity during acceleration.

Peak Hip Angle

Following the swing through of the recovery leg, a 'high knee' position—approximately 90°; Figures 2.10 and 2.11; Mann, Kotmel, Herman, Johnson, & Schultz, 1984—facilitates the subsequent downward velocity toward the ground to produce an active foot-strike.

It is feasible that Newton's third angular analogue may be influential to knee height in this situation. That is, the torque created by the hip of the contact leg rotating forward into and during ground contact may determine the torque of the opposite leg and the extent to which it rotates backward (i.e. knee lift). Increasing hip power through strength training may therefore be of importance to achieving a high knee position.

Spatiotemporal Variables

Contact Time

During the acceleration phase, ground contact times typically range between 0.12 s and 0.20 s with the early and late stages of acceleration at the higher and lower end of this range, respectively. During acceleration, contact time is highly related to contact length (Wild et al., 2021) and thus a longer contact time will nearly always result in longer contact lengths. This may be beneficial if a longer step length is being sought and while longer ground contact times clearly allow an athlete more time to produce force—leading to greater impulse production—the ultimate aim of any sprint is to cover a specific horizontal distance in the shortest time possible, and so it may not be favourable to achieve increases in impulse through simply increasing contact time.

Therefore, it may be possible that an optimal contact time exists during acceleration: one which is sufficiently long to allow athletes to produce large horizontal forces, without being so long that overall sprint time is sacrificed, or that the leg is extended beyond the point during which large forces can be produced (Bezodis, Salo, & Trewartha, 2009). Nevertheless, a contact time of greater than 0.20 s during early acceleration, to 0.12 s toward the end of the acceleration phase, is not favourable.

Regarding the maximum velocity phase, there is a large amount of research which demonstrates that shorter contact times are linked to better sprint performance (e.g. Weyand, Sternlight, Bellizzi, & Wright, 2000; Mann & Herman, 1985) and have typically been found to range between 0.09 s and 0.12 s (Figure 3.5).

Smaller ground contact times, however, allow less time to apply force during stance for impulse generation and so a change in an athlete's velocity. The mechanisms responsible for increasing the amount of force produced during these shorter ground contact times are therefore important to sprinting performance. This raises some important issues when selecting sprint specific strength exercises (e.g. consideration of the contact times during different plyometric exercises).

Flight Time

Flight time is typically a function of take-off velocity angle and the horizontal sprinting velocity of the athlete. Spending too long in the air during the early phases of acceleration mean it is not going to be possible to accrue horizontal impulse to accelerate the athlete's centre of mass in the forward direction.

However, enough flight time is needed to enable an athlete to recycle their limb ready for the next step. It has been theorised that, in acceleration, a favourable flight time is one which is just long enough for repositioning of the lower limbs and that if an athlete can reposition their limbs more quickly, then a lower relative vertical impulse is sufficient, and all other 'strength reserves' should be applied horizontally (Hunter et al., 2005). As contact times decrease, flight times increase with each step and as already discussed, being airborne is typically more beneficial during the maximum velocity phase compared to the early acceleration phase.

Step Length and Step Frequency

Step length is the combination of an athlete's contact and flight lengths—i.e. the horizontal distance between consecutive ground contacts—whereas step frequency is the combination of an athlete's contact and flight times (i.e. how quickly do they complete their steps).

An athlete's running velocity is a product of their step length and step frequency and historically there has been much debate as to which variable is more important to sprint performance. It is currently not clear within the research whether one is more important than the other for sprinting performance. This is because the majority of research focusses on cross-sectional group-based studies and whilst it is possible for comparable performance to be reached across a group with slightly different sprinting actions, it is unlikely that a general consensus will be found.

Therefore, it is recommended that practitioners ought to consider longitudinally monitoring the step length and step frequencies of their athletes—and other variables of interest—individually to see how they correspond with changes in the athlete's performance.

In a study by Bezodis and colleagues over the course of five months, four elite sprinters were shown to achieve greater maximum velocities during the maximum velocity phase, when step frequency, but not step length, was higher during training (Bezodis, Kerwin, Cooper, & Salo, 2018). However, it has been shown that athletes are individually more reliant on either step length or step frequency (Salo, Bezodis, Batterham, & Kerwin, 2011). That is, individual performance is best when one of these values is high compared to the other.

Additionally, Wild et al. (2021) demonstrated that professional rugby union backs were reliant on either step length or step frequency for better initial sprint acceleration performance, and that by applying a technically focused intervention on an individual's reliance in this sprint phase can lead to even better sprinting performance. These findings highlight value in determining how step length and step frequency individually associate with sprinting performance and suggest that intentionally attempting to enhance, or, at least, prevent a negative effect on, the variable athletes are individually reliant on for better sprinting performance is important.

Establishing whether an athlete is step length or step frequency reliant involves the use of biomechanical equipment, and although some additional information on this is included within the next section in this, a detailed explanation of how to do this is outside the scope of this book. If identified, however (some coaches are able to do this without equipment) strength training should be individualised during specific training periods to enhance one of these variables more so than the other depending on which one the athlete is more reliant upon. *More information of planning strength sessions can be found in the Section 4.*

Conclusion

Knowledge of sprinting biomechanics is useful to inform strength training practices aimed at increasing an athlete's ability to sprint faster. The ground contact portion of the sprint would appear to be the most important phase of sprinting since ground reaction forces determine an athlete's velocity, and the swing phase has been identified as being provided by passive mechanisms of energy transfer rather than muscular power.

That said, the importance of the swing phase should not be discounted altogether and ultimately what happens during the swing phase will affect the ground contact phase, and vice versa. Although ground contact times change (decrease) as a sprint progresses, achieving high levels of force during short ground contact times across all sprint phases appears to be critical to sprint performance.

In addition to the magnitude of force production, the direction in which it is applied—relative to the earth's surface—during the different sprint phases should be considered, where horizontal impulse and vertical impulse seem to be more important to acceleration and maximum velocity respectively.

However, strength training methods should not attempt to mimic these directional differences at the sacrifice of overload since muscle actions do not change. Regardless of the body's orientation, the lower limb muscles will still pull on its end to rotate body segments to produce, for example, a generalised triple extension pattern.

Body orientation and differing joint angles do, however, affect the contribution of the muscles surrounding the lower limb joints to express fast segment rotations and force production, which differ depending on the joint and the sprint phase. With the exception of the activity at the hip, there is a shift in emphasis from power generating (net concentric contraction) to power dissipating (net eccentric contraction) muscular activity as a sprint progresses. Eccentric work and the effects of the SSC may therefore become increasingly important during mid-late acceleration and maximum velocity sprinting due to the larger peak vertical and horizontal braking forces experienced, whereas concentric power may be more important to the early acceleration phase.

Finally, a number of key technical markers are evident during the recovery phases of a sprint, which improves sprinting efficiency. However, it ought to be recognized that technique will differ between individuals and that unlocking what appears to be most favourable for each individual is something a coach and athlete ought to navigate together.

References

Alexander, M. (1989b). The relationship between muscle strength, sprinting kinematics and sprinting speed in elite sprinters. *Track and Field Journal, 5,* 7–12.

Baumann W. (1976). Kinematic and dynamic characteristics of the sprint start. In: Komi PV, editor. Biomech V-B. Baltimore: University Park Press; pp. 194–9.

Bezodis, I., Kerwin, D., & Salo, A. (2008). Lower-limb mechanics during the support phase of maximum-velocity sprint running. *Medicine and Science in Sports and Exercise, 40,* 707–715.

Bezodis, I., Kerwin, D., Cooper, S., & Salo, A. (2018). Sprint running performance and technique changes in athletes during periodized training: An elite training group case study. *International Journal of Sports Physiology and Performance, 13*(6), 755–762.

Bezodis, N., Salo, A., & Trewartha, G. (2009). Development, evaluation and application of a simulation model of a sprinter during the first stance. In A. J. Harrison, R. Anderson, & I. Kenny (Ed.), *In Proceedings of XXVII International Symposium on Biomechanics in Sports* (pp. 108–111). Limerick: University of Limerick Press.

Bezodis, N., Salo, A., & Trewartha, G. (2014). Lower limb joint kinetics during the first stance phase in athletics sprinting: Three elite athlete case studies. *Journal of Sports Sciences, 32*(8), 738–746.

Bhowmick, S., & Battacharyya, A. (1988). Kinematic analysis of arm movements in sprint start. *Journal of Sports Medicine and Physical FItness, 28,* 315–323.

Charalambous, L., Irwin, G., Bezodis, I., & Kerwin, D. (2012). Lower limb joint kinetics and ankle joint stiffness in the sprint start push-off. *Journal of Sports Sciences, 30*(1), 1–9.

Clark, K. P., & Weyand, P. G. (2014). Are running speeds maximized with simple-spring stance mechanics? *Journal of Applied Physiology (Bethesda, Md.: 1985), 117*(6), 604.

Clark, K., Meng, C., & Stearne, D. (2020). 'Whip from the hip': Thigh angular motion, ground contact mechanics, and running speed. *Biology Open, 9*(10).

Colyer, S., Nagahara, R., & Salo, A. (2018). Kinetic demands of sprinting shift across the acceleration phase: Novel analysis of entire force waveforms. *Scandinavian Journal of Medicine & Science in Sports, 28*(7), 1784–1792. doi:10.1111/sms.13093

Colyer, S., Nagahara, R., Takai, Y., & Salo, A. (2018). How sprinters accelerate beyond the velocity plateau of soccer players: Waveform analysis of ground reaction forces. *Scandinavian Journal of Medicine & Science in Sports, 28*(12), 2527–2535.

Cronin, J., Green, J., Levin, G., Brughelli, M., & Frost, D. (2007). Effect of starting stance on initial sprint performance. *Journal of Strength and Conditioning Research, 21*(3), 990.

Debaere, S., Vanwanseele, B., Delecluse, C., Aerenhouts, D., Hagman, F., & Jonkers, I. (2017). Joint power generation differentiates young and adult sprinters during the transition from block start into acceleration: A cross-sectional study. *Sports Biomechanics, 16*(4), 452–462.

Debaere, S., Delecluse, C., Aerenhouts, D., Hagman, F., & Jonkers, I. (2013). From block clearance to sprint running: Characteristics underlying an effective transition. *Journal of Sports Sciences, 31*(2), 137–149.

Debaere, S., Delecluse, C., Aerenhouts, D., Hagman, F., & Jonkers, I. (2015). Control of propulsion and body lift during the first two stances of sprint running: A simulation study. *Journal of Sports Sciences, 33*(19), 2016–2024.

Dorn, T. W., Schache, A. G., & Pandy, M. G. (2012). Muscular strategy shift in human running: Dependence of running speed on hip and ankle muscle performance. *The Journal of Experimental Biology, 215*(Pt 11), 1944–1956.

Deshon, D. E., & Nelson, R. C. (1963). A cinematographical analysis of sprint running. *Research Quarterly, 35*(4), 451–455.

Di Salvo, V., Baron, R., González-Haro, C., Gormasz, C., Pigozzi, F., & Bachl, N. (2010). Sprinting analysis of elite soccer players during European Champions League and UEFA cup matches. *Journal of Sports Sciences, 28*(14), 1489–1494.

Duthie, G., Pyne, D., Marsh, D., & Hooper, S. (2006). Sprint patterns in rugby union players during competition. *Journal of Strength and Conditioning Research, 20*(1), 208–214.

Fenn, W. O. (1930). Work against gravity and work due to velocity changes in running. *American Journal of Physiology, 93*, 433–462.

Frost, D., & Cronin, J. (2011). Stepping back to improve sprint performance: A kinetic analysis of the first step forward. *Journal of Strength and Conditioning Research, 25*(10), 2721–2728.

Fuduka, K., & Ito, A. (2004). Relationship between sprint running velocity and changes in the horizontal velocity of the body's center of gravity during the foot contact phase. *Japanese Journal of Physical Education, 49*, 29–39.

Gabbett, T. (2012). Sprinting patterns of national rugby league competition. *Journal of Strength and Conditioning Research, 26*(1), 121–130.

Goodwin, J., Tawiah-Dodoo, J., Waghorn, R., & Wild, J. (2018). Sprint running. In A. Turner (Ed.), *Routledge handbook of strength and conditioning* (pp. 473–505). London and New York: Routledge.

Hinrichs, R. (1987). Upper extremity function in running. II: angular momentum considerations. *International Journal of Sports Biomechanics, 3,* 242–263.

Hinrichs, R., Cavanagh, P., & Williams, K. (1987). Upper extremity function in running. I center of mass propulsion considerations. *International Journal of Sports Biomechanics, 3,* 222–241.

Hirvonen, J., Nummela, A., Rusko, H., Rehunen, S., & Härkönen, M. (1992). Fatigue and changes of ATP, creatine phosphate, and lactate during the 400-m sprint. *Canadian Journal of Sports Sciences, 17,* 141–144.

Hunter, J. P., Marshall, R. N., & McNair, P. J. (2004). Segment-interaction analysis of the stance limb in sprint running. *Journal of Biomechanics,* 1439–1446.

Hunter, J. P., Marshall, R. N., & McNair, P. J. (2005). Relationships between ground reaction force impulse and kinematics of sprint-running acceleration. *Journal of Applied Biomechanics, 21,* 31–43.

Hunter, J., Marshall, R., & McNair, P. (2004a). Reliability of biomechanical variables of sprint running. *Medicine & Science in Sport & Exercise, 36,* 850–861.

Ito, A., Fukuda, K., & Kijima, K. (2008). Mid-phase movements of Tyson Gay and Asafa Powell in the 100 metres at the 2007 World Championships in Athletics. *IAAF Nee Studies in Athletics, 23,* 39–43.

Jacobs, R., & Ingen Schenau, G. (1992). Intermuscular coordination in a sprint push-off. *Journal of Biomechanics, 25*(9), 953–965.

Johnson, M. D., & Buckley, J. G. (2001). Muscle power patterns in the mid-acceleration phase of sprinting. *Journal of Sports Sciences, 19,* 263–272.

Kawamori, N., Nosaka, K., & Newton, R. U. (2013). Relationships between ground reaction impulse and sprint acceleration performance in team sport athletes. *Journal of Strength and Conditioning Research, 27*(3), 568.

Kugler, F., & Janshen, L. (2010). Body position determines propulsive forces in accelerated sprinting. *Journal of Biomechanics, 43,* 343–348.

Lee, S. S. M., & Piazza, S. J. (2009). Built for speed: Musculoskeletal structure and sprinting ability. *Journal of Experimental Biology, 212*(22), 3700–3707.

Lockie, R., Murphy, A., Schultz, A., Jeffriess, M., & Callaghan, S. (2013). Influence of sprint acceleration stance kinetics on velocity and step kinematics in field sport athletes. *Journal of Strength and Conditioning Research; Journal of Strength and Conditioning Research, 27*(9), 2494–2503.

Luhtanen, P., & Komi, P. (1980). Force-, power-, and elasticity-velocity relationships in walking, running and jumping. *European Journal of Applied Physiology, 44,* 279–289.

Mann, R. (1981). A kinetic analysis of sprinting. *Medicine and Science in Sports and Exercise, 13,* 325–328.

Mann, R., & Herman, J. (1985). Kinematic analysis of Olympic sprint performance: men's 200 meters. *International Journal of Sport Biomechanics, 1,* 151–162.

Mann, R., & Sprague, P. (1980). A kinetic analysis of the ground leg during sprint running. *Research Quarterly for Exercise and Sport, 51*, 334–348.

Mann, R., Kotmel, J., Herman, J., Johnson, B., & Schultz, C. (1984). Kinematic trends in elite sprinters. In J. Terauds, K. Barthels, E. Kreighbaum, R. Mann, & J. Crake (Ed.), *Proceedings of International Symposium on Biomechanics in Sports* (pp. 17–33). Del Mar: Academic Publishers.

Mero, A., & Komi, P. (1992). Biomechanics of sprint running: a review. *Sports Medicine, 13*, 376–392.

Mero, A., & Komi, P. (1994). EMG, force, and power analysis of sprint-specific strength exercises. *Journal of Applied Biomechanics, 10*, 1–13.

Mero, A., Luhtanen, P., & Komi, P. (1983). A biomechanical study of the sprint start. *Scandinavian Journal of Sports Sciences, 5*, 20–28.

Morin, J., Bourdin, M., Edouard, P., Peyrot, N., Samozino, P., & Lacour, J. R. (2012). Mechanical determinants of 100-m sprint running performance. *European Journal of Applied Physiology, 112*(11), 3921–3930.

Morin, J., Gimenez, P., Edouard, P., Arnal, P., Jimenez-Reyes, P., Samozino, P., & Mendiguchia, J. (2015). Sprint acceleration mechanics: The major role of hamstrings in horizontal force production. *Frontiers in Physiology, 24*.

Morin, J., Slawinski, J., Dorel, S., de Villareal, E. S., Couturier, A., Samozino, P., & Rabita, G. (2015). Acceleration capability in elite sprinters and ground impulse: Push more, brake less? *Journal of Biomechanics, 48*(12), 3149–3154.

Murphy, A., Lockie, R., & Coutts, A. (2003). Kinematic determinants of early acceleration in field sport athletes. *Journal of Sports Science and Medicine, 2*, 144–150.

Nagahara, R., Mizutani, M., Matsuo, A., Kanehisa, H., & Fukunaga, T. (2018). Association of sprint performance with ground reaction forces during acceleration and maximal speed phases in a single sprint. *Journal of Applied Biomechanics, 34*(2), 1–110.

Payne, A., Slater, W., & Telford, T. (1968). The use of a platform in the study of athletic activities. *A preliminary investigation. Ergonomics, 2*, 123–143.

Rabita, G., Dorel, S., Slawinski, J., Saez-de-Villarreal, E., Couturier, A., Samozino, P., & Morin, J. B. (2015). Sprint mechanics in world-class athletes: A new insight into the limits of human locomotion. *Scandinavian Journal of Medicine & Science in Sports, 25*(5), 583–594.

Ross, A., Leveritt, M., & Riek, S. (2001). Neural influences on sprint running: training adaptations and acute responses. *Sports Medicine, 31*, 409–425.

Salo, A., Bezodis, I., Batterham, A., & Kerwin, D. (2011). Elite sprinting: are athletes individually step-frequency or step-length reliant? *Medicine & Science in Sport & Exercise, 43*, 1055–1062.

Salo, A., Keranen, T., & Viitasalo, J. (2005). Force production in the first four steps of sprint running. In Q. Wang (Ed.), *XXIII International Symposium on Biomechanics on Sport* (pp. 313–317). Beijing: The China Institute of Sports Science.

Samozino, P., Rabita, G., Dorel, S., Slawinski, J., Peyrot, N., Saez de Villarreal, E., & Morin, J. B.

(2016). A simple method for measuring power, force, velocity properties, and mechanical effectiveness in sprint running. *Scandinavian Journal of Medicine & Science in Sports, 26*(6), 648–658.

Schache, A., Lai, A., Brown, N., Crossley, K., & Pandy, M. (2019). Lower-limb joint mechanics during maximum acceleration sprinting. *Journal of Experimental Biology, 222*, jeb209460

Slawinski, J., Bonnefoy, A., Ontanon, G., Leveque, J. M., Miller, C., Riquet, A., et al. (2010). Segment-interaction in sprint start: analysis of 3D angular velocity and kinetic energy in elite sprinters. *Journal of Biomechanics, 43*, 1494–502.

Weyand, P., Sandell, R., Prime, D., & Bundle, M. (2010). The biological limits to running speed are imposed from the ground up. *Journal of Applied Physiology, 108*, 950–961.

Weyand, P., Sternlight, P., Bellizzi, M., & Wright, S. (2000). Faster top running speeds are achieved with greater forces not more rapid leg movements. *Journal of Applied Physiology, 89*, 1991–1999.

Veloso, A., Joao, F., Valamatos, M., Cabral, S., & Moniz-Pereira, V. (2015). Subject-specific musculoskeletal model to identify muscle contribution to the acceleration phase in elite sprinting. Paper presented at the 33rd International Conference on Biomechanics in Sport, Poitiers, France.

von Lieres Und Wilkau, H, Bezodis, N., Morin, J. B., Irwin, G., Simpson, S., & Bezodis, I. (2020). The importance of duration and magnitude of force application to sprint performance during the initial acceleration, transition and maximal velocity phases. *Journal of Sports Sciences, 38*(20), 2359–2366.

Wdowski, M., & Gittoes, M. (2020). First-stance phase force contributions to acceleration sprint performance in semi-professional soccer players. *European Journal of Sport Science, 20*(3), 366–374.

Wild, J. J., Bezodis, I. N., North, J. S., & Bezodis, N. E. (2018). Differences in step characteristics and linear kinematics between rugby players and sprinters during initial sprint acceleration. *European Journal of Sport Science, 18*(10), 1327–1337.

Wild, J., Bezodis, I., North, J., & Bezodis, N. (2021). Biomechanics and motor control during initial acceleration: A framework to enhance the short sprint distance performances of professional rugby union backs. *Unpublished PhD Thesis.*

Wood, G. (1987). Biomechanical limitations to sprint running. In B. van Gheluwe, & J. Atha (Ed.), *Medicine and Sports Science, 25*, pp. 58–71. Basel: Karger: Current Research in Sports Biomechanics.

Associations of Strength Qualities with Speed

I n Sections 1 and 2, we discussed the importance of ground reaction force impulse in the context of high sprint performance. The lower limb muscles along with the actions of gravity and inertia generate these impulses, but it is the contribution from the muscles which is the highest amongst these different contributory features. We can infer about muscle contribution to sprinting performance from the joint kinetic information derived from studies discussed in Section 2.

However, from this information alone, we are not able to confirm what the functional roles of individual muscles are during sprinting with assurance—although through musculoskeletal modelling research we are developing a better understanding—and this will be covered in this section first. This information is clearly of interest in the context of strength program design, since we can target the development of specific strength qualities within specific muscles in a way which is compatible with their functional role during sprinting.

Further insight can be gleaned from investigations which have determined relationships between strength qualities assessed during the testing of athletes and sprinting performance. This will also be explored within this section and, whilst correlation does not equal causation, the coach can be more informed about their strength program design with an understanding of these relationships in conjunction with greater knowledge of the functional role of individual muscles during sprinting.

An additional area discussed in this section, which is currently not well known, is how different strength qualities relate to different technical features adopted by athletes during sprinting. Given that athlete's movement preferences are in part shaped by their physical characteristics, a better understanding of this may help program design to facilitate changes being sought in an athlete's technique.

Functional Role of Muscles During Sprinting

Initial Investigations

To better understand the function of the hip extensor muscles of athletes during sprint acceleration, Morin and colleagues (2015) measured hip and knee joint torques using isokinetic dynamometry and, during maximum effort sprinting over 6 s on an instrumented treadmill, they obtained the horizontal ground forces and electromyographic (EMG) activity for select lower-limb muscles. Isokinetic dynamometry is used to assess the muscular forces produced at constant velocity limb movements, whereas EMG assessment is used to measure the electrical activity produced by muscles. This provides us with an understanding of the extent to which a muscle is 'activated' (the higher the EMG reading, the higher the muscle activation), although not necessarily how much force it is producing.

The authors found a significant multiple relationship between higher propulsive horizontal ground reaction forces and the combination of biceps femoris muscle activity during the late swing phase and knee flexor (hamstring) eccentric peak torque during isokinetic testing. This implies that the hamstring muscles are important for acceleration performance. However, meaningful relationships were not found between biceps femoris muscle activity during late swing in isolation and propulsive ground reaction force magnitude (Morin et al., 2015). Nor was a meaningful relationship observed between knee flexor eccentric torque in isolation and propulsive ground reaction force magnitude. They concluded that the athletes who were able to highly activate their hamstring muscles just before ground contact and who also demonstrated high levels of eccentric hamstring strength were able to produce higher propulsive forces during 6-s sprints.

When considering the initial steps only of the sprint, the authors revealed similar findings with gluteal muscles and performance over just the initial acceleration phase (Morin et al., 2015). For example, in a subanalysis of the initial acceleration phase (first ten steps), a significant relationship was found between horizontal ground reaction force production and the combination of gluteal concentric hip extension torque capability measured during isokinetic testing and gluteus maximus EMG activity during the late swing phase (Morin et al., 2015).

EMG research has been conducted by other studies in an attempt to provide information about the function of select individual muscles during sprinting. For example, one study reported that the gluteus maximus acted to actively extend the hip joint and control trunk flexion during the stance phase of sprinting (Bartlett, Sumner, Ellis, & Kram, 2014). This information is of interest, but it doesn't provide much of an insight into how muscle function influences the external kinetics of sprinting and ultimately sprinting performance.

Muscle Forces During Sprinting

Perhaps the most comprehensive investigation to explore the role of individual muscles during sprinting was the work of Pandy and colleagues (2021). To provide a better understanding of this area, they combined computational modelling of the musculoskeletal system with experimental data to determine the forces developed by individual lower limb muscles and how they contributed to the ground reaction force characteristics during the stance phase of maximal sprinting over 19 consecutive ground contacts.

The noteworthy results from their investigation showed that the gluteus maximus developed its peak force during the early portion of the stance phase across all steps, whereas the vasti muscle group and soleus muscle forces peaked near the midstance phase. The gastrocnemius and rectus femoris muscle forces then peaked during the second half of stance and the iliopsoas produced a large spike in force just prior to toe-off (Pandy, Lai, Schache, & Lin, 2021). The soleus produced the highest muscle force of all muscles (>8 times bodyweight) followed by the vasti group, which is logical if you consider that they need to act to support bodyweight and keep an athlete upright when sprinting.

Contribution of Individual Muscles to Joint Moments

The same study (Pandy et al., 2021) also showed how the individual muscles contribute to the net joint moments during the first 19 foot contacts. The gluteus maximus and hamstrings were the major contributors to the extensor moment produced at the hip joint during the first two thirds of the stance phase, while the iliopsoas and rectus femoris contributed to the majority of the hip flexion moment during the second half or final third of the stance phases investigated. The vasti group and rectus femoris were major contributors to the extensor moment produced at the knee joint, whereas the hamstrings and gastrocnemius applied relatively large knee flexor moments throughout the stance phase. At the ankle joint, the soleus and gastrocnemius combined to produce most of the plantar flexion moment developed, with the soleus being the biggest contributor of the two muscles (Pandy et al., 2021).

These findings can generally be inferred from the joint kinetic information discussed in Section 2, but provide useful information for coaches looking to enhance the sprinting capabilities of athletes since the individual muscles can be trained from a strength training standpoint in a way which is compatible with the power generation or power absorption emphases across the sprint.

Contribution of Individual Muscles to Ground Reaction Force Characteristics

Perhaps the most novel aspects of the study by Pandy and colleagues (2021), were the investigations into the contributions of individual muscles to the ground reaction force and impulse magnitudes. The gastrocnemius was shown to generate the highest propulsive force of any muscle during all foot contacts. The soleus also generated substantial propulsive force, but mainly during the first few steps of acceleration, beyond which it acted to induce a braking ground reaction force during the first half of the stance phase as sprinting velocity increased.

At the hip, the hamstrings generated peak propulsive forces during the first half of the stance phase for all foot contacts, whereas propulsion from the gluteus maximus was only present during the first half of the stance phase for steps 1 to 7. Interestingly, the gluteus medius generated greater propulsive forces than the gluteus maximus at all foot contacts.

The vasti and rectus femoris induced braking forces during the stance phases of all foot contacts, with the peak braking force applied by the vasti increasing with sprinting velocity (Pandy et al., 2021).

Regarding the vertical ground reaction forces produced, the vasti, soleus and gastrocnemius acted synergistically to generate support forces throughout the stance phase of all foot contacts. The biggest contribution to vertical support forces were from the soleus. Interestingly, the hamstrings and iliopsoas were shown to accelerate the body downward.

To summarise the main findings regarding the contribution of individual muscles to ground reaction force magnitudes (Pandy et al., 2021), the gastrocnemius contributes largely to propulsive forces and moderately to vertical support forces. The soleus contributes moderately to propulsion and largely to vertical support forces. The vasti contribute largely to braking and moderately to vertical support forces. The hamstrings contribute a reasonable amount to propulsive forces and a small amount of downward forces. The gluteus maximus and gluteus medius both contribute—albeit a relatively small amount—to propulsive forces, although the contribution of the latter muscle is greater.

The findings regarding muscle contributions to ground reaction force magnitudes logically transfer to their contributions to the impulses also produced. Pandy and colleagues (2021) discuss different functions of muscle according to their contributions to impulse production. For example, they cite the gastrocnemius, soleus, hamstrings and gluteal muscles as being 'accelerators'. The gastrocnemius and soleus are the major accelerators since they contribute the most to the propulsive impulse generated over all acceleration steps.

This is consistent with another study, where the ankle plantar flexors were shown to contribute the majority of the ground reaction force impulse generated during the first two steps of sprint when lower limb muscle forces were calculated after the block clearance of sprinters (Debaere, Delecluse, Aerenhouts, Hagman, & Jonkers, 2015). The hamstrings and gluteals tend to generate smaller propulsive impulses than the ankle plantar flexors during the first ten steps, but their contribution to propulsive forces seem to be more consistent in terms of their magnitude over all steps in acceleration (Pandy et al., 2021).

Pandy et al. (2021) refer to the vasti and rectus femoris muscles as functioning like 'brakes' since they induce braking impulses to attenuate forward momentum during each step. The researchers also refer to the soleus, gastrocnemius, vasti and rectus femoris as being 'supporters' since they contribute to vertical support impulse during each step. The major supporter was shown to be the soleus, contributing to 44% of the total vertical support impulse generated by all muscles over all steps (Pandy et al., 2021).

Understanding the individual roles of muscles during sprinting can assist the program design process in several ways. For example, in the context of altering sprinting technique, if a coach wants to increase the step length of an athlete, then it might be advisable to enhance the strength qualities of their soleus muscle since it contributes largely to vertical impulse (Pandy et al., 2021), and vertical impulse explains a large proportion of the variation in step length (Nagahara, Takai, Kanehisa, & Fukunaga, 2018). At the very least, the information on muscle function during sprinting provides an insight into how individual muscles can be conditioned through strength training methods to better prepare each muscle to withstand the specific stresses imposed on each muscle during sprinting.

Relationships Between Strength Qualities and Initial Sprint Acceleration Performance

Maximum Strength

Although there seems to be some differences in how the lower-limb moments and powers at the hip, knee and ankle relate to sprint performance across acceleration and maximum velocity (see Section 2), there is generally a shift in emphasis at the whole leg

level from power generation during the early stages of acceleration, to power absorption (dissipation) as the sprint progresses (Figure 3.1).

Accordingly, we can infer what strength qualities may be more relevant for the different phases of a sprint, which can help the design of strength programs for athletes where sprinting is important in their sport and where targeting performance in specific phases has been deemed necessary. Broadly, as a result of these joint kinetics, explosive strength qualities derived from a more net concentric muscle action appear to be more important in initial acceleration, whereas reactive strength and stiffness-like qualities and a net eccentric muscle action appear to be more important at maximum velocity.

The information which follows in this section will explore how strength qualities measure in a testing environment are related to phase specific sprint performance.

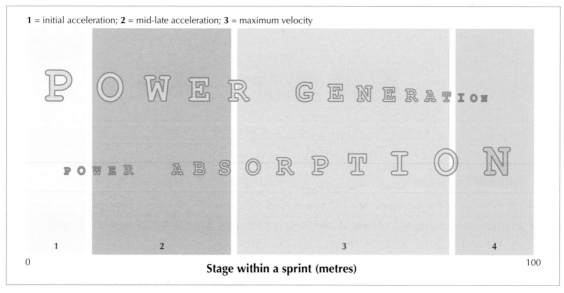

Figure 3.1. Joint kinetic emphasis according to the different phases of a sprint.

A number of studies investigating the relationships between maximum strength (isotonic muscle contraction) in the squat and initial sprint acceleration performance are shown in Figure 3.2. Broadly, the magnitude of relationships between maximum strength in the squat and initial sprint acceleration performance tend to be moderate to large although a number of findings were also trivial to small. Generally, maximum squat strength relative to body mass is more related to initial acceleration performance compared with absolute squat strength, which is logical given the necessity to produce large mass specific forces for high sprinting performance. There also seems to be a training age effect whereby a greater association is usually present between maximum squat strength and initial acceleration performance in those athletes, with a lower training age suggesting that the magnitude of relationships diminish somewhat as training age and maximum squat strength levels increase. This is discussed more in Section 4.

In Figure 3.3, several investigations which have sought to determine the relationships between maximum isometric strength and initial acceleration performance are shown. In isometric mid-thigh pull and isometric squat assessments, the magnitude of relationships between peak isometric force and initial acceleration performance are typically moderate, although they range from trivial to very large.

Although there are a relatively small number of studies, the difference in relationship magnitude between absolute and relative strength measures with initial acceleration

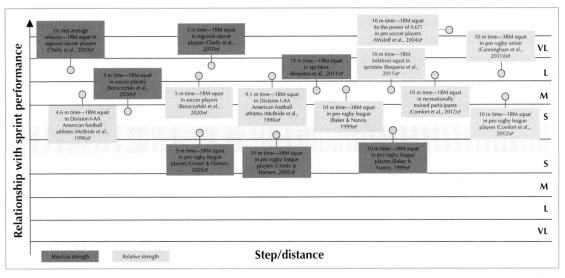

Figure 3.2. Relationships between maximum strength in a squat (isotonic muscle contraction) and initial sprint acceleration performance. Note that where the relationship magnitudes are higher than the horizontal line bisecting the shaded grey area, higher strength levels are evident with better sprinting performance and where relationship magnitudes are lower than this line, higher strength levels are evident with worse sprinting performance. Relationship magnitudes: S = small; M = moderate; L = large; VL = very large.

performance appears to be minimal. One study (Brady et al., 2019) showed there was a meaningful difference in the relationship magnitudes based on gender, whereby the strength of the associations between peak force and initial acceleration performance were lower in females generally. More research is needed to determine whether this is a consistent trend.

Relationship magnitudes between maximum strength measures and initial acceleration performance in other strength-based assessments can be found in Figure 3.4. This includes the theoretical force reached by the leg extensors during squat jump profiling (F0; Samozino et al., 2013), 1RM calf raise strength, isometric peak hip extensor torque and knee flexor and extensor concentric torque (during isokinetic dynamometry assessment). The relationship magnitudes observed in these

studies tend to be lower than those evident in Figures 3.1 to 3.3.

Again, relative strength in these measures seems to relate more to initial acceleration performance than absolute strength measures. Knee extensor, rather than flexor, concentric torque appears to be more related to initial acceleration also, which is logical given the necessity to 'push' during the initial steps.

Explosive Strength

Likely owing to the importance on the rate at which force is produced during sprinting, there are a greater number of studies which have investigated the relationships between explosive strength, rather than maximum strength, qualities and initial acceleration performance.

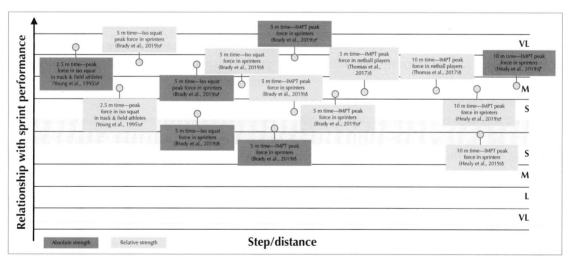

Figure 3.3. Relationships between maximum strength during an isometric mid-thigh pull (IMTP) and isometric squat (Iso squat) and initial sprint acceleration performance. Note that where the relationship magnitudes are higher than the horizontal line bisecting the shaded grey area, higher strength levels are evident with better sprinting performance and where relationship magnitudes are lower than this line, higher strength levels are evident with worse sprinting performance. Relationship magnitudes: S = small; M = moderate; L = large; VL = very large.

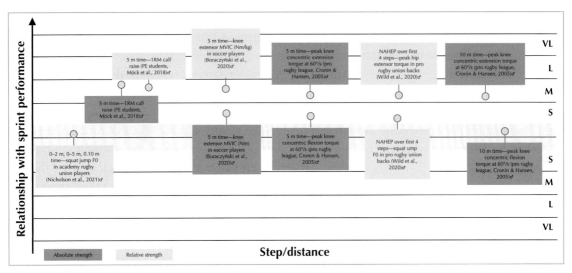

Figure 3.4. Relationships between a range of maximum strength measures and initial sprint acceleration performance. Note that where the relationship magnitudes are higher than the horizontal line bisecting the shaded grey area, higher strength levels are evident with better sprinting performance and where relationship magnitudes are lower than this line, higher strength levels are evident with worse sprinting performance. Relationship magnitudes: S = small; M = moderate; L = large; VL = very large.

Figure 3.5 shows the relationship magnitudes of squat and countermovement jump-based performances with initial acceleration performance. Generally, a higher proportion of large to very large relationship magnitudes are observed of explosive strength measures during jumps rather than maximum strength measures, with initial acceleration performance.

In Figure 3.6, relationship magnitudes between a range of explosive strength measures weightlifting performance (isometric RFD, isokinetic torques at high angular velocities) and initial sprint acceleration performance. Generally, the relationship magnitudes observed here are lower compared with those evident between jump-based performance measures and initial acceleration performance.

Of all explosive strength measures, jump height seems to be most strongly correlated to initial acceleration performance.

These relationships are typically stronger than those observed in isolated joint strength tests, suggesting that the multi-joint coordinated action of jumping may have a higher degree of transference to sprinting compared to single joint movements.

Jump-based explosive strength measures are also likely to have a stronger relationship with initial acceleration performance compared with maximum strength measures, likely as a consequence of the need to produce force at higher rates during a jump to enhance performance.

Reactive Strength and Stiffness

As discussed in Section 2, regardless of an athlete's hip and knee maximum explosive strength capabilities, the contribution of their powerful actions to propulsive ground

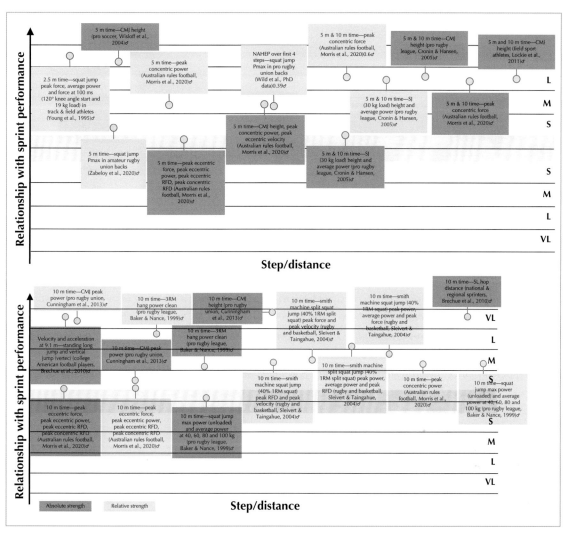

Figure 3.5. Relationships of a range of explosive strength measures during squat and countermovement jumps with initial sprint acceleration performance. Note that where the relationship magnitudes are higher than the horizontal line bisecting the shaded grey area, higher strength levels are evident with better sprinting performance and where relationship magnitudes are lower than this line, higher strength levels are evident with worse sprinting performance. Relationship magnitudes: S = small; M = moderate; L = large; VL = very large.

reaction forces is unlikely to be fully realised unless a suitably 'stiff' leg is produced during the stance phase. Therefore, reactive strength and stiffness measures are still of interest to the initial acceleration phase even though they are typically deemed more important during the maximum velocity.

Figure 3.7 shows the results from several studies which have investigated the relationships of reactive strength, vertical stiffness, jump height or contact times during drop jump or repeated rebound jumping/hopping in-place and initial acceleration performance. One potentially interesting

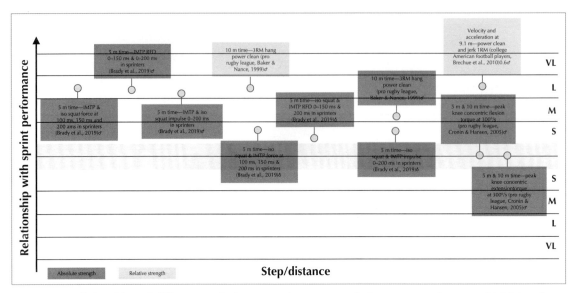

Figure 3.6. Relationships of different explosive strength measures during a range of tests and initial sprint acceleration performance. Note that where the relationship magnitudes are higher than the horizontal line bisecting the shaded grey area, higher strength levels are evident with better sprinting performance and where relationship magnitudes are lower than this line, higher strength levels are evident with worse sprinting performance. Relationship magnitudes: S = small; M = moderate; L = large; VL = very large.

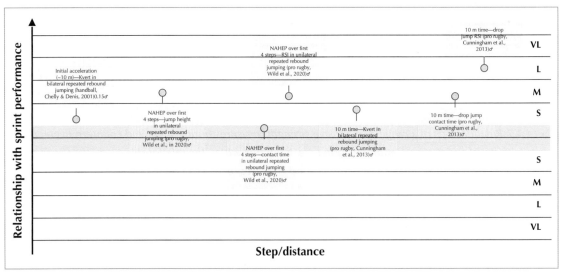

Figure 3.7. Relationships of reactive strength and stiffness measures and initial sprint acceleration performance. Note that where the relationship magnitudes are higher than the horizontal line bisecting the shaded grey area, higher strength levels are evident with better sprinting performance and where relationship magnitudes are lower than this line, higher strength levels are evident with worse sprinting performance. Relationship magnitudes: S = small; M = moderate; L = large; VL = very large.

trend evident from this research emerges from the studies which have explored the reactive strength index and the constituent parts (jump height and contact time) which make up this ratio (i.e. reactive strength index = jump height [or flight time] divided by contact time).

For instance, there seems to be a meaningful relationship between reactive strength index and initial acceleration performance. However, given that the contact times (and vertical stiffness measures which are strongly associated with contact time) are less related to initial acceleration performance, it can be deduced that the relationship between reactive strength index and initial acceleration performance can mostly be attributed to the jump heights achieved in the test.

This is typified by the findings of Cunningham and colleagues (2013) who investigated a range of strength measures and how they related to the sprinting performances of professional rugby players. They found a large relationship to exist between the reactive strength measured during drop jumps and sprint performance over 10 m. However, the relationships of contact time and vertical stiffness were lower.

Similarly, in the work of Wild et al. (2020), which explored performance measures repeated unilateral rebound jumps in-place and initial acceleration performance, reactive strength was meaningfully related to sprint performance over the first four steps, but contact time was only trivially related to sprint performance. Jump heights in the test were also shown to relate more so to initial acceleration performance than reactive

strength, although by a trivial margin. It's worth clarifying at this stage that—whilst strongly related—reactive strength and 'stiffness' are not the same thing, which is why differences in relationship magnitudes of these variables are seen with initial acceleration performance in these examples.

To summarise, for the initial acceleration phase—in terms of relationship magnitudes—explosive strength would appear to be more associated with initial acceleration performance compared with maximum strength and reactive strength (in that order) based on the findings within the research. Collectively, the information obtained from these studies would support the premise that performance in the initial steps of a sprint is dominated by large amounts of power generation.

Relationships of Strength Qualities with Late Acceleration and Maximum Velocity Performance

Leg Stiffness

One mechanism which has been identified as potentially influential to increased support forces at greater running velocities is a change in muscle activity that may alter leg stiffness (Kuitunen, Komi, & Kyrolainen, 2002).

Leg stiffness has been reported to increase as sprint velocity increases (Arampatzis, Bruggemann, & Metzler, 1999; Luhtanen & Komi, 1980), and it is thought that a stiffer system allows for more efficient elastic energy contribution, potentially enhancing force production (Farley & Morgenroth, 1999).

Leg stiffness has actually been shown to be related to maximum velocity sprinting, but not acceleration (Bret, Rahmani, Dufour, Messonnier, & Lacour, 2002; Chelly & Denis, 2001; Cunningham et al., 2013).

This is shown in Figure 3.8, whereby in Cunningham et al., 2013, vertical stiffness was more strongly related to maximum velocity sprint performance compared with initial acceleration. The same was also evident in the study by Chelly & Dennis (2001).

Lastly, although reactive strength index during a normal rebound jump was not related to later acceleration/maximum velocity performance, during an ankle rebound jump

in which the legs remain straight during repeated jumps (thus increasing leg stiffness), meaningful relationships were found of reactive strength index with late acceleration performance, but not initial acceleration performance. The study by Cunningham et al. (2013) also demonstrates how relationships of maximum and explosive strength differ through different sprint phases.

Collectively, the relationships explored in this section would appear to make sense considering the joint kinematics and kinetics already discussed, where, as a sprint progresses—with the exception of the activity at the hip—there is a shift in emphasis from power generating (net concentric contraction)

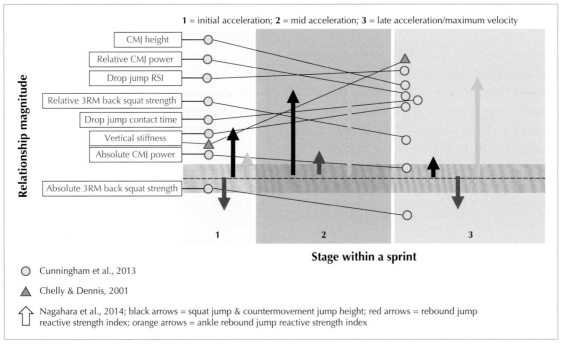

Figure 3.8. Relationships of a range of strength measures and performance in different sprint phases. Note that where the relationship magnitudes are higher than the horizontal line bisecting the shaded grey area, higher strength levels are evident with better sprinting performance and where relationship magnitudes are lower than this line, higher strength levels are evident with worse sprinting performance. Relationship magnitudes: S = small; M = moderate; L = large; VL = very large.

to power dissipating (net eccentric contraction) muscular activity. Eccentric work and the effects of the SSC may therefore become increasingly important during mid-late acceleration and maximum velocity sprinting, due to the larger peak vertical and horizontal braking forces experienced.

These findings suggest the ability to resist applied stretch, thus leg stiffness, during stance is more pertinent during maximum velocity as ground contacts become shorter. During early acceleration, however, concentric power appears to be more applicable to performance (Bret, Rahmani, Dufour, Messonnier, & Lacour, 2002; Sleivert & Taingahue, 2004). That said, ankle joint stiffness is still a very important quality during acceleration.

Driving Technical Changes Through Specific Strength Training

Proponents of an ecological-psychology approach to skill acquisition would contend that human movement—and thus the optimal movement strategies adopted by athletes during sprinting—is produced from the interaction of various subsystems within the task, environment and performer (Davids, Button, & Bennett, 2007). It is purported that these subsystems self-organise spontaneously to yield the most favourable and efficient movement solution for the specific task at hand (Newell, 1986; Thelan, 1989).

For skilled coaches, it is possible to manipulate various constraints during training in an attempt to affect the emergent coordinated behaviour of an athlete. In a sprinting context, for example, a strength-based manipulation

would endeavour to change the human system and alter the organismic constraints and would suggest that an athlete's movement preferences may, in part, be shaped by their strength-related qualities.

The concept that the sprinting action is, to a degree, reflexively generated without conscious effort is supported by the field of neuroscience (e.g. Hultborn & Nielsen, 2007; McCrea & Rybak, 2008).

Following initial central input, genetically determined central organisation in the spinal cord (central pattern generator) is thought to send rhythmic oscillating instructions to the musculature to produce locomotion even in the absence of afferent inputs (McCrea & Rybak, 2008). Sensory feedback from the limbs is necessary, however, to refine the motor pattern. For example, sensory input from lower limb extensors during ground contact can modify the timing and magnitude of muscle activities of the limbs to the speed of locomotion (Rossignol, Dubic, & Gossard, 2006).

It is plausible therefore that these modifications are to an extent involuntarily constrained by the affordances (possible actions) available to an individual (Michaels, 2003), partly resulting from an individual's strength-related qualities. Accordingly, it is possible that the strength capabilities of an athlete are associated with technical markers identified by coaches.

For instance, one likely outcome from a smaller touchdown distance is shorter ground contact time. If an athlete's contact times shorten, however, there is less time to produce force, and so the impulses which determine an athlete's change in velocity. Potentially, they would therefore need to increase the amount of force produced into the floor in the shorter ground contact times to avoid sacrificing other factors such as stride length, since otherwise a reduction in impulse will be evident.

One way to increase the amount of force produced in a shorter period of time may be to target specific strength qualities. For example, increasing reactive strength and leg stiffness may offer a strategy by which, over time, athletes can reflexively minimise touchdown distances and contact times during maximum velocity sprinting without sacrificing stride length. Initial research suggests there may be relationships between different strength qualities and a number of technical markers during the different sprint phases (Wild, 2011). Few investigations have explored this area, although some research has begun to emerge during the initial acceleration phase (Wild, Bezodis, North, & Bezodis, 2021).

Relationships Between Strength Qualities and Technical Features During Acceleration

Changes in organismic (athlete) constraints will affect the way performers interact with their environment (Fajen, Riley, & Turvey, 2008), and knowledge of the way strength-based qualities relate to technical features adopted during the initial steps of a sprint provide further insight into how different movement strategies observed in this sprint phase may be influenced. With this in mind, Wild and colleagues (2020) set out to determine how strength-based qualities relate to the technical features of athletes. The following information can therefore help inform the training of athletes aimed at directly enhancing their lower limb strength capacities and/or movement strategies to improve sprint acceleration performance.

Initially, the researchers measured sprint acceleration performance and a range of technical features of professional rugby union backs during the initial steps of sprinting. They then obtained a range of strength-based measures from the same athletes. The strength-based measures obtained were based on the joint kinetic information available, which has been shown to be important to performance in this sprint phase (see Section 2).

The tests undertaken consisted of:

1. an amended squat-jump profiling method based on the work of Samozino and colleagues (2013). From this assessment, the peak power capabilities of the leg extensors were determined as were the theoretical maximum force and velocity capabilities of the leg extensors;

2. an amended hip extensor torque test based on the work of Goodwin & Bull (2021). From this assessment, the peak torque relative to body mass was obtained;

3. an amended repeated in-place unilateral hop test based on the work of Comyns and colleagues (2019). From this assessment, the reactive strength, contact times and jump heights were retained for analysis.

A practically perfect relationship was found between vertical stiffness relative to body mass and contact time. By scanning the QR code below, it is possible to view these tests being conducted, and some of the measures which can be obtained.

Having conducted this testing, the researchers then determined how different strength-based measures related to initial acceleration performance. The results from this analysis are shown in Figure 3.9.

As can be seen, hip extensor torque, peak power during squat jump profiling and reactive strength and jump height were all moderately related to sprint performance. This would suggest that sufficient levels of these strength qualities may be worth considering as part of an athlete's strength training program.

The magnitudes of relationships of contact times, theoretical maximal leg extension strength and velocity with initial acceleration performance were either trivial or small. However, considering strength-based variables in isolation and how they relate to sprinting performance may be somewhat reductionist, and understanding how strongly combinations of strength qualities interact with each other in relation to sprinting performance may be more informative.

For example, contact times (vertical stiffness) were shown not to relate to initial acceleration performance in isolation. However, when contact time data is visualised in tandem with hip extensor torque amongst the athlete cohort, some interesting patterns began

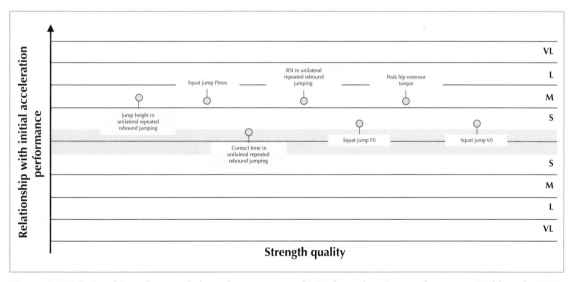

Figure 3.9. Relationships of strength-based measures and initial acceleration performance (Wild et al., 2020). Note that where the relationship magnitudes are higher than the horizontal line bisecting the shaded grey area, higher strength levels are evident with better sprinting performance and where relationship magnitudes are lower than this line, higher strength levels are evident with worse sprinting performance. Relationship magnitudes: S = small; M = moderate; L = large; VL = very large.

to emerge. This is shown in Figure 3.10, where the vertical and horizontal axes are bisected using a median split based on the hip torque and contact times achieved by the athletes in the study. Each data point represents the hip torque and contact times achieved by an individual athlete and the size of the data point represents how fast they are (i.e. the larger the circle, the greater the initial acceleration performance).

As can be seen by the four quadrants created by splitting the axes, high acceleration performance is achieved with varying combinations of hip torque and contact time. In fact, the fastest athlete (largest circle in the bottom left quadrant) achieves the second shortest contact times, but the lowest hip torque. This suggests that some athletes may still be able to accelerate well with low hip extensor torque capabilities, but that they will also likely need to possess high levels of vertical stiffness.

Given the initial acceleration performances in the bottom right quadrant of the figure, the results from the analysis would also suggest that low vertical stiffness (long contact times during the repeated in-place unilateral jump test) and low hip extensor torque is not a desirable combination.

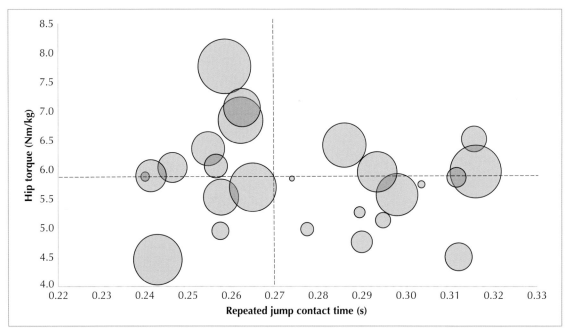

Figure 3.10. Interaction between hip torque, repeated contact time and acceleration performance during the first four steps of professional rugby union backs (Wild et al., 2020). The centre of each data point represents the mean of these strength measures for an individual. Dotted lines divide axes according to a median split to form quadrants. The size of the marker depicts the relative sprinting performance of each participant over the first four steps, with marker sizes increasing in proportion to the rank order of a given participant's performance (i.e. largest marker size = highest acceleration).

Whilst the results of their research outlining the relationships of strength qualities with initial acceleration performance is of interest, the main aim of the investigation (Wild et al., 2020) was to establish how strength-related qualities associated with different sprint technique variables. These relationships are shown in Table 3.1. A list of the technical features measured which were averaged over the first fours steps, and definitions, where necessary, are as follows:

- Spatiotemporal variables:
  - Step length—horizontal displacement between the toe tips at adjacent touchdowns (m)
  - Step rate—the reciprocal of step duration, which was determined as the sum of contact time and the subsequent flight time (Hz)
  - Contact time—duration of the contact phase (from touchdown to toe-off; s)
  - Flight time—duration of the flight phase (from toe-off to touchdown; s)
- Linear kinematic variables:
  - Touchdown distance—horizontal distance between the toe and whole-body centre of mass at the instant of touchdown (with positive values representing the toe ahead of the centre of mass; m)
  - Toe-off distance—horizontal distance between the toe and whole-body centre of mass at the instant of toe-off (with positive values representing the toe ahead of the centre of mass; m)
  - Contact length—horizontal distance the centre of mass travelled during stance (m)
  - Flight length—horizontal distance the centre of mass travelled during the flight phase (m)

- Touchdown and toe-off angular kinematics:
  - Ankle, knee, and hip joint angles (°) at touchdown and toe-off
  - Shank and trunk angles (°; with respect to the horizontal) at touchdown and toe-off
  - Peak ankle dorsiflexion angle—minimum ankle angle (°) during the stance phase
  - Ankle dorsiflexion ROM—magnitude of ankle dorsiflexion range of motion (°) during the stance phase
  - Hip touchdown angular velocity—hip extension angular velocity at the instant of touchdown (°/s)
  - Stance mean hip angular velocity—difference between the angular position of the stance hip at touchdown and toe-off divided by ground contact time (°/s)

The following technical variables were analysed in their dimensionless form (Hof, 1996) to remove the effect that stature would have on relationship magnitudes: step length, step rate, contact time, flight time, touchdown distance, toe-off distance, contact length, hip touchdown angular velocity and stance mean hip angular velocity.

The following provides a summary of the findings where meaningful and statistically significant relationships were evident.

Regarding spatiotemporal variables, results would suggest that athletes with higher vertical stiffness (lower repeated jump contact time) achieved greater step rate and those who produced shorter contact times over the first four steps also achieved greater hip extensor torque, greater reactive strength and higher levels of vertical stiffness.

Table 3.1. Relationships (correlation coefficients) between a range of strength-based measures and the initial sprint acceleration (first four steps) technical features of professional rugby union backs (Wild et al., 2020). For all correlation coefficients, the strength of observed relationships was defined as: (±) < 0.1, trivial; 0.1 to < 0.3, small; 0.3 to < 0.5 moderate, 0.5 to < 0.7 large, 0.7 to < 0.9 very large and ≥ 0.9, practically perfect (Hopkins, 2002). Correlation coefficients in bold represent relationship magnitudes which are practically meaningful, and asterisks depict relationships which were found to be statistically significant.

	Relationship between strength-based variable and initial acceleration performance						
	Sprint acceleration technical feature	**Squat jump profiling**			**Hip extensor torque test**	**Repeated unilateral jump test**		
		F0 N/kg	**V0 (m/s)**	**Pmax (W/kg)**	**Peak torque (Nm/kg)**	**RSI**	**Jump height (m)**	**Contact time (s)**
Spatiotemporal variables[a]	Step length	–0.01	0.10	0.05	**–0.28**	–0.11	0.09	**0.34**
	Step rate	0.11	–0.19	–0.06	0.17	0.16	–0.11	**–0.47***
	Contact time	–0.21	0.14	–0.17	**–0.42***	**–0.42***	–0.20	**0.43***
	Flight time	0.17	0.17	**0.26**	0.27	**0.35**	**0.39**	–0.03
Linear kinematics[a]	Touchdown distance	–0.01	0.20	0.15	**–0.51***	**–0.37**	–0.13	**0.45***
	Toe-off distance distance	0.09	0.06	0.14	**0.36**	0.23	0.01	**–0.37**
	Contact length	–0.05	0.11	0.04	**–0.49***	**–0.34**	–0.09	**0.46***
	Flight length	0.03	0.04	0.02	0.17	0.24	0.24	–0.04

Table 3.1. (Continued)

		Relationship between strength-based variable and initial acceleration performance						
	Sprint acceleration technical feature	Squat jump profiling			Hip extensor torque test	Repeated unilateral jump test		
		F0 N/kg	V0 (m/s)	Pmax (W/kg)	Peak torque (Nm/kg)	RSI	Jump height (m)	Contact time (s)
Touchdown angular kinematics (contact leg)	Shank angle (°)	**−0.35**	−0.09	**−0.34**	**−0.46***	**−0.33**	−0.18	**0.29**
	Trunk angle (°)	−0.07	0.15	−0.14	−0.03	0.04	−0.06	−0.16
	Ankle angle (°)	**−0.31**	−0.28	**−0.46***	−0.07	−0.01	−0.10	−0.13
	Peak ankle dorsiflexion angle (°)	−0.15	**−0.48***	**−0.56***	−0.14	0.20	−0.06	**−0.40***
	Ankle dorsiflexion ROM (°)	**0.30**	0.04	0.26	0.04	−0.02	−0.06	−0.04
	Knee angle (°)	**−0.45***	−0.20	**−0.50***	0.02	−0.08	−0.19	−0.16
	Hip angle (°)	−0.20	−0.18	**−0.31**	0.24	0.15	−0.08	**−0.37**
	Hip touchdown angular velocity[a]	−0.27	−0.33	**−0.47***	−0.09	−0.04	−0.14	−0.15
	Stance mean hip angular velocity[a]	**0.34**	**0.35**	**0.57***	**0.31**	0.24	**−0.49***	0.27

Table 3.1. (Continued)

		Relationship between strength-based variable and initial acceleration performance							
	Sprint acceleration technical feature	Squat jump profiling			Hip extensor torque test	Repeated unilateral jump test			
		F0 N/kg	V0 (m/s)	Pmax (W/kg)	Peak torque (Nm/kg)	RSI	Jump height (m)	Contact time (s)	
Toe-off angular kinematics (contact leg)	Shank angle (°)	–0.12	–0.14	–0.2	**0.42***	–0.03	–0.13	0.17	
	Trunk angle (°)	0.14	0.05	0.14	0.09	0.02	0.04	0.00	
	Ankle angle (°)	**–0.30**	–0.07	–0.29	–0.16	**–0.29**	**–0.43***	–0.12	
	Knee angle (°)	**–0.34**	0.05	–0.2	**0.27**	–0.05	0.09	0.18	
	Hip angle (°)	–0.07	0.11	0.03	0.09	0.01	0.18	0.22	

[a]Variables are in their dimensionless form (Hof, 1996).

In relation to linear kinematics, smaller touchdown distances and contact lengths were achieved with higher levels of hip extensor torque and greater vertical stiffness. For touchdown angular kinematics, peak power during squat jump profiling was the strength-based variable most related to the sprint technique variables.

Ankle and knee joints of athletes were more flexed at touchdown, and hip angular velocities were smaller at touchdown and larger when averaged during the stance phase, with higher level of squat jump peak power. Greater hip extensor peak torques were also typically associated with more and less horizontal oriented shank angles at touchdown and toe-off, respectively.

Conclusion

Generally, the associations between strength qualities and the performances of athletes during different sprint phases are logical based on the joint kinetic information presented in Section 2. Broadly, strength-based qualities demonstrating high levels of power generation or power absorption are more related to sprint acceleration and maximum velocity sprint performance respectively.

Whilst the information presented in this section which details these relationships is of interest, it is important to remember that correlation does not equal causation and that a large percentage of variation in sprinting performance will be explained by other factors. That said, it would appear important to ensure athletes meet a 'minimum threshold' of a variety of strength qualities to help remove the possibility of these physical constraints preventing higher levels of sprinting performance.

Lastly, it is important to remember that it is possible for some physical qualities (like strength) can be manipulated to help facilitate technical changes coaches may seek to make within individuals since physical constraints will in part shape the movement preferences of athletes. Whilst there is a lack of information on this area, some of the research presented in this section may begin to provide some initial direction.

Through Sections 1–3, some pertinent issues have been discussed which inform the program design process. In Section 4, the strength program design process will be covered in detail to help coaches maximise the effectiveness of their interventions.

References

Arampatzis, A., Bruggemann, G., & Metzler, V. (1999). The effect of speed on leg stiffness and joint kinetics in human running. *Journal of Biomechanics, 32*, 1349–1353.

Baker, D., & Nance, S. (1999). The relation between running speed and measures of strength and power in professional rugby league players. *Journal of Strength & Conditioning Research, 13*(3).

Bartlett, J., Sumner, B., Ellis, R., & Kram, R. (2014). Activity and functions of the human gluteal muscles in walking, running, sprinting, and climbing. *American Journal of Physical Anthropology, 153*(1), 124–131.

Boraczyński, M., Boraczyński, T., Podstawski, R., Wójcik, Z., & Gronek, P. (2020). Relationships between measures of functional and isometric lower body strength, aerobic capacity, anaerobic power, sprint and countermovement jump performance in professional soccer players. *Journal of Human Kinetics, 75*(1), 161–175.

Bosch, F., & Klomp, R. (2005). Running: Biomechanics and Exercise Physiology Applied in Practice. London: Elsevier.

Brady, C. J., Harrison, A. J., Flanagan, E. P., Haff, G. G., & Comyns, T. M. (2019). The relationship between isometric strength and sprint acceleration in sprinters. *International Journal of Sports Physiology and Performance, 15*(1), 1–45.

Brechue, W. F., Mayhew, J. L., & Piper, F. C. (2010). Characteristics of sprint performance in college football players. *Journal of Strength and Conditioning Research, 24*(5), 1169–1178.

Bret, C., Rahmani, A., Dufour, A., Messonnier, L., & Lacour, J. (2002). Leg strength and stiffness as ability factors in 100 m sprint running. *Journal of Sports Medicine and Physical Fitness, 42*, 274–281.

Chelly, S., & Denis, C. (2001). Leg power and hopping stiffness: relationship with sprint running performance. *Medicine and Science in Sports and Exercise, 33*, 326–333.

Comyns, T., Flanagan, E., Fleming, S., Fitzgerald, E., & Harper, D. (2019). Inter-day reliability and usefulness of reactive strength index derived from two maximal rebound jump tests. *International Journal of Sports Physiology and Performance*, 1–17.

Cronin, J. B., & Hansen, K. T. (2005). Strength and power predictors of sports speed. *Journal of Strength and Conditioning Research, 19*(2), 349–357.

Cunningham, D. J., West, D. J., Owen, N. J., Shearer, D. A., Finn, C. V., Bracken, R. M., & Kilduff, L. P. (2013). Strength and power predictors of sprinting performance in professional rugby players. *Journal of Sports Medicine and Physical Fitness, 53*(2), 105–111.

Debaere, S., Delecluse, C., Aerenhouts, D., Hagman, F., & Jonkers, I. (2015). Control of propulsion and body lift during the first two stances of sprint running: A simulation study. *Journal of Sports Sciences, 33*(19), 2016–2024.

Fajen, R., Riley, M., & Turvey, M. (2008). Information, affordances, and the control of action in sport. *International Journal of Sports Psychology, 40*, 79–107.

Farley, C., & Morgenroth, D. (1999). Leg stiffness primarily depends on ankle stiffness during human hopping. *Journal of Biomechanics, 32*, 267–273.

Goodwin, J., & Bull, A. M. (2021). Novel assessment of isometric hip extensor function: Reliability, joint angle sensitivity, and concurrent validity. *Journal of Strength and Conditioning Research*, ahead-of-print.

Healy, R., Smyth, C., Kenny, I., & Harrison, A. (2019). Influence of reactive and maximum strength indicators on sprint performance. *Journal of Strength and Conditioning Research, 33*(11), 3039–3048.

Hof, A. L. (1996). Scaling gait data to body size. *Gait & Posture, 4*(3), 222–223.

Hopkins, W. (2002). A scale of magnitudes for effect statistics. Retrieved from http://www.sportsci.org/resource/stats/effectmag.html

Kuitunen, S., Komi, P., & Kyrolainen, H. (2002). Knee and ankle joint stiffness in sprint running. *Medicine and Science in Sports and Exercise, 34*, 166–173.

Lockie, R. G., Murphy, A. J., Knight, T. J., & Janse de Jonge, X. (2011). Factors that differentiate acceleration ability in field sport athletes. *Journal of Strength and Conditioning Research, 25*(10), 2704–2714.

Luhtanen, P., & Komi, P. (1980). Force-, power-, and elasticity-velocity relationships in walking, running and jumping. *European Journal of Applied Physiology, 44*, 279–289.

McBride, J., Blow, D., Kirby, T. J., L Haines, T., M Dayne, A., & Travis Triplett, N. (2009). Relationship between maximal squat strength and five, ten, and forty-yard sprint times. *Journal of Strength and Conditioning Research, 23*, 1633–1636.

Möck, S., Hartmann, R., Wirth, K., Rosenkranz, G., & Mickel, C. (2018). Correlation of dynamic strength in the standing calf raise with sprinting performance in consecutive sections up to 30 meters. *Research in Sports Medicine, 26*(4), 474–481.

Morin, J., Gimenez, P., Edouard, P., Arnal, P., Jimenez-Reyes, P., Samozino, P., & Mendiguchia, J. (2015). Sprint acceleration mechanics: The major role of hamstrings in horizontal force production. *Frontiers in Physiology, 24*, 1–16.

Morris, C., Weber, J., & Netto, K. (2020). Relationship between mechanical effectiveness in sprint running and force-velocity characteristics of a countermovement jump in Australian rules football athletes. *Journal of Strength and Conditioning Research*, ahead-of-print.

Nagahara, R., Naito, H., Miyashiro, K., Morin, J., & Zushi, K. (2014). Traditional and ankle-specific vertical jumps as strength-power indicators for maximal sprint acceleration. *Journal of Sports Medicine and Physical Fitness, 54*(6), 691–699.

Nagahara, R., Takai, Y., Kanehisa, H., & Fukunaga, T. (2018). Vertical impulse as a determinant of combination of step length and frequency during sprinting. *International Journal of Sports Medicine, 39*, 282–290.

Pandy, M., Lai, A., Schache, A., & Lin, Y. (2021). How muscles maximize performance in accelerated sprinting. *Scandinavian Journal of Medicine & Science in Sports, 31*(10), 1882–1896.

Samozino, P., Edouard, P., Sangnier, S., Brughelli, M., Gimenez, P., & Morin, J. (2013). Force-velocity profile: Imbalance determination and effect on lower limb ballistic performance. *International Journal of Sports Medicine, 35*(6), 505–510.

Sleivert, G., & Taingahue, M. (2004). The relationship between maximal jump-squat power and sprint acceleration in athletes. *European Journal of Applied Physiology, 91*, 46–52.

Thomas, C., Comfort, P., Jones, P. A., & Dos'Santos, T. (2017). A comparison of isometric midthigh-pull strength, vertical jump, sprint speed, and change-of-direction speed in academy netball players. *International Journal of Sports Physiology and Performance, 12*(7), 916–921.

Wild, J., Bezodis, I., North, J., & Bezodis, N. (2021). Characterising initial sprint acceleration strategies using a whole-body kinematics approach. *Journal of Sports Sciences*, ahead-of-print, 1–12.

Wild, J., Bezodis, I., North, J., & Bezodis, N. (2020). Relationships between strength qualities and initial sprint acceleration technique. Unpublished PhD data.

Wisloff, U., Castagna, C., Helgerud, J., Jones, R., & Hoff, J. (2004). Strong correlation of maximal squat strength with sprint performance and vertical jump height in elite soccer players. *British Journal of Sports Medicine, 38*(3), 285–288.

Young, W., McLean, B., & Ardagna, J. (1995). Relationship between strength qualities and sprinting performance. *Journal of Sports Medicine and Physical Fitness, 35*, 13–19.

Zehr, P., & Stein, R. (1999). What functions do reflexes serve during human locomotion? *Progress in Neurobiology, 58*, 185–205.

Designing Individual Training Sessions

When designing an individual training session, there are numerous variables which need to be considered. Each of these variables will vary according to the stage an athlete is in with regards to their annual training plan, their training age and a number of other factors relating to that individual. As previously discussed, the way in which these variables are manipulated should be based upon the specific adaptation(s) being targeted.

With this objective in mind, consideration ought to be given to the type of stress required to elicit these adaptations. This should be reflected within the session by the type of exercises selected, the order they are completed by an athlete, the intensity they are performed at and the degree of rest employed, amongst other factors.

Training Age

One of the key considerations when designing an individual training session is the training status of the participant. For the purposes of this book, an athlete's training age is determined by the length of time an individual has consistently been exposed to well-structured strength training (Table 4.1).

Ascertaining an athlete's training age is important for two reasons. Firstly, from a safety perspective this is essential so as to avoid applying too great a stress to an

Table 4.1. Determining an athlete's strength training age.

Training age*	Time exposed to well-structured strength training
Beginner	Less than 1.5 years
Intermediate	Between 1.5 and 3 years
Advanced	Greater than 3 years

*The three training ages exist on a continuum and cannot be definitively described.

individual's musculoskeletal system, which may lead to injury. With this in mind, it is important for an athlete to progress gradually over time in terms of the intensities and volumes they encounter when training. This allows for the muscles and connective tissues to adapt in preparation for greater training loads as an athlete's training status progresses. However, the intensity and volume parameters targeted will be dictated by the training age of the athlete and should change over time (see Tables 4.2 to 4.8).

Determining an athlete's training age is also important to ensure the optimal doses of the training variables are prescribed to maximise strength gains (Peterson, Rhea, & Alvar, 2005). The strength training dose-response relationship will be explored in more detail later in this section.

Session Design for the Development of Different Strength Qualities

The Force-Velocity Relationship

Before exploring the optimal strength training dosage to elicit the adaptations necessary to develop specific strength qualities, attaining an understanding of the force-velocity relationship is important to inform individual session design.

The force-velocity curve (Figure 1.6) depicts an inverse relationship between the force and velocity during concentric muscle contraction. This curve implies that maximal force can only occur at zero or low velocities, and the greatest velocities can only be attained under conditions of zero or low loading. In simple terms, the lighter the load being lifted, the faster it is possible to move it. It should also be noted that it is possible to move heavy loads quickly during certain exercises (e.g. Olympic weightlifting), and it is also possible to produce large forces when travelling at high velocities (e.g. sprinting).

Theoretically, after prolonged maximal strength-only training, the adaptations elicited will improve an athlete's ability to achieve higher velocities of movement under high loads, but lower velocities under low loads. Conversely, velocity-centred only training with low loads will result in an athlete's ability to achieve higher velocities of movement under low loads and lower velocities under higher loads. A long-term combination of training approaches is thought to raise both velocity and force capabilities along the whole curve.

Maximum Strength

Maximum strength training with submaximal efforts—often referred to as base strength, hypertrophy or strength endurance training—is an effective means of developing muscle and connective tissue tolerance in preparation for future more intense strength training. This type of training is recommended as a starting point for most beginner athletes, whatever the stage the athlete is in with regards to their annual sport season. For intermediate and advanced athletes, this type of training is usually carried out early in pre-season, following a period of active rest from the previous season (Section 5: Periodisation). Typically, hypertrophic gains are made with this type of training.

Maximum strength training with maximal loads is primarily incorporated to increase relative strength. As such, the strength gains made through this type of training are more related to neural adaptations. The optimal training variable parameters can be found in Table 4.2. The optimal strength training dosage has been shown to alter depending on an athlete's training age. When examining the results of a number of different studies, it is evident that a dose-response continuum exists, whereby increases in strength training dosage should accompany increases in training age (Peterson, Rhea, & Alvar, 2005). Simply put, the strength training dose which elicits maximum strength gains varies according to training age, and this has been reflected in Table 4.2.

The exercises typically used in maximum strength training sessions are compound multi-joint lifts. A suggested number of these exercises are listed in Table 4.3 and can be found in Section 6: Exercise Library. Note that these exercises are appropriate across all training ages, provided they are performed with sound technique.

During the concentric phase of the lift, the intention from the exerciser should be to lift the weight explosively and lower the weight (eccentric phase) more steadily and under control. This explosive intent, regardless of the actual velocity of movement, has been shown to be more favourable for RFD (Behm & Sale, 1993). As with any new exercise, load should gradually be introduced only when an athlete has learnt to perform the exercises correctly and safely.

Explosive Strength

As previously identified, due to the time constraints of sprinting, how quickly an athlete can apply force is potentially more important than the maximum amount of force they can produce. Explosive strength (ballistic) exercises require an athlete to accelerate throughout the entire movement to the point of release or take-off, and as such negate any deceleration phase of a lift (Newton, Kraemer, Hakkinen, Humphries, & Murphy, 1996). Therefore, the antagonist muscles are trained to delay the rate at which they decelerate the concentric movement of the action. As a result, concentric velocity, force, power and muscle activation are higher during an explosive strength exercise in comparison to a similar maximal strength exercise (Cormie, McCaulley, Triplett, & Mcbride, 2007; Newton, Kraemer, Hakkinen, Humphries, & Murphy, 1996).

Furthermore, power has also been shown to be improved across a range of loading conditions during explosive strength training (Cormie, McCaulley, Triplett, & Mcbride, 2007; McBride, Triplett-McBride, Davie, & Newton, 2002), allowing for athletes of all training ages to improve power production. It also means that power can be developed at various points along the force-velocity curve (see Figure 2.6). These ranges have been accounted for within the suggested guidelines in Table 4.4.

Under heavy loads, explosive strength training is more likely to facilitate recruitment of high-threshold motor units similar to maximum strength training, and enhance RFD at the 'force end' of the force-velocity curve when compared to lifting with lighter loads. Under lighter loads, explosive strength training is more favourable for reducing antagonist co-contraction and RFD at the 'velocity end' of the force-velocity curve (see Figure 2.6). The adaptations shared between training under heavier and lighter

Table 4.2. Individual session program design training variables for maximum strength development.

Training for maximum strength development	
Submaximal loads	**Maximal loads**
Typical objectives: Base strength/work capacity/hypertrophy **Adaptations:** Increased muscle physiological cross-sectional area/tissue conditioning	**Typical objectives:** Maximal force expression **Adaptations:** Enhanced recruitment of fast twitch motor units & muscle fibres; enhanced rate coding; preferential hypertrophy of type II muscle fibres

Beginner athlete

	No. of exercises	RM	%1RM	Rep range	Sets	Set rest (min)
Submaximal loads	6–8	12	67	10–12	2–4	1 to 1.5
		11	70	9–11		
		10	75	8–10		
	5–6	9	77	7–9		1.5 to 2
		8	80	6–8		
Maximal/ near maximal loads	3–4	7	83	5–7	2–4	2 to 2.5
		6	85	4–5		
		5	87	3–4		

Intermediate athlete

	No. of exercises	RM	%1RM	Rep range	Sets	Set rest (min)
Submaximal loads	6–8	10	75	9–10	3	1.5 to 2
		9	77	8–9		
	5–6	8	80	6–8	3–5	2 to 2.5
		7	83	5–7		
Maximal/ near maximal loads	4–5	6	85	4–6	3–5	2.5
		5	87	3–5		
		4	90	2–3		3

Advanced athlete

	No. of exercises	RM	%1RM	Rep range	Sets	Set rest (min)
Submaximal loads	5–7	8	80	7–8	3–6	2
		7	83	6–7		
		6	85	5–6		2 to 2.5
Maximal/ near maximal loads	4–6	5	87	4–5	4–6	2.5 to 3
		4	90	3–4		3 to 4
		3	93	2–3		
		2	95	1–2		3.5 to 4
		1	100	1		5+

Table 4.3. Suggested exercises for the development of maximum strength.

Lower body (bilateral)	Lower body (unilateral)	Upper body pulling	Upper body pushing
Back squat	Step up	Bent over row	Bench press
Front squat	Lunge	Chin ups	Incline bench press
Overhead squat	Single leg squat	Pull ups	
Leg press	Split squat	Single arm row	Dumbbell bench press
Deadlift	Bulgarian split squat	Inverted row	Incline dumbbell bench press
Hip thrust	Single leg press	Seated cable row	Barbell shoulder press
Romanian deadlift (RDL)	Single leg hip thrust		Dumbbell shoulder press
Nordic curls	Single leg RDL		Press up
Glute-ham raise	Single leg calf raise		Loaded press up

loads (Table 4.4) will also be specific to the force-velocity training conditions.

Consequently, explosive strength training under lighter loads may be more related to sprinting performance, where high power output during fast movements against low external is required. The optimal load, however, which elicits maximal power production, has been shown to differ according to the type of movement involved.

For example, the optimal load typically to elicit maximal power in the countermovement jump has been shown to be 0% of 1RM back squat (Cormie, McCaulley, Triplett, & Mcbride, 2007). However, 70–80% 1RM in Olympic weightlifting exercises (namely the clean and the snatch) has been shown to produce maximal power when performing these types of lifts (Cormie, McCaulley, Triplett, & Mcbride, 2007).

A suggested number of explosive strength exercises are listed in Table 4.5 and can be found in Section 6: Exercise Library. These types of exercises should be performed with maximal explosive intent.

The explosive strength training modalities included so far are traditional forms of explosive strength training. However, this strength can also be developed using specific isometric-based training (e.g. Kordi et al., 2020; Lum, Barbosa, Joseph, & Balasekaran, 2021; Lum, Barbosa, & Balasekaran, 2021).

Whilst there are a number of ways in which isometric exercises can be performed, one of the more common approaches is known as

Table 4.4. Individual session program design training variables for explosive strength development.

Training for explosive strength development						
Heavy loads			**Moderate loads**		**Light loads**	
Adaptations: Enhanced recruitment of type II motor units; enhanced rate coding; RFD at moderate to high velocities; Intermuscular coordination			**Adaptations:** Earlier recruitment of type II motor units; enhanced rate coding; RFD at high to moderate velocities; Intermuscular coordination; reduced antagonist co-contraction		**Adaptations:** Earlier recruitment of type II motor units; increased rate coding; RFD at very high velocities; Intermuscular coordination; reduced antagonist co-contraction	
Beginner						
	No. of exercises	RM	%1RM	Rep range	Sets	Set rest (min)
Heavy	3–4	9	77	5–6	2–4	2.5
		8	80	4–5		
		7	83	3–4		2.5 to 3
Moderate	3–4	–	30	3–4	2–4	2.5 to 3.5
		–	45			
		–	60			
Light	3–4	–	0	1–6	2–4	2.5 to 3.5
		–	10			
		–	20			
Intermediate						
	No. of exercises	RM	%1RM	Rep range	Sets	Set rest (min)
Heavy	3–4	9	77	5–6	3–5	2.5
		8	80	4–5		
		7	83	3–4		3
		6	85	2–3	4–5	3 to 3.5
Moderate	3–4	–	30	3–4	3–4	2.5 to 3.5
		–	45			
		–	60			3.5 to 4
		10	75			
Light	3–4	–	0	1–8	3–4	2.5 to 4
		–	10			
		–	20			
		–	30			

Table 4.4. Individual session program design training variables for explosive strength development. (Continued)

	No. of exercises	RM	%1RM	Rep range	Sets	Set rest (min)
			Advanced			
Heavy	3–5	8	80	4–5	3–5	3 to 3.5
		6	85			
		4	90	2–3		3 to 4
		2	95	1–2	4–6	3.5 to 4
		1	100	1		4 to 5
Moderate	3–5	–	35	3–6	3–5	2.5 to 4
		–	45			
		–	60			3 to 5
		10	75			
Light	3–4	–	0	1–8	3–5	2.5 to 5
		–	10			
		–	20			
		–	30			

'pushing' isometrics (Schaefer & Bittmann, 2017). This essentially involves the athlete attempting to move ('push') an immoveable surface or object, such as an Olympic bar. This form of isometric exercise may be best suited to the early acceleration phase of sprinting where there is a greater power generation and 'concentric' muscle action emphasis. This is because 'pushing' isometrics are essentially an attempt to produce a concentric muscle action.

Consider Figure 4.1, which shows an athlete undertaking a test that measures the strength qualities of their hip extensors (see Section 3), but it can also 'double up' as an exercise in its own right. In this set up, the athlete's hips are fixed beneath an immoveable bar. With one leg raised off the ground, the athlete 'drives' the heel of the other leg into the ground as if trying to 'push' the bar toward the ceiling. Since it is not possible for the athlete to move the bar upward (i.e. the load on the bar exceeds the maximum force capabilities of the athlete's hip

extensors), no movement takes place, thus joint angles remain the same and there is no (or very little) change in muscle-tendon lengths. Where relatively short explosive efforts are made to move the bar/surface and incorporated within the training of athletes, increases in explosive strength have been observed.

It is important to note that the duration and intensity of 'pushing' for each repetition should be short and high respectively. However, as with introducing any new form of training stimulus, it is important that the athlete starts with a lower intensity (i.e. 'pushing' with submaximal intent) and builds to maximum intent after a period of time. Therefore, a phase of training where 'pushing' with lower intensity and for longer durations is recommended before undertaking maximum effort isometric exercises.

That said, this form of training will typically result in less fatigue compared with other

Table 4.5. Suggested exercises for the development of explosive strength.

Loading condition	Exercises*
Heavy	Clean Hang clean Clean from hip Snatch Hang snatch Snatch from hip Power pull Hang pull Hip pull Jerk
Moderate	**All of the above exercises, plus the following:** Squat jump Countermovement jump Explosive step up Medball heave (upward) Bench throw Sled runs
Light	Medball heave (upward) Medball heave (backward) Medball heave (forward) Standing long jump Squat jump Countermovement jump Explosive Bulgarian split squat

*The exercises listed should only be introduced following a period of technical work and base strength development.

more dynamic forms of strength training. Table 4.6 provides some program design variable recommendations for the use of 'pushing' isometric exercises to elicit explosive strength gains. Multiple different exercises can be used to develop explosive strength through isometric training. The exercises chosen are dependent on the muscle-tendon units in which the athlete/coach wishes to develop these explosive strength qualities.

Figure 4.1 provides an example of how hip extensor explosive strength qualities can be developed. To develop knee extensor explosive strength qualities through isometric exercises, a squat rack/smith machine can be used where the barbell is positioned on the rack such that if the athlete was going to unload the bar, their knee and hip joint angles are in a position specific to the angles which may be prevalent in an aspect of their sport when explosive strength of the muscles crossing those joints is important. If the bar is loaded high enough, then it will not be possible for the athlete to move it and they can attempt to 'squat' the bar up from the racks toward the ceiling, although in reality they will not move it.

A similar approach can be used with a leg press machine. The machine can be fixed such that the knee joint is at a specific and desired angle and loaded so that it is not possible for the athlete to 'push' the foot plate away. The leg press or a squat rack/smooth machine can also be used in a similar way to train the ankle plantar flexors isometrically also.

Another form of isometric training which can induce similar, but slightly different explosive strength qualities, are known as 'holding' isometrics (Schaefer & Bittmann, 2017).

Figure 4.1. An athlete undertaking a hip extensor torque test.

Although research is limited in this area, 'holding' isometrics may elicit slightly different training adaptations than holding isometrics. Whereas 'pushing' isometrics are an attempt to apply a concentric muscle action, 'holding' isometrics are an attempt to resist an eccentric muscle action. This may provide beneficial explosive strength qualities, for example, during the stance phase of maximum velocity sprinting where the ability to attenuate braking forces and produce high levels of eccentric RFD (see Section 2) are key.

In 'holding' isometrics, similar exercises can be used as those employed during 'pushing' isometrics, but rather than the athlete 'pushing' against an immoveable surface or object, they hold against a weight they could lower (eccentric action) although not necessarily lift (concentric action).

Again, consider Figure 4.1. Imagine the same set up, but the bar was loaded equivalent to the athlete's single leg 1RM. The athlete would then lift the bar by just a few inches off the ground using both legs, but then lift one leg off the ground and attempt to hold the bar in place (i.e. a few inches off the ground).

As another example, using a leg press machine the athlete positions themself such that the balls of their feet are in contact with the foot plate they would normally push against, but their heel is positioned below the plate. They then load the leg press machine to a load equivalent to the athlete's single leg 1RM calf raise in the leg press and push the plate away initially so that the athlete's legs are straight. Holding this position, they then remove one leg, requiring the plantar flexor muscles to resist ankle dorsiflexion in order to keep the foot plate in place for a specified duration.

Table 4.7 provides some program design variable recommendations for the use of 'holding' isometric exercises to elicit explosive strength gains.

Another option for developing explosive strength qualities is through power endurance training to enhance repeat power ability (Natera, Cardinale, & Keogh, 2020). As mentioned in Section 1, this type of training can be fatiguing due to the high intensities and high-volume conditions of this training. Therefore, it should only be limited to intermediate to advanced level athletes and when this training is included within their training week ought to be considered carefully.

Some example schemes for this type of training according to training age are included in Tables 4.8 and 4.9. In these examples, the suggested exercise is a squat jump.

Table 4.6. Example 4-week blocks when using 'pushing' isometric exercises for the development of explosive strength according to training age (note a 'de-load' week is included in week 4).

Training age	Progression	Week 1			Week 2			Week 3			Week 4		
		Reps[a]	Sets[b]	% effort[c]	Reps[a]	Sets[b]	% effort[c]	Reps[a]	Sets[b]	% effort[c]	Reps[a]	Sets[b]	% effort[c]
Beginner	Block 1	10/5 ramp [2]	2 (1 min rest)	75% at peak	10/5 ramp [2]	3 (1 min rest)	75% at peak	10/5 ramp [2]	3 (1 min rest)	75% at peak	10/5 ramp [2]	2 (1 min rest)	75% at peak
	Block 2	10/5 ramp [2]	2 (1 min rest)	80% at peak	10/5 ramp [2]	4 (1 min rest)	80% at peak	5/5 ramp [3]	3 (1 min rest)	85% at peak	10/5 ramp [2]	2 (1 min rest)	80% at peak
	Block 3	10/5 ramp [2]	2 (1 min rest)	85% at peak	5/5 ramp [3]	3 (2 min rest)	90% at peak	5/5 ramp [3]	4 (2 min rest)	90% at peak	10/5 ramp [2]	2 (1 min rest)	85% at peak
Intermediate	Block 1	10/5 ramp [2]	2 (1 min rest)	85% at peak	5/5 ramp [3]	3 (1 min rest)	90% at peak	5/5 ramp [3]	4 (2 min rest)	90% at peak	10/5 ramp [2]	2 (1 min rest)	85% at peak
	Block 2	5/5 ramp [3]	3 (2 min rest)	90% at peak	5/5 ramp [3]	3 (2 min rest)	95% at peak	5/5 ramp [3]	3 (2.5 min rest)	100% at peak	5/5 ramp [3]	2 (1 min rest)	90% at peak
	Block 3	5/5 ramp [3]	3 (1 min rest)	90% at peak	5/5 ramp [3]	4 (2 min rest)	100% at peak	3/3 max [3]	3 (3 min rest)	100%	5/5 ramp [3]	2 (1 min rest)	90% at peak
Advanced	Block 1	5/5 ramp [3]	3 (2 min rest)	90% at peak	5/5 ramp [3]	4 (2.5 min rest)	95% at peak	3/3 max [3]	3 (3 min rest)	95% at peak	5/5 ramp [3]	2 (1 min rest)	90% at peak
	Block 2	3/3 max [3]	3 (3 min rest)	100%	3/3 max [3]	4 (3 min rest)	100%	3/3 max [3]	5 (3 min rest)	100%	5/5 ramp [3]	2 (1 min rest)	90% at peak
	Block 3	3/3 max [3]	3 (3 min rest)	100%	2/5 max [3]	4 (3 min rest)	100%	1/5 max [3]	5 (3 min rest)	100%	5/5 ramp [3]	2 (1 min rest)	90% at peak

a push duration/within repetition rest [n] (i.e. pushing for 'x' s and then resting for 'y' s = 1 rep [no. reps per set]; note this works well when using single leg exercises as the athlete can alternate between left and right sides for each rep)

b number in brackets = rest duration between sets

c based on the maximum effort in trying to move the surface/bar/object

Ramp = gradually build up the intensity and then apply the prescribed intensity during the last 3–5 s of the rep

Max. = maximum explosive intent from the outset of the rep.

Table 4.7. Example suggested program design variable ranges when using 'holding' isometric exercises for the development of explosive strength according to training age and joint used.

Training age	Single leg iso hip thrust hold			Single leg knee or ankle leg press hold		
	Reps[a]	Sets[b]	Load[c]	Reps[a]	Sets[b]	Load[d]
Beginner	10/5 − 3/3 [2–3]	2–3 (1–2 min)	5–20%	10/5 − 3/3 [2–3]	2–3 (1–2 min)	50–100%
Intermediate	8/5 − 3/3 [2–4]	2–5 (1.5–3 min rest)	up to ~30%	8/5 − 3/3 [2–3]	2–5 (1.5–3 min rest)	Up to ~200%
Advanced	5/5 − 3/3 [2–4]	3–5 (2–4 min rest)	up to ~ 45%	5/5 − 3/3 [2–4]	3–5 (2–4 min rest)	Up to ~300%

[a] holding duration/within repetition rest [n] (i.e. holding for 'x' s and then resting for 'y' s = 1 rep [no. reps per set]; note this works well when using single leg exercises as the athlete can alternate between left and right sides for each rep)
[b] number in brackets = rest duration between sets
[c] based on the athlete's %1RM bilateral hip thrust to inform load during the single leg iso hip thrust hold (as in Figure 4.1, but with the bar lifted a few inches off the ground)
[d] based on the athlete's %1RM single leg, leg press to inform load during a single leg press hold with the knee angle at approximately 140° or a calf raise hold with knees extended and ankle joint at approximately 90°.

Reactive Strength

On the basis that the activities which most resemble sprinting with regards to their force-velocity and movement pattern characteristics have the highest carryover to sprint performance, reactive strength exercises through the use of plyometric exercises are likely to have the greatest transfer of training effect.

Plyometric training predominantly involves performing bodyweight jumping-type exercises using the SSC muscle action (see Section 2). The SSC enhances the ability of the neural and musculotendinous systems to produce maximal force in the shortest amount of time. Training through the use of plyometric training is seen as a 'bridge' between maximum strength and speed (Chmielewski, Myer, Kauffman, & Tillman, 2006).

Plyometric training is generally high in terms of intensity. While some low intensity exercises exist which are suitable for all training ages, other exercises are very stressful on the nervous and musculoskeletal system. Alongside the development of good joint alignment and exercise technique, a solid strength base should be developed before commencing certain plyometric exercises.

Table 4.10 lists a number of suggested plyometric exercises, their relative intensity levels and prerequisite strength targets, according to their intensity classification. It is prudent to start training with low intensity plyometric exercises before progressing onto higher intensity ones. Note that a more comprehensive plyometric exercise framework can be found in Section 6: Exercise Library.

When performing plyometric exercises, a number of rules should be adhered to:

Table 4.8. Example 4-week block when using the squat jump exercise to develop repeat power for an athlete with an intermediate training age (note a 'de-load' week is included in week 4).

Training age	Block	Sets	Reps	Week 1 Intensity (%1RM back squat)	Week 1 Set rest	Week 2 Reps	Week 2 Intensity (%1RM back squat)	Week 2 Set rest	Week 3 Reps	Week 3 Intensity (%1RM back squat)	Week 3 Set rest	Week 4 Reps	Week 4 Intensity (%1RM back squat)	Week 4 Set rest
Intermediate	1	1	5	0	2 min	5	0	2 min	5	0	2 min	5	0	2 min
		2	5	0	2 min	5	0	2 min	5	0	2 min	5	0	2 min
		3	8	0	2 min	8	0	2 min	8	0	2 min	–	–	–
		4	8	0	2 min	8	0	2 min	8	0	2 min	–	–	–
		5	8	0	2 min	8	0	2 min	8	0	2 min	–	–	–
	2	1	5	10	2 min	5	0	2 min	5	0	2 min	5	10	2 min
		2	5	10	2 min	5	0	2 min	5	0	2 min	5	10	2 min
		3	8	10	2 min	8	0	2 min	8	0	2 min	–	–	–
		4	8	10	2 min	8	0	2 min	8	0	2 min	–	–	–
		5	8	10	2 min	8	0	2 min	8	0	2 min	–	–	–
	3	1	5	20	2 min	5	20	2 min	5	20	2 min	5	20	2 min
		2	5	20	2 min	5	20	2 min	5	20	2 min	5	20	2 min
		3	8	20	2 min	8	20	2 min	8	20	2 min	–	–	–
		4	8	20	2 min	8	20	2 min	8	20	2 min	–	–	–
		5	8	20	2 min	8	20	2 min	8	20	2 min	–	–	–
	4	1	5	30	2 min	5	30	2 min	5	30	2 min	5	30	2 min
		2	5	30	2 min	5	30	2 min	5	30	2 min	5	30	2 min
		3	8	30	2 min	8	30	2 min	8	30	2 min	–	–	–
		4	8	30	2 min	8	30	2 min	8	30	2 min	–	–	–
		5	8	30	2 min	8	30	2 min	8	30	2 min	–	–	–

Table 4.9. Example 4-week block when using the squat jump exercise to develop repeat power for an athlete with an advanced training age (note a 'de-load' week is included in week 4).

Training age	Block	Sets	Reps	Week 1			Week 2			Week 3			Week 4		
				Intensity (%1RM back squat)	Set rest	Reps	Intensity (%1RM back squat)	Set rest	Reps	Intensity (%1RM back squat)	Set rest	Reps	Intensity (%1RM back squat)	Set rest	Reps
Advanced	1	1	5	0	2 min	5	0	2 min	5	0	2 min	5	0	2 min	5
		2	5	0	2 min	5	0	2 min	5	0	2 min	5	0	2 min	5
		3	10	0	2 min	10	0	2 min	10	0	2 min	10	–	–	–
		4	10	0	2 min	10	0	2 min	10	0	2 min	10	–	–	–
		5	10	0	2 min	10	0	2 min	10	0	2 min	10	–	–	–
		6	10	0	2 min	10	0	2 min	10	0	2 min	10	–	–	–
		7	10	0	2 min	10	0	2 min	10	0	2 min	10	–	–	–
	2	1	5	10	2 min	5	10	2 min	5	10	2 min	5	10	2 min	5
		2	5	10	2 min	5	10	2 min	5	10	2 min	5	10	2 min	5
		3	10	10	2 min	10	10	2 min	10	10	2 min	10	–	–	–
		4	10	10	2 min	10	10	2 min	10	10	2 min	10			
		5	10	10	2 min	10	10	2 min	10	10	2 min	10			
		6	10	10	2 min	10	10	2 min	10	10	2 min	10	–	–	–
		7	10	10	2 min	10	10	2 min	10	10	2 min	10	–	–	–
	3	1	5	20	2 min	5	20	2 min	5	20	2 min	5	20	2 min	5
		2	5	20	2 min	5	20	2 min	5	20	2 min	5	20	2 min	5
		3	10	20	2 min	10	20	2 min	10	20	2 min	10	–	–	–
		4	10	20	2 min	10	20	2 min	10	20	2 min	10	–	–	–
		5	10	20	2 min	10	20	2 min	10	20	2 min	10	–	–	–
		6	10	20	2 min	10	20	2 min	10	20	2 min	10	–	–	–
		7	10	20	2 min	10	20	2 min	10	20	2 min	10	–	–	–

Table 4.9. Example 4-week block when using the squat jump exercise to develop repeat power for an athlete with an advanced training age (note a 'de-load' week is included in week 4). (Continued)

Training age	Block	Sets	Reps	Week 1		Week 2			Week 3			Week 4		
				Intensity (%1RM back squat)	Set rest	Reps	Intensity (%1RM back squat)	Set rest	Reps	Intensity (%1RM back squat)	Set rest	Reps	Intensity (%1RM back squat)	Set rest
Advanced	4	1	5	30	2.5 min	5	30	2.5 min	5	30	2.5 min	5	30	2.5 min
		2	5	30	2.5 min	5	30	2.5 min	5	30	2.5 min	5	30	2.5 min
		3	10	30	2.5 min	10	30	2.5 min	10	30	2.5 min	5	30	2.5 min
		4	10	30	2.5 min	10	30	2.5 min	10	30	2.5 min	–	–	–
		5	10	30	2.5 min	10	30	2.5 min	10	30	2.5 min	–	–	–
		6	10	30	2.5 min	10	30	2.5 min	10	30	2.5 min	–	–	–
		7	10	30	2.5 min	10	30	2.5 min	10	30	2.5 min	–	–	–
	5	1	5	40	2-3 min	5	40	2-3 min	5	40	2-3 min	5	40	2-3 min
		2	5	40	2-3 min	5	40	2-3 min	5	40	2-3 min	5	40	2-3 min
		3	12	40	2-3 min	12	40	2-3 min	12	40	2-3 min	5	40	2-3 min
		4	12	40	2-3 min	12	40	2-3 min	12	40	2-3 min	–	–	–
		5	12	40	2-3 min	12	40	2-3 min	12	40	2-3 min	–	–	–
		6	12	40	2-3 min	12	40	2-3 min	12	40	2-3 min	–	–	–
		7	12	40	2-3 min	12	40	2-3 min	12	40	2-3 min	–	–	–

Table 4.10. Intensity classification and prerequisites for a variety of plyometric exercises.

Exercise intensity	Low	Medium	Medium high	High to very high
Prerequisites	Good technique	Good technique	Good technique	Good technique
	Able to squat (no external load) with good technique	Able to squat a load equal to bodyweight	Able to squat a load equal to 1.3 × bodyweight	Able to squat a load equal to 1.75 × bodyweight
	–	Able to perform 5 squats in 6 s using a load equal to 30% of bodyweight	Able to perform 5 squats in 5 s using a load equal to 50% of bodyweight	Able to perform 5 squats in 5 s using a load equal to 60% of bodyweight
	–	Minimum of several months' experience with maximum strength training methods	Minimum of several months' experience with medium level intensity plyometric training	Minimum of several months' experience with medium high-level intensity plyometric training
Example exercises	Pogos (aiming for low jump height and minimum contact time)	Pogo (rhythmic, medball overhead)	Hops	Hop hurdle hop (high hurdle)
	Submaximal hops	Acceleration bound	Bounding (double arm, rolling start)	Drop jump (high box)
	Skips for height	Hurdle rebound jump (low hurdle)	Repeated broad jump	
	Skips for distance			

- Focus should be on quality of movement rather than quantity. As soon as quality of movement (i.e. technique) and/or speed break down, the set should be stopped
- Each repetition should be performed explosively and maximally
- At the point of landing, weight should be balanced toward the front half of the foot rather than landing on the toes of heels
- Minimum ground contact time should be a main priority
- Exercises should be performed on a soft yet firm surface—grass, sprung floor and some running tracks are suitable

Plyometric volume during an individual session is determined by the type and complexity of the exercise(s) being performed, and is typically defined by the number of foot contacts and/or reps.

Table 4.11 lists the 'optimal' dosages for the development of reactive strength, taking into account the considerations already mentioned. The way in which a foot contact or repetition is defined may differ depending on the type of exercise being performed. Definitions have been provided in Table 4.12.

Exercise Selection: General-Specific Continuum

Any change or adaptation in the body's muscles, organs and systems will be very specific to the type of training (stress) undertaken. This relates to the training principle of specificity, which in simple terms means that if an athlete wants to improve their sprinting speed, they need to practice sprinting. This begs the question: why not just practice sprinting, since this is the most specific way to improve sprint performance? This is, after all, why the majority of training undertaken to improve running speed should be spent sprinting.

However, there is a limit to the amount of overload which can be applied to the sprinting action, and therefore fewer adaptations are likely to occur from simply practicing sprinting itself. Therefore, less specific activities (such as strength training) are carried out so that more significant overload can be applied, providing the adaptations elicited in an athlete by this type of training are still transferable to their sprinting performance.

A general-specific continuum of activities therefore exists, upon which strength exercises

can be placed based on their mechanical specificity to sprinting. Although strength exercises of a more general nature may form the foundation of an athlete's strength training schedule, selecting exercises that have a greater dynamic correspondence to sprinting is important at certain times. When these exercises should be employed as part of a training plan will be discussed in Section 5: Periodisation.

The biomechanical differences identified between accelerative and maximum velocity sprinting in Section 3 suggest that exercise selection is important to maximise the transfer of strength training effects to a specific sprint phase. There are numerous strength training exercises which may be suitable to develop both phases of sprinting. The strength exercises within this book are classified in a hierarchy, according to the degree to which they correspond dynamically to accelerative and maximum velocity sprinting (Table 4.13).

Stage 1 Exercises

Stage 1 exercises (Table 4.13; also see Section 6: Exercise Library) produce high forces against the ground, and are generally used to develop neuromuscular adaptations such as motor unit recruitment and firing frequency (Hakkinen, et al., 2003; Moritani & DeVries, 1979; Narici, Roi, Landoni, Minetti, & Cerretelli, 1989).

These exercises are related to the ability to produce force through a triple extension (hips, knees and ankles) movement pattern (Carroll, 2001; Delecluse, et al., 1995; Harris, Cronin, Hopkins, & Hansen, 2008). As such, high

Table 4.11. Individual session program design variables for reactive strength development.

Training for reactive strength development					
Bodyweight			**Very light loads**		
Adaptations: Enhanced utilisation of SSC cycle; RFD at very high velocities; increased stiffness; Intermuscular coordination; reduced antagonist co-contraction					
Beginner					
No. of exercises	**Intensity**	**Session foot contacts**	**Rep range per set**	**Sets**	**Rest between sets (min)**
2–4	L	30–80	4–10	2–4	1 to 3
	M	20–60	3–5		
Intermediate					
No. of exercises	**Intensity**	**Session foot contacts**	**Rep range per set**	**Sets**	**Rest between sets (min)**
3–5	L	30–100	4–10	3–4	1 to 2
	M	30–80	4–6		2 to 3
	MH	20–60	3–6		2 to 4
Advanced					
No. of exercises	**Intensity**	**Session foot contacts**	**Rep range per set**	**Sets**	**Rest between sets (min)**
3–6	L	30–150+	4–10	3–6	1 to 2
	M	30–120	4–8		2 to 3
	MH		3–8		2 to 4
	H	20–100	3–6		3 to 5
	VH		3–5		

force maximum strength exercises (e.g. squats and deadlifts) and high force, high velocity exercises (e.g. cleans and snatches) may induce neural adaptations, which enable the athlete to recruit larger motor units (fast twitch) more effectively for the similar movement patterns observed in sprinting (Haff, Whitley, & Potteiger, 2001).

Stage 2 Exercises

Although stage 1 exercises do not necessarily closely replicate the kinematics of sprinting, it is not until more specific preparatory phases of training that exercises bearing greater resemblance to sprinting are implemented, to help direct the strength

Table 4.12. Foot contact and repetition classification according to exercise type.

1 foot contact defined as	Exercise	1 rep determined by	Rest between reps
2 consecutive unilateral ground contacts (i.e. touchdown and take-off with 1 foot followed by the other)	Speed bound Bounding	Coverage of a set distance (typically 20 to 60 m)	Slow walk back recovery; work : rest ratio—1:10
1 bilateral ground contact (i.e. touchdown and take-off with both feet simultaneously)	Repeated broad jump Drop jump	1 jump	None None 5–15 s
	Hurdle rebound jump	A prescribed number of jumps (typically 4 to 8) or a single rebound jump	Slow walk back recovery; work : rest ratio—1:10
1 ground contact with each leg (e.g. 5 hops/ jumps on the right leg followed by 5 hops/jumps on the left leg would equate to 5 foot contacts in total)	Hops	Coverage of set distance or 1 hop	
	Single leg depth jump	1 jump	5 to 10 s

increases gained from stage 1 exercises toward the sprinting action.

Stage 2 exercises are typically used to increase RFD and reactive strength, so as to enhance the ability to apply force more quickly during the ground contact phase of sprinting. The relatively short ground contact times during sprinting constrains an athlete's ability to sprint quickly. The time it takes to develop large amounts of force in the lower limbs far exceeds the time available during the ground contact phase of a sprint (Harridge, et al., 1996). With this in mind it would appear that strategies to increase RFD should supersede those implemented to increase maximum strength during more specific phases of training.

A large percentage of stage 2 exercises increase the rate that force can be produced, through an enhanced utilisation of the SSC (Cavagna, Dusman, & Margaria, 1968; Turner & Jeffreys, 2010). The duration of contact during activities reflect the type of SSC function taking place. It has been suggested that the SSC can be classified as fast if the contact times are less than 0.25 s, and slow if they are greater (Schmidtbleicher, 1992).

Although the understanding of the SSC mechanisms remains incomplete, different

Table 4.13. Classification of exercises based on their mechanical specificity to sprint running.

Acceleration specific	Maximum velocity specific	Acceleration specific	Maximum velocity specific	Acceleration specific	Maximum velocity specific
Clean and Snatch variations	Standing long jump	Hurdle rebound jumps	Sled sprints	Speed bounding	
Lunge and split squat variations	Standing triple jump	Depth/drop jumps	Hill sprints	Weighted vest sprints	
Squat and Deadlift variations	Medball heave (forwards)				
Stage 1 exercises	Stage 2 exercises		Stage 3 exercises		
Low mechanical specificity		High mechanical specificity			

adaptations are likely to result from the fast and slow SSC (Bobbert, Huijing, & van Ingen Schenau, 1987), and so training with slow SSC may not be suited to activities that involve a fast SSC and vice versa.

The ground contact times during all phases of a sprint imply that a fast SSC occurs. As already identified, however, there are clearly differences in contact time as a sprint progresses, and simply classifying all contact into the same 'fast SSC' category may be misleading, since contact times during early acceleration can be around double those observed during maximum velocity Where possible, exercises with contact times at the shorter end of the 'fast SSC' continuum should be selected for maximum velocity and the longer end for acceleration, although in reality there may be few exercises (namely plyometric exercises) where the ground contact times are less than 0.16 s (Young, 1992).

Even though there is a disparity between contact time during plyometric exercises and sprinting, greater forces are typically produced during a number of plyometric exercises (Mero & Komi, 1994). As a result, in exercises such as bounding and hopping where ground contact times are longer than those during sprinting, one could speculate that they are still likely to have a positive transfer effect due to the higher levels of force production and the similar leg extension patterns adopted.

The stage 2 exercises listed as suitable to all sprint phases within Table 4.13 appear to provide a transition from stage 1 to more specific stage 2 exercises, and allow for a logical progression of training. To a great extent they do not correspond dynamically to one phase or another but are suggested to have mechanical similarities to both phases of a sprint, and so can be classified as stage 2 exercises for developing sprint performance.

The stage 2 exercises suggested for the development of acceleration (Table 4.13) place an emphasis on the development of explosive concentric strength, previously identified as important during this phase. A major consideration in regard to the type of exercises selected during maximum velocity specific training are the increased braking forces evident as a sprint progresses from early acceleration toward maximum velocity. The explosive power generating (net concentric) action of muscles about the knee and ankle during acceleration make way for greater eccentric strength demands, which becomes increasingly important as velocity increases. This is due to the increased negative vertical velocity which an athlete must reverse upon contact, which is evident from the increased power dissipation (net eccentric work) observed about the ankle and knee joints as a sprint progresses.

The exercises suggested in Table 4.13 for the development of maximum velocity sprint running are typically characterised by vertical force production, smaller displacements at the ankle, knee and hip, and a greater emphasis on power dissipation (eccentric strength) requirements when compared to acceleration.

Stage 3 Exercises

Stage 3 exercises overload a mechanical element of a sprint phase and thus replicate the movement patterns of sprinting more closely. There are fewer exercises to choose from in stage 3, and resisted sprinting and various plyometric exercises are typically used for improving sprint performance in this phase (Costello, 1985; Donati, 1996; Faccioni, 1993a; Faccioni, 1993b; Young, 1992).

Sled towing, with low loads, is a stage 3 exercise for accelerative sprinting, purported to lead to greater levels of adaptation by recruiting more muscle fibres through increasing the load on the leg extensors (Clark, Stearne, Walts, & Miller, 2010; Faccioni, 1993a). A load which represents 10% of body mass is said to be optimal for sled towing (Alcaraz, Palao, & Elvira, 2009; Maulder, Bradshaw, & Keogh, 2008; Murray, et al., 2005). Similarly, it has been suggested that acceleration velocity should be decreased by no greater than 10% as a result of towing a load (Jakalski, 1998).

These guidelines should not prohibit the use of heavier loads at times during training, especially early on in the annual training plan. Hill (uphill) running is also suggested to improve accelerative sprint performance (Costello, 1981; Dintiman, 1964; Faccioni, 1993a). Research regarding an optimal gradient to use is scarce, but as a stage 3 exercise it is recommended that slopes do not exceed 3° (Dintiman, 1964; Paradisis & Cooke, 2001; Paradisis & Cooke, 2006).

Utilising weighted vests whilst sprinting has been suggested as a means to improve maximum velocity sprint running speed (Alcaraz, Palao, Elvira, & Linthorne, 2008; Clark, Stearne, Walts, & Miller, 2010; Cronin, Hansen, Kawamori, & McNair, 2008; Sands, et al., 1996). While limited research exists in this area, guidelines for the optimal load given for sled towing already mentioned should be followed.

Bounding exercises have been shown to produce similar force-time characteristics to that of maximum velocity sprinting (Mero & Komi, 1994; Young, 1992), and are performed unilaterally in a cyclical manner whilst generating high forces, which are marked by large flight times when compared to sprinting at maximum velocity. For these reasons, bounding exercises would appear to be mechanically specific to maximum velocity sprinting, while remaining favourable in terms of the principle of overload.

Trunk Training

Definition and Structure

The trunk is an important consideration for sprint running athletes. For the purposes of this book and for simplicity, if you discount the arms and legs, the trunk is what remains. Before discussing the function of the trunk in sprinting, an understanding of its structure is necessary. Broadly speaking, the trunk musculature is composed of three different layers—deep, middle and outer.

The deep muscle layer of the trunk consists of a number of 'position sense' muscles which cross from one vertebral segment to another. They are responsible for controlling accessory movement at the segmental level of the spine (Figure 4.2).

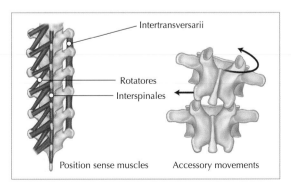

Figure 4.2. Deep layer trunk muscles.

For example, when the hip is powerfully flexed and extended during a sprint, although the spine may outwardly appear to be fixed in its position, small accessory movements will be taking place at each vertebral segment. Depending on the task at hand, each segment will rotate, flex and slide on top of one another. Position sense muscles are important in controlling these movements and to prevent excess displacement, which could lead to injury.

Middle layer muscles include the transversus abdominis, internal obliques, lumbar multifidus, diaphragm and pelvic floor (Figure 4.3). As these muscles contract, they create a non-compressible cylinder where the spine is stabilised. This helps to provide a working foundation from which the legs and arms can function optimally during a sprint.

The outer layer muscles of the trunk include the rectus abdominis, external obliques, erector spinae, latissimus dorsi, the gluteals and the adductors (Figure 4.4). These muscles contribute to the ability to maintain an optimal working relationship between joints and intermuscular coordination to integrate the various body segments when sprinting.

Function of the Trunk

During sprinting, the primary role of the trunk is to transfer force from the lower extremities upon ground contact to an athlete's centre of mass. The trunk as a whole therefore provides an anchor point from which the limbs can exert force. A weak trunk is likely to result in less than optimal limb mechanics during a sprint, which in turn will result in

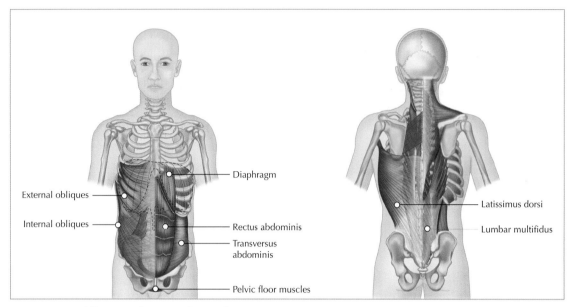

Figure 4.3. Middle/outer layer trunk muscles.

reduced ground reaction forces and wasted energy through compensatory movements.

For example, during ground contact the hip flexors of the contact leg will at some point activate to decelerate hip extension, ready to swing the leg forward into the next step. This hip flexor activation will create a pulling force on the lumbar spine and pelvis. If the trunk muscles are not strong enough to withstand this force, then this is likely to result in an excessive anterior pelvic tilt and an increased lumbar curvature (Figure 4.5). Such an excessive movement may predispose an athlete to low back injury and will result in poor efficiency when recovery the leg ready for the next step.

Based on the discussion so far, the goals of trunk training should be aimed at improving

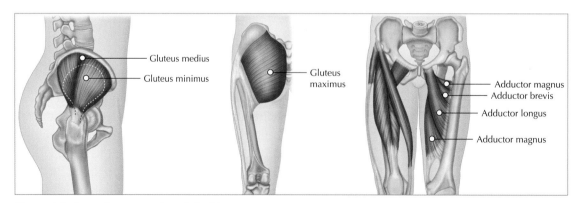

Figure 4.4. Outer layer muscles of the hips.

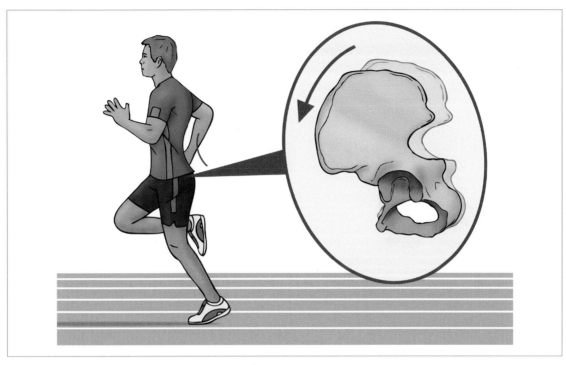

Figure 4.5. Lumbo-pelvic control during ground contact.

the ability of the trunk muscles to transmit forces and to handle high forces safely. Predominantly—when sprinting—the trunk musculature is used isometrically, i.e. there isn't a great deal of movement from the trunk. The trunk is 'stiffened' to provide a stable foundation, so that force can be transferred from the lower extremities to the athlete's centre of mass.

Although sessions consisting only of trunk exercises are not uncommon, a number of trunk exercises (typically 2 to 4) are positioned at the end of a strength training session and performed as part of a circuit. A select number of trunk exercises may also be placed as part of a warm-up to activate key muscles before the main part of the session.

Tables 4.14–4.18 provide a list of suitable exercises based on their difficulty, and include the appropriate program design variable to improve trunk strength, stabilisation and stiffness. All of these exercises are shown below.

Trunk

FLEXION STABILISATION (EASY)		
Plank	**Phase**	**Teaching Points**
	Start	• Lie face down with forearms on floor • Elbows directly below shoulders • Head in neutral position
	Ascent	• Take a breath in and hold • Tighten abdominals • Raise torso off floor, keeping the body aligned from the head to feet
	Position	• Head, shoulders, hips, knees and ankles all aligned • Tight abdominals • Head in neutral position • Breathe naturally

Side Plank	**Phase**	**Teaching Points**
	Start	• Lie on your side with your upper body supported by your forearm • Elbow aligned under shoulder • One leg on top of the other • Non-supporting arm placed on your hip
	Ascent	• Breathe in and hold • Tighten abdominals and glutes • Raise hips off floor
	Position	• Head, shoulders, hips, knees and ankles aligned • Elbow aligned under shoulder • Wrist aligned with elbow • Tight abdominals and glutes • Head and back in neutral position • Breathe naturally

Swiss Ball Plank	**Phase**	**Teaching Points**
	Start	• Kneel with ball placed slightly in front of you • Lean on top of ball with your forearms • Head in neutral position • Maintain neutral position of spine
	Ascent	• Extend at the knee and step back, one leg followed by the other • Lean forward slightly, bringing shoulders in line above elbows • Tighten abdominals
	Position	• Head, shoulders, hips, knees and ankles aligned • Straight back • Elbows directly below shoulders • Tighten abdominals • Head in neutral position • Breathe naturally

FLEXION STABILISATION (INTERMEDIATE)		
Press-up Plank with Rotation	**Phase**	**Teaching Points**
	Start	• Feet hip-width apart • Ankles, knees, hips and shoulders aligned • Hands shoulder-width apart with shoulder, elbow and wrist aligned • Hands flat on floor; fingers pointing forward • Head in neutral position • Tighten abdominals
	Exercise	• Rotate at hips and shoulders to bring one hand off floor • Keep both feet on floor • Arm extended with wrist, elbow, shoulder and back aligned • Head in neutral position • Rotate to return to start position and repeat with other arm

One Leg Plank	Phase	Teaching Points
	Start	• Lie face down on floor • Forearms on floor • Elbows directly below shoulders • Head in neutral position
	Ascent	• Take a breath in and hold • Tighten abdominals • Raise torso off floor, keeping body aligned from head to feet
	Position	• Raise one leg off floor • Maintain neutral position of hips (no tilt) • Tighten abdominals • Head and back in neutral position • Breathe naturally

One Arm Plank	Phase	Teaching Points
	Start	• Lie face down with forearms on floor • Elbows directly below shoulders • Head in neutral position
	Ascent	• Take a breath in and hold • Tighten abdominals • Raise torso off floor, keeping body aligned from head to feet
	Position	• Raise one arm off floor • Extend arm at elbow and shoulder • Arm at shoulder height • Maintain neutral position of shoulders and hips (no tilt) • Head, shoulders, hips, knees and ankles aligned • Tighten abdominals • Head and back in neutral position • Breathe naturally

Modified Renegade Row	**Phase**	**Teaching Points**
	Start	• Feet positioned on a block so that ankles, hips, shoulders and head are aligned when arms are fully extended • Hands flat on floor; fingers pointing forward • Arms directly below shoulders • Shoulders, elbows and wrists all aligned • Head in neutral position • Straight back • Tighten abdominals
	Exercise	• Perform a rowing movement, flexing at the elbow • Elbow pointing toward ceiling • Extend at elbow, returning to floor • Repeat with other arm • Maintain tight abdominals • Maintain alignment at head, shoulders, hips, knees and ankles • Minimise trunk sway • Perform in a controlled manner

FLEXION STABILISATION (HARD)		
Dumbbell Renegade Row	**Phase**	**Teaching Points**
	Start	• Feet positioned on a block so that ankles, hips, shoulders and head are aligned when arms are fully extended • Hands gripped around dumbbell; dumbbells rest on floor • Arms directly below shoulders • Shoulders, elbows and wrists all aligned • Head in neutral position • Straight back • Tighten abdominals

Dumbbell Renegade Row	Phase	Teaching Points
	Exercise	• Perform a rowing movement, flexing at elbow, bringing dumbbell toward side of body • Elbow pointing toward ceiling • Extend at elbow, returning to floor • Repeat with other arm • Maintain tight abdominals • Maintain alignment at head, shoulders, hips, knees and ankles • Minimise trunk sway • Perform in a controlled manner

Press-up Walk Out	Phase	Teaching Points
	Start	• Feet hip-width apart • Ankles, knees, hips and shoulders aligned • Hands shoulder-width apart with shoulder, elbow and wrist aligned • Hands flat on floor, fingers pointing forward • Head in neutral position • Tighten abdominals
	Walk out	• "Walk" hand out away from body • Repeat until your hands are as far away as possible while maintaining good alignment • Keep straight body alignment head to toe
	End	• Tight abdominals • Ankles, knees, hips and shoulders aligned • Head and back in neutral position
	Walk in	• "Walk" hands back to the start position • Maintain good body alignment • Keep back in neutral position

One Arm One Leg Plank	Phase	Teaching Points
	Start	• Lie face down with forearms on floor • Elbows directly below shoulders • Head in neutral position
	Ascent	• Take a breath in and hold • Tighten abdominals • Raise torso off floor, keeping body aligned from head to feet
	Position	• Raise one leg and opposite arm off floor simultaneously • Maintain neutral position of shoulders and hips (no tilt) • Tighten abdominals • Head and back in neutral position • Breathe naturally

FLEXION STRENGTH AND POWER (EASY)		
Lower Abdominal 1	**Phase**	**Teaching Points**
	Start	• Lie on back and flex knees with feet flat on floor • Feet hip-width apart • Head in neutral position (looking toward ceiling) • Place hands under lower back (directly below navel) • Tighten abdominals and tilt pelvis so lower back applies pressure on hands • Maintain this pressure on hands throughout
	Exercise	• Flex at hip, bringing knee toward chest • Maintain knee angle • Maintain pressure on hands from lower back • Other foot remains flat on floor • Extend at hip, moving knee away from chest and foot back to floor • Repeat with other leg

Lower Abdominal 2	**Phase**	**Teaching Points**
	Start	• Lie on back and flex knees and hips so feet begin in the air • Toes pointing toward ceiling • Head in neutral position (looking toward ceiling) • Place hands under lower back (directly below the navel) • Tighten abdominals and tilt pelvis so lower back applies pressure on hands • Maintain this pressure on hands throughout
	Exercise	• Extend at hip, bringing one foot toward the floor • Maintain knee angle • Maintain pressure on hands from lower back • Other leg remains in start position • Continue lowering leg until foot is placed on floor • Flex at hip, moving leg back to start position • Repeat with other leg

Swiss Ball Crunches	**Phase**	**Teaching Points**
	Start	• Lie on ball so arch of back is supported by ball • Relax head back • Place hands on temples • Feet hip-width apart • Feet flat on floor
	Ascent	• Breathe in • Tighten abdominals and raise upper back and shoulders off ball • Flex at trunk • Head in neutral position • Ball remains in same place on floor

Medball Swiss Ball Crunch Throw	Phase	Teaching Points
	Start	• Lie on ball so back is supported by ball • Shoulders not in contact with the ball • Hold medicine ball above hips, higher than head height • Tighten abdominals, glutes and legs to hold this position • Head in neutral position • Feet hip-width apart, flat on floor
	Counter-movement	• Breathe in • Extend back and shoulders to bring shoulders in contact with ball and medball over your head toward the floor • Weight shifts backward • Lower back still in contact with ball
	Throw	• Raise upper back off ball • Simultaneously throw medball • Release medball when it is above chest • Lower back remains in contact with ball • Exhale when performing throw

Swiss Ball Roll Out	Phase	Teaching Points
	Start	• Kneel up with ball placed slightly in front of you • Clasp hands together and lean on top of ball with side of hands and wrists • Head and spine in neutral position • Head, shoulders and hips all aligned
	Roll out	• Tighten abdominals • Extend at knees • Extend at shoulders and elbows to allow arms to roll over ball and ball to move forward • Head, shoulders, back, hips and knees all aligned • Extend as far forward as possible while maintaining good posture

Swiss Ball Roll Out	Phase	Teaching Points
	Roll in	• Flex at knees, shoulders and elbows, bringing the ball backward • Maintain good body alignment • Keep back in neutral position • Finish in start position

FLEXION STRENGTH AND POWER (INTERMEDIATE)

Lower Abdominal 3	Phase	Teaching Points
	Start	• Lie on back and flex knees and hips so feet begin in mid-air • Toes pointing toward ceiling • Head in neutral position (looking towards ceiling) • Place hands under lower back (so that they are directly below navel) • Tighten abdominals and tilt pelvis so lower back applies pressure on hands • Maintain this pressure on hands throughout
	Exercise	• Extend at hips, bringing feet towards floor • Maintain knee and ankle angle • Maintain pressure on hands from lower back • Keep legs and feet together • Continue lowering legs until feet are placed on floor • Flex at hips, returning legs to start position

V-sits	Phase	Teaching Points
	Start	• Lie on back • Elbows, shoulders, hips and knees extended • Arms shoulder-width apart • Forearms and palms facing the ceiling • Head in neutral position (looking toward ceiling) • Toes pointing toward ceiling

V-sits	Phase	Teaching Points
	Ascent	• Tighten abdominals • Take breath in • Simultaneously lift legs and back off the floor, bringing feet toward shoulders and upper body toward feet • Flex at shoulder, bringing arms up and over head • Keep a straight back • Keep feet and legs together • Maintain straight elbows and knees • Maintain head in neutral position
	Top	• Upper and lower body symmetrical • Straight back • Arms reached forward toward toes • Head in neutral position
	Descent	• Simultaneously lower legs and back towards the floor • Also extend at shoulder to bring arms back towards floor and overhead • Back to start position • Exhale

FLEXION STRENGTH AND POWER (HARD)

Medball V-sits	Phase	Teaching Points
	Start	• Lie on back • Extension at elbows, shoulders, hips and knees • Arms shoulder-width apart • Hold medball in line with top of head • Head in neutral position (looking toward ceiling) • Toes pointing toward ceiling

Medball V-sits	**Phase**	**Teaching Points**
	Ascent	• Tighten abdominals • Take breath in • Simultaneously lift legs and back off floor, bringing feet toward shoulders and upper body toward feet • Flex at shoulder, bringing medball up and over head • Keep feet and legs together • Keep elbows and knees straight
	Top	• Upper and lower body symmetrical • Touch medball to feet
	Descent	• Simultaneously lower legs and back toward the floor • Also extend at shoulder to bring medball back toward floor and overhead • Back to start position • Exhale

Hanging Leg Raise	**Phase**	**Teaching Points**
	Start	• Extend at shoulders and elbows to grip the bar overhead • Grip shoulder-width apart. Use overhand grip • Ankles, knees, hips shoulders and head all aligned • Straight back • Head in neutral position • Hang from bar

Hanging Leg Raise	Phase	Teaching Points
	Ascent	• Tighten abdominals • Flex ("hinge") at the hips, bringing your legs up in front of you • Keep legs straight and together • Maintain position of upper body. Avoid "swinging" the body • Arms remain extended • Move legs as high as possible whilst maintaining good body alignment
	Descent	• Extend at hips, lowering legs back down to neutral position • Maintain good body alignment • Return to hang position

Lower Abdominal 4	Phase	Teaching Points
	Start	• Lie on back and flex at hips to 90° • Extend at knees • Head in neutral position (looking toward ceiling) • Place hands under lower back (directly below navel) • Tighten abdominals and tilt pelvis so low back applies pressure on hands • Maintain this pressure on hands throughout
	Exercise	• Extend at hips, bringing feet toward the floor • Maintain straight legs • Maintain pressure on hands from low back • Keep legs and feet together • Continue lowering legs until heels touch floor • Flex at hips, moving legs back to start position whilst maintaining the same amount of pressure on hands from the low back

ROTATIONAL STRENGTH AND POWER (EASY)

Swiss Ball Russian Twist	Phase	Teaching Points
	Start	• Lie on ball so head, shoulders and upper back are supported by ball • Tighten abdominals and lower back • Keep a straight back • Head, shoulders, hips and knees aligned • Feet hip-width apart • Extend at elbows and bring palms of hands together above your chest
	Exercise	• Twist at trunk, rotating to one side • Only shoulder and upper back of one side in contact with the ball • Head in neutral position • Keep feet flat on floor • Twist at trunk all the way through to the other side

Medball Reverse Chop	Phase	Teaching Points
	Start	• Feet slightly wider than shoulder-width apart • Toes, knees and hips pointing forward • Weight shifted to side while ball is being held • Hold ball above and slightly in front of knee with trunk rotated • Arms extended • Head looking forward
	Exercise	• Rotate at trunk to move the ball up and across body • Shift weight laterally across to other leg • Ball finishes above head height • Arms stay extended • Straight back
	Recovery	• Rotate trunk back to starting position, bringing ball down and across your body • Shift weight across to other leg

Cable Reverse Chop	Phase	Teaching Points
	Start	• Position body so pulley handle is slightly above knee height and in front of you • Feet slightly wider than shoulder-width apart • Toes pointing slightly outward • Weight shifted to same side as pulley • Hold pulley with both hands, arms straight • Head looking forward
	Exercise	• Rotate at shoulders and trunk to pull handle upward and across body • Shift weight laterally across to other leg • Handle finishes above head height • Arms straight throughout • Straight back
	Recovery	• Rotate shoulders, trunk and hips back to starting position • Shift weight back toward leg closest to pulley

Cable Chop	Phase	Teaching Points
	Start	• Position body so pulley handle is above shoulder height and in front of you • Feet slightly wider than shoulder-width apart • Toes pointing slightly outward • Weight shifted to same side as pulley • Hold pulley with both hands • Head looking forward
	Exercise	• Rotate at shoulders and trunk to pull handle downward and across body • Shift weight laterally across to other leg • Handle finishes above knee • Arms straight throughout • Straight back
	Recovery	• Rotate shoulders and trunk back to starting position • Shift weight back toward leg closest to pulley

Medball Seated Rotation	Phase	Teaching Points
	Start	• Sit with knees slightly flexed and heels in contact with floor • Lean back slightly at hips • Keep straight back • Head in neutral position • Hold ball above knees
	Exercise	• Rotate at the trunk to one side, bringing the ball across the body and down toward floor • Touch ball on floor • Keep straight back • Head looking forward • Keep glutes and heels on floor • Hips, knees and ankles remain in starting position • Rotate all the way through to other side

ROTATIONAL STRENGTH AND POWER (INTERMEDIATE)

Medball Swiss Ball Russian Twist	Phase	Teaching Points
	Start	• Lie on ball so that head, shoulders and upper back are supported • Tighten abdominals • Keep straight back • Head, shoulders, hips and knees aligned • Feet hip-width apart • Extend at elbows and hold medball above your chest
	Exercise	• Rotate at trunk to one side • Keep feet flat on floor • Head in neutral position • Only the shoulder and upper back of one side in contact with ball • Rotate at trunk to other side

Medball Explosive Chops	Phase	Teaching Points
	Start	• Stand with feet shoulder-width apart • Toes pointing forward • Hold medball at hip height and slightly to one side of navel • Head looking straight ahead
	Counter-movement	• Rotate at trunk, shoulders and hips to take medball upward and across the body • Weight shifted toward same side as medball • Medball finishes in line with shoulder and above the head
	Throw	• Rotate at trunk, shoulders and hips to take the medball downward and across the body • Shift weight laterally across your body • Extend elbows to throw medball so that it lands in line with knee, slightly in front of you • Counter-movement and throw performed as a fluent, explosive action

Medball Explosive Reverse Chops	Phase	Teaching Points
	Start	• Stand with feet shoulder-width apart • Toes pointing forward • Hold medball at shoulder height and in line with shoulder (to one side) • Head looking straight ahead
	Counter-movement	• Rotate at trunk, shoulders and hips to take medball downward and across body • Weight shifted toward same side as medball • Medball finishes between knee and hip height • Toe, knee, hip, shoulder and head aligned

Medball Explosive Reverse Chops	Phase	Teaching Points
	Throw	• Rotate at trunk, shoulders and hips to take medball upward and across body • Shift weight laterally across body • Extend elbows to throw medball, releasing it when in line with shoulder and above head height • Counter-movement and throw performed as a fluent, explosive action

ROTATIONAL STRENGTH AND POWER (HARD)

Barbell Russian Twist	Phase	Teaching Points
	Start	• Stand with feet shoulder-width apart • Toes pointing forward • Weight evenly distributed either side of barbell • Grip barbell at head height, one hand above the other • Arms extended • Stand far enough away from barbell so it is slightly leaning toward you when you grip • Tighten abdominals • Straight back
	Rotate to right	• Rotate at shoulders, trunk, hips, knees and ankles to take barbell downward and across the body • Decelerate the movement keeping abdominals tight • Weight shifted toward same side as barbell • Arms remain extended • Knees flexed • Head in neutral position • Straight back
	Rotate to left	• Rotate explosively all the way through to other side • Continue rotating side to side with no break for desired number of repetitions

Medball Wall Rebound Rotations	Phase	Teaching Points
	Start	• Stand side on, approximately 1 m away from wall • Feet shoulder-width apart • Toes pointing forward • Hold medball at chest height • Flex at the knees • Good body alignment
	Counter-movement	• Rotate trunk away from the wall • Medball moves across and down body • Flex knees • Weight shifts away from wall
	Throw	• Rotate trunk toward wall • Extend at knees • Shift weight toward wall • Move medball upward and across the body and throw to wall
	Catch and recovery	• Begin to rotate back to start position • Catch ball • Immediately continue into counter-movement phase as above and repeat throw • Continue without a break for required number of repetitions

EXTENSION STABILISATION AND STRENGTH (EASY)		
Prone Hold	**Phase**	**Teaching Points**
	Start	• Lie on a bench with end of bench resting under crease of hips • Hands placed on floor, shoulder-width apart • Ankles, knees, hips and shoulders aligned • Head in a neutral position (looking down)
	Position	• Either partner holds down legs or hook feet under a fixed object to keep you stationary • Tighten lower back and abdominals • Take hands off floor and cross across chest • Ankles, knees, hips and shoulders aligned • Head and back in neutral position • Hold for desired length of time
	Descent	• Place hands back on floor

Back Hyperextensions	**Phase**	**Teaching Points**
	Start	• Lie flat on your front • Feet, knees, hips, shoulders and head aligned • Head looking at floor • Hands on temples • Toes in contact with floor
	Ascent	• Lift head, shoulders and chest off floor by hyperextending back • Keep hips and toes in contact with floor • Head in neutral position
	Descent	• Lower chest and shoulders toward the floor • Maintain good body alignment

EXTENSION STABILISATION AND STRENGTH (INTERMEDIATE)

Swiss Ball Back Extensions	Phase	Teaching Points
	Start	• Ball positioned under hips • Place feet against wall • Feet hip-width apart • Slight flexion at knees • Upper body curved over ball • Head in neutral position • Hands on temples
	Ascent	• Tighten lower back • Lift head, shoulders and chest off ball by extending back • Keep hips in contact with ball • Keep toes in contact with wall • Ankles, knees, hips and shoulders aligned • Head in neutral position • Ball remains in same place on floor
	Descent	• Lower abdomen, chest and shoulders toward floor • Maintain good body alignment • Curve your body around ball, as in start position

Medball Prone Hold	Phase	Teaching Points
	Start	• Lie on a bench with end of bench resting under top of thighs • Hands placed on floor, shoulder-width apart • Ball between arms • Ankles, knees, hips and shoulders aligned • Head in neutral position (looking down)
	Position	• Either partner holds down legs or hook ankles under a fixed object to keep you stationary • Tighten lower back and abdominals • Pick up ball and hold to chest • Ankles, knees, hips and shoulders aligned • Head in neutral position
	Descent	• Drop ball and place hands back on floor

EXTENSION STABILISATION AND STRENGTH (HARD)

Barbell Isometric Romanian Deadlift Hold	Phase	Teaching Points
	Start	• Feet hip-width apart, toes pointing forward • Shoulder blades pulled back and down • Chest up and out • Straight back • Head up (look straight ahead) • Grip bar outside of legs, both hands in overhand grip • Weight evenly distributed
	Descent	• Slight flexion at knee. Maintain this degree of flexion throughout descent • Flex ("hinge") at hips, lowering bar towards floor • Maintain neutral position of lower back (lordotic curve)
	Position	• Maintain neutral position of low back • Head up (looking straight ahead) • Flexion at hips • Slight flexion at knees • Chest and shoulders over bar • Arms extended at elbow • Hold position
	Ascent	• Extend at hip and knees • Maintain neutral (straight) lower back position • Return to start position

Plate Prone Hold	Phase	Teaching Points
	Start	• Lie on a bench so end of bench rests at crease of hips • Ankles, knees, hips and shoulders aligned • Head in neutral position (looking down)

Plate Prone Hold	Phase	Teaching Points
	Position	• Partner holds down legs • Tighten lower back and abdominals • Pick up plate and hold to chest • Ankles, knees, hips and shoulders aligned • Head in neutral position • Hold for required length of time
	Descent	• Lower plate and place hands back on floor

GLUTE ACTIVATION AND STRENGTH (EASY)

Reverse Hyperextensions	Phase	Teaching Points
	Start	• Lie flat on your front • Feet, knees, hips, shoulders and head aligned • Head looking at floor • Hands resting on top of each other • Forehead resting on hands • Toes in contact with floor
	Ascent	• Tighten lower back and abdominals • Lift legs up and off floor • Legs remain straight • Hips in contact with floor
	Descent	• Lower legs back to floor

Bodyweight Single Leg Romanian Deadlift	Phase	Teaching Points
	Start	• Feet hip-width apart, toes pointing forward • Shoulder blades pulled back and down • Chest up and out • Straight back • Head up (look straight ahead)

Bodyweight Single Leg Romanian Deadlift	Phase	Teaching Points
	Descent	• One hand placed on top of the other • Slight flexion at the knee • Maintain this degree of flexion throughout descent in supporting knee • Flex ("hinge") at hips, taking one leg behind you • Maintain neutral position of lower back (lordotic curve)
	Position	• Lie flat on your front • Feet, knees, hips, shoulders and head aligned • Head looking at floor • Hands resting on top of each other • Forehead resting on hands • Toes in contact with floor
	Ascent	• Tighten lower back and abdominals • Lift legs up and off floor • Legs remain straight • Hips in contact with floor
	Descent	• Lower legs back to floor

Single Leg Hip Extension	Phase	Teaching Points
	Start	• Lie down on your back • Flex at knees and place feet on floor • Feet hip-width apart • Arms placed along either side of your body • Head in neutral position (looking up) • Lift one leg off the floor and extend at knee
	Ascent	• Tighten glutes • Lift hips and low back off floor • Shoulders and hips aligned • Straight back • Supporting leg remains in start position
	Descent	• Lower low back and glutes to floor • One leg remains off floor

GLUTE ACTIVATION AND STRENGTH (INTERMEDIATE)

Medball Single Leg Romanian Deadlift	Phase	Teaching Points
	Start	• Feet hip-width apart, toes pointing forward • Shoulder blades pulled back and down • Hold ball hip height, slightly in front of you • Chest up and out • Straight back • Head up (look straight ahead)
	Descent	• Slight flexion at the knee. Maintain this degree of flexion throughout descent in supporting knee • Flex ("hinge") at hips, taking one leg behind you • Ball moves toward the floor • Maintain a neutral position of lower back (lordotic curve)
	Position	• Maintain neutral position of lower back • Head up (looking straight ahead) • Flexion at hips • Slight flexion at knee • Arms extended at elbow • Wrist, elbow and shoulder aligned • Hold position • Hinge at hips as much as possible whilst maintaining neutral position of spine
	Ascent	• Extend at hip and knees • Maintain neutral (straight) low back position • Return to start position

Swiss Ball Reverse Hyperextensions	Phase	Teaching Points
	Start	• Lie with ball positioned under your hips • Hands placed on floor shoulder-width apart • Head looking at floor • Head, shoulders and hips aligned • Straight back • Toes in contact with floor

Swiss Ball Reverse Hyperextensions	Phase	Teaching Points
	Ascent	• Tighten lower back • Push navel and hips into ball • Lift legs up and off floor • Ball remains in the same place • Upper body position remains the same • Legs remain straight • Hips in contact with ball
	Descent	• Lower legs back to floor

GLUTE ACTIVATION AND STRENGTH (HARD)		
Swiss Ball Single Leg Hip Extensions	**Phase**	**Teaching Points**
	Start	• Lie on ball so head, shoulders and upper back are supported by ball • Flex at knees and place feet on floor • Tighten lower back and glutes • Shoulders and hips aligned • Straight back • Arms placed on chest • Head in neutral position (looking up) • Lift one leg off floor and extend at knee
	Descent	• Flex at hips • Glutes move toward floor • One leg remains off floor
	Ascent	• Tighten glutes • Push hips back up toward ceiling to start position

Medball Reverse Hyperextensions	Phase	Teaching Points
	Start	• Lie flat on your front • Feet, knees, hips, shoulders and head aligned • Head looking at floor • Hands resting on top of each other • Forehead resting on hands • Toes in contact with floor • Medball between feet
	Ascent	• Squeeze medball between feet • Tighten lower back • Push navel and hips to floor • Lift legs up and off floor • Medball remains between feet • Legs remain straight • Hips in contact with floor
	Descent	• Lower legs back to floor

Training Principles

Training to Failure

Training to failure can be described as the inability to complete a repetition due to fatigue or a breakdown in proper technique. While it is important to ensure each set provides a stimulus sufficiently strong enough to elicit training adaptations, research shows it is not necessary to lift as many repetitions as possible (i.e. to failure) at a given load in a set to optimise strength gains (Peterson, Rhea, & Alvar, 2005). During maximal strength training, typically a buffer of two to three repetitions should be allowed for before failure is reached in a set for a beginner. Over time as an athlete gains more experience and strength, a buffer of one to two repetitions or training to failure is appropriate.

During speed strength exercises, training to failure is not recommended since speed of movement is likely to be sacrificed. During this type of training, a low number of

Table 4.14. Program design variables for the development of trunk flexion stabilisation.

Main focus	Difficulty	Exercise	Reps	Duration of hold	Sets	Rest between sets
Flexion stabilisation	Easy	Plank	1	up to 90 s	2–4	30–60 s
		Side plank	1 each side	up to 90 s	2–4	30–60 s
		SB plank	1	up to 90 s	2–4	30–60 s
	Intermediate	Press up plank with rot.	up to 12 each side	–	2–4	30–60 s
		1 leg plank	up to 6 each side	up to 12 s each side	2–4	30–60 s
		1 arm plank	up to 6 each side	up to 12 s each side	2–4	30–60 s
		Modified renegade row	up to 12 each side	–	2–4	30–60 s
	Hard	DB renegade row	up to 12 each side	–	2–4	30–60 s
		Press up walk-out	up to 12 each side	–	2–4	30–60 s
		1 arm 1 leg plank	up to 6 each side	up to 12 s each side	2–4	30–60 s

repetitions are typically required to maintain high movement velocities. This is important to ensure velocity-specific strength adaptations are elicited by the actual velocity utilised during training (Moss, Refsnes, Abildgaard, Nicolaysen, & Jensen, 1997). As a result, the set should be stopped if velocity of movement slows down during the exercise being performed.

Warm-up

It is common knowledge that a warm-up should be carried out at the start of a training session. The main purpose of a warm-up is to prepare both physically and mentally for the ensuing session. An effective warm-up provides a number of physiological benefits including an increase in core body

Table 4.15. Program design variables for the development of trunk flexion strength and power.

Main focus	Difficulty	Exercise	Reps	Duration of hold	Sets	Rest between sets
Flexion strength and power	Easy	Lower abdominal 1	up to 12 each side	–	2–4	30–60 s
		Lower abdominal 2	up to 12 each side	–	2–4	30–60 s
		SB crunches	up to 20	–	2–4	30–60 s
		MB SB crunch throw	up to 8	–	2–5	60–120 s
		SB roll out	up to 12	–	2–4	30–60 s
	Intermediate	Lower abdominal 3	up to 15	–	2–4	30–60 s
		V-sits	up to 10	–	2–5	60–120 s
		Kneeling BB roll outs	up to 12	–	2–4	60–120 s
	Hard	MB V-sits	up to 10	–	2–5	60–120 s
		Hanging leg raise	up to 12	–	2–4	60–120 s
		Lower abdominal 4	up to 12	–	2–4	60–120 s

temperature, which will increase blood supply and provide more oxygen to the tissues and working muscles. Warming up should not be too intense because physical performance may be impaired for the rest of the session. The onset of sweating is generally indicative of the effectiveness of a warm up sequence. Warming up before a strength training session can be completed in three separate stages.

Stage 1

The main aim of this stage is to elevate body temperature, heart rate, respiration rate, blood flow and circulation of fluid within the joint via low intensity exercise. There are many activities from which to choose in order to elicit these physiological changes—e.g. jogging, rowing, cycling or more athletic

Table 4.16. Program design variables for the development of rotational trunk strength and power.

Main focus	Difficulty	Exercise	Reps	Duration of hold	Sets	Rest between sets
Rotational strength and power	Easy	SB russian twist	up to 12 each side	–	2–4	30–60 s
		MB reverse chops	up to 12 each side	–	2–4	30–60 s
		Cable reverse chop	up to 12 each side	–	2–4	30–60 s
		Cable chop	up to 13 each side	–	2–4	30–60 s
		MB seated rot.	up to 12 each side	–	2–4	30–60 s
	Intermediate	MB SB russian twist	up to 12 each side	–	2–4	30–60 s
		MB explosive chops	up to 6 each side	–	3–5	120–180 s
		MB explosive reverse chop	up to 6 each side	–	3–5	120–180 s
	Hard	BB russian twist	up to 6 each side	–	3–5	120–180 s
		MB wall rebound rot.	up to 6 each side	–	3–5	120–180 s

movements which more closely resemble the activities being undertaken in the main session (albeit at a lower intensity)—but emphasis should be placed on a gradual increase in intensity for approximately 5 to 8 minutes.

Stage 2

The aim of this stage is to activate key muscle groups and mobilise key joints, moving through ranges associated with the exercises being performed in the main part of the session. This phase includes a number of exercises and a series of dynamic stretches carried out to provide the mobilisation needed for the strength session.

The following exercises show a suggested number of activities which can be used as part of this phase:

Table 4.17. Program design variables for the development of rotational trunk strength and power.

Main focus	Difficulty	Exercise	Reps	Duration of hold	Sets	Rest between sets
Extension stability and strength	Easy	Prone hold	1	up to 90 s	2–4	60–90 s
		Back hyperextensions	up to 20	–	2–4	30–60 s
	Intermediate	SB back extensions	up to 20	–	2–4	30–60 s
		MB prone hold	–	up to 90 s	2–4	60–90 s
	Hard	BB isometric RDL hold	–	up to 30 s	2–4	60–90 s
		Plate prone hold	–	up to 60 s	2–4	60–90 s

Table 4.18. Program design variables for the development of glute activation and strength.

Main focus	Difficulty	Exercise	Reps	Duration of hold	Sets	Rest between sets
Glute activation and strength	Easy	Reverse hyperextensions	up to 20	–	2–4	30–60 s
		BW SL RDL	up to 12 each side	–	2–4	30–60 s
		SL hip extension	up to 12 each side	–	2–4	30–60 s
	Intermediate	MB SL RDL	up to 12 each side	–	2–4	30–60 s
		SB reverse hyperextensions	up to 20	–	2–4	30–60 s
	Hard	SB SL hip extensions	up to 12 each side	–	2–4	30–60 s
		MB reverse hyperextensions	up to 15	–	2–4	30–60 s

WARM UP

Press-up Position Calves

Teaching Points
- Performed in press-up position
- Back in neutral position
- Head looking toward floor
- Alternate pushing each heel toward the floor

Squats

Teaching Points
- Feet shoulder-width apart
- Back in neutral position
- Chest up and out
- Pull shoulder blades back and down
- Looking forward
- Cross arms so hands rest on front of shoulders
- Squat until thighs break parallel to floor
- Knees over the line of the big toe
- Heels remain on floor
- Back remains in a neutral position, chest up and out

Walking Lunge with Hamstrings Stretch

Teaching Points
- Toes aligned, pointing directly forward
- Knee pointing out along the line of the big toe in the lunge
- Hips aligned and facing forward
- Straighten front leg until stretch is felt in hamstrings of front leg, then step forward into next lunge

Walking Lunge with Reach Back

Teaching Points
- Toes aligned, pointing directly forward
- Knee pointing out along the line of the big toe in the lunge
- Hips aligned and facing forward
- Stretch up and back until stretch is felt in quads of the front leg, then step forward into the next lunge

Single Leg Glute Bridge

Teaching Points
- Tighten glutes
- Lift hips and low back off floor
- Shoulders and hips aligned
- Straight back
- Supporting leg remains in start position
- Palms facing up

Press-up Plank Rotation

Teaching Points
- Ankles, knees, hips and shoulders aligned
- Tighten abdominals
- Rotate at hips and shoulders to bring one hand off the floor
- Head in a neutral position

Iron Cross

Teaching Points

- Lie on your back with arms at shoulder height, forming a "T" shape with your body
- Ankles, knees, hips and shoulders aligned
- Rotate at trunk and hips, taking the foot to opposite hand
- Return back to start position and repeat with other leg
- Shoulders remain on floor
- Other leg remains on floor
- Looking toward ceiling

Scorpion's Tail

Teaching Points

- Lie on your front with ankles, knees, hips and shoulders aligned
- Rotate at the trunk and hips, taking foot to opposite side of body at hip height
- Other leg remains on floor

Forwards and Backwards Shoulder Rotations

Teaching Points

- Stand with feet together, ankles, knees, hips and shoulders aligned
- Chest up and out
- Looking forward
- Circle arms backward for one and a half rotations then one and a half rotations forward

Activity	Repetitions
Press up position calves	x 8 each leg
Squats	x 8
Lunge with hamstrings stretch	x 5 each leg
Lunge with reach back	x 5 each leg
Single leg glute bridge	x 5 each side
Press up plank rotations	x 5 each side
Iron cross	x 5 each side
Scorpion's tail	x 5 each side
Forward and backward shoulder rotations	x 5

Stage 3

Warm-up sets are performed prior to the target sets of each specific exercise, and should be carried out without creating unnecessary fatigue. It is difficult to provide an exact prescription of the reps, sets and intensity of warm up sets because this will depend on the weight being lifted, the exercise performed and the intensity and reps of the main target sets.

As a guideline, the following warm up sets should be carried out ahead of the main target set.

When main target sets are at an intensity of 12RM or more:

- No warm up sets needed

When main target sets are at an intensity of 8–10RM:

- 6 reps at approximately 75% of weight for target set

When main target sets are at an intensity of 5–7RM:

- 6 reps at approximately 60% of weight for target set
- 5 reps at approximately 70% of weight for target set
- 4 reps at approximately 80% of weight for target set

When main target sets are at an intensity of 3–4RM:

- 6 reps at 50 % of weight for target set
- 5 reps at 60 % of weight for target set
- 3 reps at 70% of weight for target set
- 2 reps at 80% of weight for target set

When main target sets are at an intensity of 1–2RM:

- 6 reps at 50% of weight for target set
- 5 reps at 70% of weight for target set
- 3 reps at 80% of weight for target set
- 1 reps at 90% of weight for target set

Exercise Order

Exercise order is an important consideration when designing an individual session. While most sessions will have a main focus, more than one strength quality is likely to be focussed on.

For example, if the main objective for a session was to develop lower limb explosive strength, it would still be feasible to include some maximum strength and trunk training exercises. This approach helps to maintain a number of physical qualities across a long-term training plan. When performing sessions which combine different training methods, it is important to consider the order in which each activity is performed, so as to maximise the effectiveness of the session.

Session Framework

Table 4.19 provides a session design framework and order in which to perform the various activities which could make up a session. It is important to note that performing all the types of activity listed within Table 4.19 in the same session would be ineffective. It is likely that the training effect would be diluted across all the strength qualities. Significant development in any of these physical attributes would not therefore be possible. The strength qualities being

Table 4.19. Session framework.

Activity order	Activity type
1	Warm-up
2	Reactive strength exercises (e.g. bounding)
3	Explosive strength exercises (e.g. snatch)
4	Bilateral lower limb max. strength exercises (e.g. back squat)
5	Unilateral lower limb max. strength exercises (e.g. step up)
6	Bilateral upper limb max. strength exercises (e.g. bench press)
7	Unilateral upper limb max. strength exercises (e.g. single arm shoulder press)
8	Trunk training exercises (e.g. v-sit)

targeted will depend on the stage an athlete is in with regards to their overall training plan and annual cycle (see Section 5: Periodisation).

Traditionally there are two main session structures: (1) total body sessions, which involve exercises stressing all major muscle groups, and (2) lower/upper body split sessions, which involve performance of lower body exercises during one workout and upper body exercises during another. The main difference between these session structures is the magnitude of concentration on muscle groups during each training session.

For example, three to four exercises for a specific muscle group may be performed during a lower/upper body split session, as opposed to one to two exercises for a specific muscle group in a total body session. A larger magnitude of concentration on specific muscle groups is generally more demanding for an athlete, and so lower upper body split sessions are generally more appropriate for intermediate to advanced athletes, whereas a total body session approach is more suitable for beginner athletes.

General Principles

There are a number of general principles which should be adhered to when structuring a strength training session:

Maximum Strength Only Session

- Large muscle group multi-joint exercises should be performed before small muscle groups single joint exercises

- Perform higher intensity exercises (i.e. higher percentage of 1RM) before lower intensity exercises

Speed Strength Only Session

- Higher-velocity exercises should be performed before lower-velocity exercises
- Where velocity of movement is similar, the exercises with the greatest load should be performed first

Multiple Strength Qualities Session

- Exercises should be performed from right to left on the force-velocity curve (i.e. highest to lowest movement-velocity). However, for experienced athletes, performing exercises to the left of the force-velocity curve may potentiate and enhance the performance of subsequent higher velocity exercises.

Sample Programs

Program Template

The following program template (Table 4.20) can be used to program individual strength sessions and will be used for the remainder of this book for sample strength training sessions.

Exercise column—each exercise is listed in the rows within this column.

Tempo column—this relates to the speed each repetition of the exercise should be performed

at. The first number represents the eccentric phase of the lift (lowering of the weight), the second details the length of time the position at the end of the eccentric phase should be held for (isometric contraction), and the third represents the concentric phase of the lift (i.e. lifting of the weight).

In the example given in the above program template, the athlete should take approximately 2 s to descend into the squat (first number). At the bottom of the squat, the athlete should immediately start to ascend, i.e. no hold at the bottom (second number). They should then take approximately 1 s to ascend fully (third number).

Rest column—the length of the rest period between each set for each exercise is listed in the rows within this column.

Intensity—the intensity for each exercise is recorded as a repetition maximum (RM). In the example given in the program template above, the athlete is required to select a weight that they could perform a maximum of 6 repetitions of in the back-squat exercise.

Reps and load—the number of repetitions for each set are listed under the 'reps' columns. In the example given in the above program template, the athlete is required to perform 4 sets of 5 repetitions. A space is provided for the athlete to enter the load being lifted next to each repetition number.

An example program which is designed for an athlete with an intermediate age which focuses on explosive and reactive strength can be found in Table 4.21.

Table 4.20. Sample program template.

Exercise	Tempo	Rest	Intensity	Target sets					
				Reps	Load	Reps	Load	Reps	Load
Back squat	2,0,1	2.5 min	6RM	5		5		5	

Table 4.21. An example program aimed at developing explosive and maximum strength qualities of an athlete with an intermediate training age

Exercise	Tempo	Rest	Intensity	Target sets							
				Reps	Load	Reps	Load	Reps	Load	Reps	Load
Hang snatch	XXX	2.5 min	65% 1RM	5		5		5		5	
Standing long jump	XXX	2 min	BW	4		4		4			
Deadlift	201	2.5 min	7RM	6		6		6		6	
Seated cable row	201	2.5 min	7RM	6		6		6		6	
Bulgarian split squat	201	2.5 min	7RM	6		6		6		6	
Single leg iso hip extensor push	5/5 ramp	2 min	90% at peak	5/5 ramp [2]		5/5 ramp [2]		5/5 ramp [2]			

Conclusion

There are numerous factors to consider when designing an individual strength program. Firstly, the training age of the athlete should influence the type of exercise and program design variables prescribed within an individual session. This is important from a safety perspective and to ensure that the correct dose-response is provided to the individual carrying out the training program. Gradual and progressive overload over time is important to avoid stagnation and plateau in strength gains.

Training sessions designed to improve maximum strength through compound lifts such as the squat are important to elicit the physiological adaptations which lay the foundation for enhanced force production and power capabilities. Maximal strength training with submaximal loads is recommended as a starting point for most beginner athletes, whatever stage the athlete is in with regards to their annual sport season.

For intermediate and advanced athletes, this type of training is usually carried out early in the pre-season phase, following a period of active rest from the previous season. The optimal strength training dosage has been shown to alter, however, depending on an athlete's training age. Consequently, a dose-response continuum exists, whereby increases in strength dosage should accompany increases in training age. Typically, maximal strength training with maximal loads is more effective in eliciting strength gains in more experienced athletes.

Having high levels of maximum strength, while important for sprint performance, will only be effective during a sprint if it can be expressed quickly during a sprint. For this reason, speed strength (including explosive and reactive strength) is arguably more important. Explosive strength is developed primarily through the use of ballistic exercises such as the clean. The type of adaptations elicited during explosive training is influenced by the magnitude of the load lifted.

For example—under heavy loads—it is more likely to facilitate recruitment of high-threshold motor units similar to maximum strength training, and enhance RFD at the 'force end' of the force-velocity curve when compared to lifting with lighter loads. Under lighter loads, explosive strength training is more favourable for reducing antagonist co-contraction and RFD at the 'velocity end' of the force-velocity curve. Reactive strength is developed primarily through the use of plyometric exercises such as the depth jump. This type of training takes advantage of the SSC to enhance the ability of the neural and musculotendinous systems, to produce maximal force in the shortest amount of time.

Regardless of the type of strength targeted, it is important to select the correct volumes, intensities and exercises according to the training age of the athlete, their strengths and weaknesses, and the stage of the season the athlete is in. Adhering to the guidelines outlined in this section will help ensure that training is appropriate to the individual and that it can be progressed over the long term while targeting the type of adaptation required at the time of training.

Another consideration when constructing a strength training program for an athlete looking to enhance their sprinting ability is that of mechanical specificity. Although strength exercises of a more general nature may form the foundation of an athlete's strength training schedule, selecting exercises that have a greater dynamic correspondence to sprinting is important at certain times.

Stage 1 exercises identified in this section produce high forces against the ground and are generally used to develop neuromuscular adaptations such as motor unit recruitment and firing frequency; neural adaptations which enable the athlete to recruit larger motor units (fast twitch) more effectively for the similar movement patterns observed in sprinting. On the surface however, they are not mechanically similar to the sprinting action.

Stage 2 exercises are more explosive in nature or utilise the SSC to a greater extent than stage 1 exercises. They are generally more specific to the running action (although still largely general in nature) and as a result are more likely to transfer over to sprinting performance.

Stage 3 exercises overload a mechanical element of a sprint phase and thus replicate the movement patterns of sprinting more closely. There are fewer exercises to choose from in stage 3, and resisted sprinting and various plyometric exercises are typically used to for improving sprint performance in this phase.

During all training phases, the extent to which mechanical specificity is important should be considered. The different stages of the exercises outlined in this section offer a general-specific continuum of exercises from which the athlete or coach can select to optimise the adaptations required during individual training sessions.

In addition to developing limb strength through the exercises detailed in the specific exercise stages and for an athlete to sprint successfully, they need to have a strong torso which can transmit forces from the lower limbs to the centre of mass. The trunk as a whole provides an anchor point from which the limbs can exert force. A weak trunk is likely to result in less than optimal limb mechanics during a sprint, which in turn will result in reduced ground reaction forces and wasted energy through compensatory movements. Focus should therefore be placed on developing a strong and 'stiff' trunk, alongside the development of general lower limb strength.

Regardless of the type of strength training approach adopted, a warm-up should be carried out during every session. This provides a number of physiological benefits such as an increase in core body temperature, which will increase blood supply and provide more oxygen to the tissues and working muscles. A framework from which a warm-up can be constructed has been given in this section, so as to optimise the quality of the ensuing training session.

Finally, careful thought ought to be given to the order in which exercises are carried out within a session. As a general rule of thumb, large muscle group multi-joint exercises and those performed at high velocities should be carried out prior to exercise of a lower velocity and those which target single joints. Where multiple strength qualities are worked on during a single session, exercises should be performed from right to left on the force-velocity curve (i.e. highest to lowest movement-velocity).

The correct design of individual training sessions is important to maximise the effectiveness of training time. However, how these sessions are planned longer term—i.e. within the week, month, year or more—and in conjunction with the non-strength training sessions—i.e. the sport the athlete competes in—is perhaps more important. Failure to plan effectively for the longer term can result in overtraining, fatigue, decreased motivation and poor training responses. Managing a training plan across the year forms the focal point for Section 6 in this book.

References

Alcaraz, P., Palao, J., & Elvira, J. (2009). Determining the optimal load for resisted sprint training with sled towing. *Journal of Strength and Conditioning Research, 23*, 480–485.

Behm, D., & Sale, D. (1993). Intended rather than actual movement velocity determines velocity-specific training response. *Journal of Applied Physiology, 74*, 359–368.

Bobbert, M., Huijing, P., & van Ingen Schenau, G. (1987). Drop jumping. The influence of jumping technique on the biomechanics of jumping. *Medicine and Science in Sports and Exercise, 19*, 332–338.

Carroll, T. (2001). Neural adaptations to resistance training: Implications for movement control. *Sports Medicine, 31*, 829–840.

Cavagna, G., Dusman, B., & Margaria, R. (1968). Positive work done by a previously stretched muscle. *Journal of Applied Physiology, 24*, 21–32.

Chmielewski, T., Myer, G., Kauffman, D., & Tillman, S. (2006). Plyometric exercise in the rehabilitation of athletes: physiological responses and clinical application. *The Journal of Orthopedic Sports Physical Therapy, 36*, 308–319.

Clark, K., Stearne, D., Walts, C., & Miller, A. (2010). The longitudinal effects of resisted sprint training using weighted sleds vs. weighted vests. *Journal of Strength and Conditioning Research, 24*, 3287–3295.

Cormie, P., McCaulley, G., Triplett, N., & McBride, J. (2007). Optimal loading for maximal power output during lower-body resistance exercises. *Medicine and Science in Sports and Exercise, 39*, 340–349.

Costello, F. (1981). Resisted and assisted training to improve speed. *Track and Field, 81*, 27.

Costello, F. (1985). Training for speed using resisted and assisted methods. *National Strength and Conditioning Association Journal, 7*, 74–75.

Cronin, J., Hansen, K., Kawamori, N., & McNair, P. (2008). Effects of weighted vests and sled towing on sprint kinematics. *Sports Biomechanics, 7*, 160–172.

Delecluse, C., van Coppenolle, H., Williems, E., Van Leemputte, M., Diels, R., & Goris, M. (1995). Influence of high-resistance and high-velocity training on sprint performance. *Medicine and Science in Sports and Exercise, 27*, 1203–1209.

Dintiman, G. (1964). Effects of various training programs on running speed. *Research Quarterly for Exercise and Sport, 35*, 456–463.

Donati, A. (1996). The association between the development of strength and speed. *New Studies in Athletics, 11*, 51–58.

Faccioni, A. (1993a). Resisted and assisted methods for speed development. *Strength and Conditioning Coach, 1*, 7–10.

Faccioni, A. (1993b). Resisted and assisted methods for speed development. Part 2. *Strength and Conditioning Coach, 1*, 10–11.

Haff, G., Whitley, A., & Potteiger, J. (2001). A brief review: explosive exercises and sports performance. *Strength and Conditioning Journal, 23*, 13–20.

Hakkinen, K., Alen, M., Kraemer, W., Gorostiaga, E., Izquierdo, M., Rusko, H., Paavolainen, L. (2003). Neuromuscular adaptations during concurrent strength and endurance training versus strength training. *European Journal of Applied Physiology, 89*, 42–52.

Harridge, S., Bottinelli, R., Canepari, M., Pellegrino, M., Reggiani, C., Esbjornsson, M., & Saltin, B. (1996). Whole-muscle and single-fibre contractile properties and myosin heavy chain isoforms in humans. *European Journal of Physiology, 432*, 913–920.

Harris, N., Cronin, J., Hopkins, W., & Hansen, K. (2008). Relationship between sprint times and the strength/power outputs of a machine squat jump. *Journal of Strength and Conditioning Research, 22*, 691–698.

Jakalski, K. (1998). The pros and cons of using resisted and assisted training methods with high school sprinters: parachutes, tubing and towing. *Track Coach, 144*, 4585–4589.

Kordi, M., Folland, J., Goodall, S., Menzies, C., Patel, T., Evans, M., Howatson, G. (2020). Cycling-specific isometric resistance training improves peak power output in elite sprint cyclists. *Scandinavian Journal of Medicine & Science in Sports, 30*(9), 1594–1604.

Lum, D., Barbosa, T., & Balasekaran, G. (2021). Sprint kayaking performance enhancement by isometric strength training inclusion: A randomized controlled trial. *Sports (Basel), 9*(2), 16.

Lum, D., Barbosa, T., Joseph, R., & Balasekaran, G. (2021). Effects of two isometric strength training methods on jump and sprint performances: A randomized controlled trial. *Journal of Science in Sport and Exercise, 3*(2), 115–124.

Maulder, P., Bradshaw, E., & Keogh, J. (2008). Kinematic alterations due to different loading schemes in early acceleration sprint performance from starting blocks. *Journal of Strength and Conditioning Research, 22*, 1992–2002.

McBride, J., Triplett-McBride, T., Davie, A., & Newton, R. (2002). The effect of heavy- vs. light-load jump squats on the development of strength, power and speed. *Journal of Strength and Conditioning Research, 16*, 75–82.

Mero, A., & Komi, P. (1994). EMG, force, and power analysis of sprint-specific strength exercises. *Journal of Applied Biomechanics, 10*, 1–13.

Moritani, T., & DeVries, H. (1979). Neural factors versus hypertrophy in the same course of muscle strength gain. *American Journal of Physical Medicine, 58*, 115–130.

Moss, B., Refsnes, P., Abildgaard, A., Nicolaysen, K., & Jensen, J. (1997). Effects of maximal effort strength training with different loads on dynamic strength, cross-sectional area, load-power and load-velocity relationships. *European Journal of Applied Physiology and Occupational Physiology, 75*, 193–199.

Murray, A., Aitchison, T., Ross, G., Sutherland, K., Watt, I., McLean, D., & Grant, S. (2005). The effect of towing a range of relative resistances on sprint performance. *Journal of Sports Sciences, 23*, 927–935.

Narici, M., Roi, G., Landoni, L., Minetti, A., & Cerretelli, P. (1989). Changes in force, cross-sectional area and neural activation during strength training and detraining of the human quadriceps. *European Journal of Applied Physiology and Occupational Physiology, 59*, 310–319.

Natera, A., Cardinale, M., & Keogh, J. (2020). The effect of high volume power training on repeated high-intensity performance and the assessment of repeat power ability: A systematic review. *Sports Medicine (Auckland), 50*(7), 1317–1339.

Newton, R., Kraemer, W., Hakkinen, K., Humphries, B., & Murphy, A. (1996). Kinematics, kinetics, and muscle activation during explosive upper body movements. *Journal of Applied Biomechanics, 12*, 31–43.

Paradisis, G., & Cooke, C. (2001). Kinematic and postural characteristics of sprint running on sloping surfaces. *Journal of Sports Sciences, 19*, 149–159.

Paradisis, G., & Cooke, C. (2006). The effects of sprint running training on sloping surfaces. *Journal of Strength and Conditioning Research, 20*, 767–777.

Peterson, M., Rhea, M., & Alvar, B. (2005). Applications of the dose-response for muscular strength development: a review of meta-analytic efficacy and reliability for designing training prescription. *Journal of Strength and Conditioning Research, 19*, 950–958.

Sands, W., Poole, C., Ford, H., Cervantez, R., Irwin, R., & Major, J. (1996). Hypergravity training: Women's track and field. *Journal of Strength and Conditioning Research, 10*, 30–34.

Schaefer, L., & Bittmann, F. (2017). Are there two forms of isometric muscle action? results of the experimental study support a distinction between a holding and a pushing isometric muscle function. *BMC Sports Science, Medicine & Rehabilitation, 9*(1), 11.

Schmidtbleicher, D. (1992). Training for power events. In P. Komi, *The Encyclopedia of Sports Medicine: Strength and Power in Sport* (pp. 169–179). Oxford: Blackwell.

Turner, A., & Jeffreys, I. (2010). The stretch-shortening cycle: mechanisms and proposed enhancement. *Strength and Conditioning Journal, 10*, 87–99.

Young, W. (1992). Sprint bounding and the sprint bound index. *National Strength & Conditioning Association Journal, 14*, 18–21.

Periodisation

The term 'periodisation' is widely used for the planning and organising of training, rest, recovery and competition into blocks or phases throughout a given period of time. Where these training blocks are placed across the specified time period, and what their content is, will depend on the arrangement of the sporting season—typically off-, pre- and in-season—and its competition structure. Without longer term planning, the anticipated physiological adaptations elicited from individual training sessions may not come to fruition.

It is impossible, for example, for an athlete to train at high intensities and volumes week on week across the whole season without variation and expect to be fresh for competition. Whilst training stress and fatigue are necessary to initiate adaptation, training variation, rest and recovery are all required elements to realise gains in fitness and thus enhanced performance.

The aim of this section is to pull together information from the previous sections in this book to provide the reader with an effective periodisation structure based on training age and status.

Periodisation Terminology

Some of the terminology frequently used when discussing periodisation is listed below.

Macrocycle

Typically, the term 'macrocycle' refers to a whole competition and training year, although it can also represent a longer time period— for example, a 4-year cycle is often termed a macrocycle for an Olympic athlete. The end point of a macrocycle will usually culminate in the main competition for which an athlete is preparing. The beginning of the macrocycle is the point at which you start to train for this main competition.

Seasonal Structure

The seasonal structure is the organisation of the sport around its competition schedule In a team sport (e.g. rugby union), this typically involves a number of phases, such as in the examples given in Figure 5.1:

Month	May	Jun	Jul	Aug	Sep	Oct	Nov	Dec	Jan	Feb	Mar	Apr
Seasonal structure	Transition	Pre-season										
	Off-season			In-season								

Figure 5.1. A typical seasonal structure for rugby union.

- **Transition period**. Focus is placed on recovery from the previous season and light exercise in the form of general activities and cross-training (i.e. taking part in activities that are not necessarily specific to the sport in which the athlete competes)
- **Off-season**. Emphasis is placed on general training (e.g. developing max. strength and muscle hypertrophy through maximum strength training under submaximal and maximal loads could be a priority during this phase) to lay the physical foundation for the development of more specific means of training later in the season
- **Pre-season**. Greater emphasis is placed on training for the sport, although physical training will still form an important part of this phase. This phase ends when the first match takes place
- **In-season (competition)**. Starts with the first game of the season and ends with the last. Usually during this phase, physical training is reduced to a minimum to avoid unnecessary amounts of fatigue, which may affect performance. Strength training emphasis is generally based around maintaining the fitness gains made during the previous phases.

In an individual sport such as athletics—while the general progression from general training to more specific methods is similar—the terminology often used to describe the seasonal structure may often just be broken down into 'off-season' and 'in-season', although within each of these periods there will be different training phases which have specific objectives (Figure 5.2):

- **General preparation phase (GPP)**. Period characterised by training which develops general physical qualities, work capacity and improves technical aspects and basic tactical skills
- **Special preparation phase (SPP)**. Transition from more general forms of training to a mechanically more specific approach
- **Competition phase (CP)**. All the training factors are consolidated to allow the athlete to compete successfully in the main competition(s)

Month	Oct	Nov	Dec	Jan	Feb	Mar	Apr	May	Jun	Jul	Aug	Sep
Seasonal structure	Off-season				In-season (winter indoors)	Off-season			In-season (summer outdoors)			Off-season
Phase	GPP 1		SPP 1		CP 1	GPP 2	SPP 2		CP 2			TP

Figure 5.2. A typical seasonal structure for a sprinter competing in a number of winter and summer competitions.

- **Transition phase (TP).** The focus of this phase is the same as that in the transition period identified in the aforementioned typical seasonal structure for a team sport

Mesocycle

The macrocycle is normally broken down into a series of training blocks or phases called mesocycles. Usually these training blocks will be between three and eight weeks in length and contain specific training objectives.

Microcycle

The microcycle is usually one week in length: sometimes it may be slightly shorter or longer.

Tapering

Tapering refers to the reduction in overall training load approaching competition so that the adaptations can be elicited from a previous block(s) of training, and to ensure that the athlete is fresh to compete. Essentially, this process allows the accumulated strength (and all fitness) gains to be exploited in a planned manner.

Peaking

Closely linked with tapering, this term refers to the process of being in the best condition mentally, physically and competitively at a particular point of time within the macrocycle. Peaking is made possible through a well-structured periodised program, in which

training stress has been appropriately cycled across a specific time period, concluding with a taper period in order to reach the best possible state—both physically and mentally—at a certain point in time.

The Structuring of Training Phases

There are numerous effective ways in which to structure strength training to maximise speed development. The approach outlined in this section is one way in which a strength program for speed can be periodised, and is based on a combination of empirical research, experience and anecdotal evidence.

Influence of Training Age on General and Special Preparation Training Phase Distribution

As a universal rule—during the general preparation phase—more time is spent developing maximum strength (under submaximal and maximal loads) than explosive and reactive strength. Stage 1 exercises are therefore predominantly used during this phase of the season.

As the season progresses toward the competition period, stage 2 and 3 exercises are implemented more than stage 1 exercises, to bring about the speed strength physiological adaptations likely to have a greater carry-over to sprint performance. Aside from the structure of the season and the strength quality deficits an athlete may possess, the amount of time spent during the general or special preparation phases will differ according to training age.

Broadly speaking, individuals with an advanced training age and high maximum strength levels have superior power production capabilities than those who are weaker and with a lower training age (Baker & Newton, 2006; Cormie, McGuigan, & Newton, 2010). The current maximum strength level of an athlete will dictate the upper limit of their potential to generate power, since the ability to generate force quickly is of little benefit if maximal force is low.

Additionally, research has shown that maximal strength training under heavy loads involving moderately trained participants results in an increase in power output, as well as maximal strength (Cormie, McGuigan, & Newton, 2010; Kaneko, 2004). For these reasons, it appears that maximum strength training should form a significant part of an athlete's overall strength program, as it is clearly an influential quality to maximal power production.

However, the degree of this influence diminishes to an extent when an athlete already possesses a high level of maximum strength (Kraemer & Newton, 2000). Rises in maximal strength will result in a concomitant reduction in the window of adaptation for further enhancements in maximum strength

development. As a result, the associated increases in maximal power output as maximal strength increases are thought to be lower in stronger athletes and more velocity-specific— i.e. the changes would impact primarily on the high-force end of the force-velocity relationship (see Figure 2.6; Newton & Kraemer, 1994).

It would seem, therefore, that training during general preparation periods plays an important role in initial improvements in the ability to express force quickly, but not beyond the time in which a reasonable level of strength is reached. For these reasons a number of suggestions, such as those in Figure 5.3, can be made as to the proportion of time spent within a macrocycle in general and special preparation periods leading toward competition.

Structuring the General Preparation Period

As already alluded to, the general preparation phase is used to develop base and maximum strength levels. The mean intensity of strength training will typically increase across each mesocycle during this period. For example, the general preparation phase in Figure 5.4

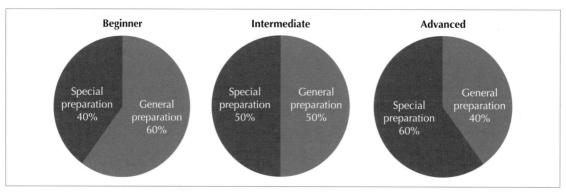

Figure 5.3. The suggested proportion of time spent in general and specific preparation within a macrocycle based on training age and existing strength levels.

Month		October				November				December			
Microcycle no.		1	2	3	4	5	6	7	8	9	10	11	12
Seasonal structure		Off-season											
Phase		General Preparation 1											
Mesocycle		1				2				3			
Average lifting intensity (%1RM)	Athlete A	70%				75%				80%			
	Athlete B	77%				80%				85%			
	Athlete C	83%				87%				90%			

Figure 5.4. Average lifting intensity across a series of mesocycles during a general preparation period of training. Athlete A has a beginner training age, athlete B an intermediate training age, and athlete C an advanced training age.

lasts 12 weeks and has been divided into four-week blocks, where the average lifting intensity across each mesocycle progresses from one to the other and is different based on the training age of the athlete.

Although there is a general increase in intensity across a general preparation phase, average weekly lifting intensities should vary for athletes with an intermediate or advanced training age. This provides higher and lower intensity weeks to vary the stimuli the body is exposed to, and helps prevent stagnation and fatigue. This is not always necessary for athletes with a beginner training age, since the loads they are lifting initially will be low relative to those with higher training ages, and so they will not be placing their body under as much stress.

The lack of variation in intensity for beginners also allows them time to develop better technique and to increase the number of reps performed, or increase the weight being lifted as the training phases progress. (It is likely that the loads being lifted for a given % 1RM would increase relatively quickly.) Figure 5.5 shows microcycle variation in lifting intensities across an example general preparation period of training.

Although the changes to lifting intensity may be relatively subtle within each mesocycle,

Month		October				November				December			
Microcycle no.		1	2	3	4	5	6	7	8	9	10	11	12
Seasonal structure		Off-season											
Phase		General Preparation 1											
Mesocycle		1				2				3			
Mesocycle average lifting intensity (%1RM)	Athlete A	70%				75%				80%			
	Athlete B	77%				80%				83%			
	Athlete C	83%				87%				90%			
Weekly average lifting intensity (%1RM)	95-100%1RM												
	90-95%1RM												
	85-90%1RM												
	80-85%1RM												
	75-80%1RM												
	70-75%1RM												
	65-70%1RM												

Figure 5.5. Average lifting intensity across a series of mesocycles during a general preparation period of training. Athlete A (blue line) has a beginner training age, athlete B (green line) an intermediate training age and athlete C (red line) an advanced training age.

a gradual increase in intensity across the general preparation phase is evident. As fatigue accumulates across a series of sessions and weeks, it becomes important to vary the volume of training, so as to cycle the overall training load each week in order to allow physiological progress.

Strength training volume load—and thus session training load—can typically be calculated by multiplying the total number of sets performed in a session by the load lifted in each rep. When planning a training phase however, it is not always possible to predict the amount of weight that can be lifted. Multiplying the total number of reps performed by the % 1RM values planned in each session provides a way in which to plan appropriate loading patterns.

For example, performing 4 sets of 3 reps with a load equivalent to 85% 1RM would equate to a volume load of 1020 (arbitrary units): $(4 \times 3) \times 85 = 1020$.

Figure 5.6 depicts training load distribution for athletes of different training ages across a general preparation period.

For athletes with a beginner or intermediate training age, a suggested training load pattern is one in which volume load increases gradually over the course of 3 weeks with a 'deload' week during week 4. This reduction in volume load should take place typically through a reduction in the number of sets, exercises and/or training sessions performed. Advanced athletes do not always need this gradual build-up of training load and can therefore tolerate higher training loads earlier in the mesocycle, especially if the last week in the previous mesocycle has been a deload week. Because of the greater training loads that can be tolerated, advanced athletes should also ensure that lower training load weeks are factored into their mesocycle structure, more so than athletes with lower training ages.

Month		October				November				December			
Microcycle no.		1	2	3	4	5	6	7	8	9	10	11	12
Seasonal structure		Off-season												
Phase		General Preparation 1												
Mesocycle		1				2				3				
Mesocycle average lifting intensity (%1RM)	Athlete A	70%				75%				80%				
	Athlete B	77%				80%				83%				
	Athlete C	83%				87%				90%				
Weekly average lifting intensity (%1RM)	95-100%1RM													
	90-95%1RM													
	85-90%1RM													
	80-85%1RM													
	75-80%1RM													
	70-75%1RM													
	65-70%1RM													
Weekly volume load	Very high													
	High													
	Medium high													
	Medium													
	Medium low													
	low													

Figure 5.6. Average lifting intensity and total volume across a series of mesocycles during a general preparation period of training. Athlete A (blue line) has a beginner training age, athlete B (green line) an intermediate training age and athlete C (red line) an advanced training age.

Where a ratio of 3 or 4 medium-high to 1 medium-low training load week arrangement is appropriate for beginner and intermediate level athletes, a 2 high-very high to 1 training load weekly arrangement would be more appropriate for an athlete with a very experienced training age. Figure 5.7 completes the general preparation period overview with suggested exercises and training prescription.

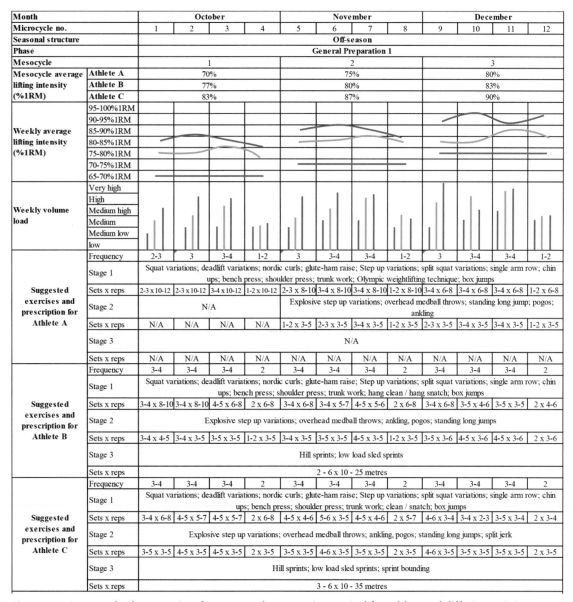

Figure 5.7. A strength plan overview for a general preparation period for athletes of differing training ages. Athlete A (blue line) has a beginner training age, athlete B (green line) an intermediate training age and athlete C (red line) an advanced training age.

The recommended frequency of strength sessions completed by an athlete during the general preparation phase is 3 to 4 per week. A minimum period of 48 to 72 hours should be allowed following a strength training session before completing a subsequent session focussing on the same muscle groups. Generally, the higher the volume load and intensity, the greater amount of rest needed between sessions. Less time is needed between sessions focussing on different muscle groups. It is possible, for example, to complete lower body and upper body sessions in the same day.

Structuring the Special Preparation Period

Moving into the special preparation period, there is a shift in emphasis more toward explosive and reactive strength, with the latter strength quality taking precedence as this period progresses toward competition. Small gains in maximum strength are typically made during this period, although athletes with a beginner age may continue to make significant gains in maximum strength during this phase.

Aside from the traditional lifts during this training period, measuring intensity as a % 1RM is not always applicable. For example, when performing bodyweight plyometric exercises, this method of calculating intensity does not work, since bodyweight is the only resistance being used to overload the body. The intensity and volumes of such exercise sessions should, however, be factored into the monitoring system an athlete or coach uses to program strength training. This is necessary, since these types of exercises require large forces to be produced (Bobbert, Huijing, & van Ingen Schenau, 1987; Wallace, et al., 2010) at high velocities, thus subjecting the musculoskeletal system to relatively high levels of stress (Potach & Chu, 2000).

Additionally, such exercises can produce peak vertical ground reaction forces several times on an athlete's bodyweight (Wallace, et al., 2010). Thus, using bodyweight alone—or the weight of a medicine ball for example—when calculating volume load in these exercises is not necessarily reflective of the demands placed on the athlete's body.

In Table 5.1, these exercises have been classified relative to their perceived stress on the body as either 'low', 'medium', medium high', 'high' or 'very high' and have been assigned a hypothetical corresponding % 1RM intensity rating. In order to calculate volume load, the number of repetitions performed should then be calculated by the corresponding % 1RM intensity rating.

For example, box to box depth jumps using medium height boxes have been classified as high intensity. In order to calculate the volume load for these exercises, the total number of repetitions should be multiplied by 90 (this exercise has been given an intensity rating of 90%). This method allows the coach or athlete to integrate plyometric and various explosive exercises into an effective monitoring system.

Broadly speaking, the strength training intensities are generally higher during the special preparation phase (Figure 5.8) than in the general preparation phase. A greater emphasis will be placed on stage 3 exercises as the special preparation period progresses.

Table 5.1. Intensity classification of example plyometric exercises.

Example exercises	Exercise intensity classification	Corresponding % 1RM rating
Box to box depth jumps (high to high box heights) High hurdle rebound jumps Single leg depth jumps (≥ 35cm box height)	Very high	90–100
Bounding Box to box depth jump (high to low or medium to medium box heights) Medium hurdle rebound jumps	High	90–100
Box to box depth jump (low to high box heights) Repeated long jumps Medium hurdle jumps with bounce Vest sprints with a load equal to 10% of bodyweight Hops (maximal)	Medium high	85–87+
Box to box depth jump (low to low box heights) Low hurdle rebound jumps Repeated countermovement jumps Sprint bounding	Medium	80–83+
Ankling, low hurdle jumps with bounce Hops (submaximal)	Low	75–77+

As mentioned already, athletes with a beginner training will still focus more on general development than an athlete with an advanced training age. Typically, volume of strength training is less during this phase to allow for a greater emphasis on sprinting and sport specific skills so as to avoid accumulating high levels of fatigue, which may negatively affect their development.

The recommended frequency of sessions per week can vary during this phase in the region of 1 to 5, but typically around 3 to 4 for the most part.

During the last few weeks approaching competition, stage 1 maximum strength exercises are reduced significantly within the program to allow time for the strength gains made to transfer to sprinting performance. Maximum strength sessions elicit high levels of fatigue, which in turn may interfere with speed strength development and sprinting speed.

Additionally, the stronger the athlete, the longer they can go without performing maximum strength exercises before their maximum strength levels decline significantly. This time reduces the weaker the athlete is. This needs to be considered when programming for athletes with different training ages.

In the last 1 to 2 weeks, the frequency of sessions per week will be low compared to

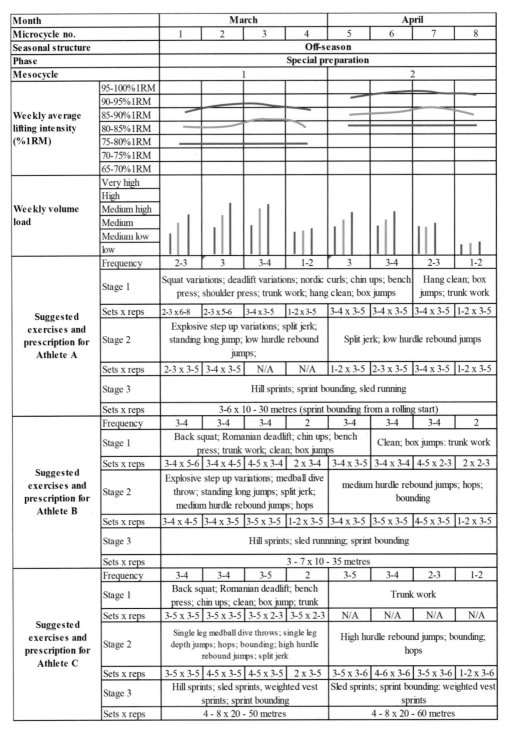

Month		March				April			
Microcycle no.		1	2	3	4	5	6	7	8
Seasonal structure		Off-season							
Phase		Special preparation							
Mesocycle		1				2			
Weekly average lifting intensity (%1RM)	95-100%1RM								
	90-95%1RM								
	85-90%1RM								
	80-85%1RM								
	75-80%1RM								
	70-75%1RM								
	65-70%1RM								
Weekly volume load	Very high								
	High								
	Medium high								
	Medium								
	Medium low								
	low								
Suggested exercises and prescription for Athlete A	Frequency	2-3	3	3-4	1-2	3	3-4	2-3	1-2
	Stage 1	Squat variations; deadlift variations; nordic curls; chin ups; bench press; shoulder press; trunk work; hang clean; box jumps						Hang clean; box jumps; trunk work	
	Sets x reps	2-3 x6-8	2-3 x5-6	3-4 x 3-5	1-2 x 3-5	3-4 x 3-5	3-4 x 3-5	3-4 x 3-5	1-2 x 3-5
	Stage 2	Explosive step up variations; split jerk; standing long jump; low hurdle rebound jumps;				Split jerk; low hurdle rebound jumps			
	Sets x reps	2-3 x 3-5	3-4 x 3-5	N/A	N/A	1-2 x 3-5	2-3 x 3-5	3-4 x 3-5	1-2 x 3-5
	Stage 3	Hill sprints; sprint bounding, sled running							
	Sets x reps	3-6 x 10 - 30 metres (sprint bounding from a rolling start)							
Suggested exercises and prescription for Athlete B	Frequency	3-4	3-4	3-4	2	3-4	3-4	3-4	2
	Stage 1	Back squat; Romanian deadlift; chin ups; bench press; trunk work; clean; box jumps				Clean; box jumps: trunk work			
	Sets x reps	3-4 x 5-6	3-4 x 4-5	4-5 x 3-4	2 x 3-4	3-4 x 3-5	3-4 x 3-4	4-5 x 2-3	2 x 2-3
	Stage 2	Explosive step up variations; medball dive throw; standing long jumps; split jerk; medium hurdle rebound jumps; hops				medium hurdle rebound jumps; hops; bounding			
	Sets x reps	3-4 x 4-5	3-4 x 3-5	3-5 x 3-5	1-2 x 3-5	3-4 x 3-5	3-5 x 3-5	4-5 x 3-5	1-2 x 3-5
	Stage 3	Hill sprints; sled runnning; sprint bounding							
	Sets x reps	3 - 7 x 10 - 35 metres							
Suggested exercises and prescription for Athlete C	Frequency	3-4	3-4	3-5	2	3-5	3-4	2-3	1-2
	Stage 1	Back squat; Romanian deadlift; bench press; chin ups; clean; box jump; trunk				Trunk work			
	Sets x reps	3-5 x 3-5	3-5 x 3-5	3-5 x 2-3	3-5 x 2-3	N/A	N/A	N/A	N/A
	Stage 2	Single leg medball dive throws; single leg depth jumps; hops; bounding; high hurdle rebound jumps; split jerk				High hurdle rebound jumps; bounding; hops			
	Sets x reps	3-5 x 3-5	4-5 x 3-5	4-5 x 3-5	2 x 3-5	3-5 x 3-6	4-6 x 3-6	3-5 x 3-6	1-2 x 3-6
	Stage 3	Hill sprints; sled sprints, weighted vest sprints; sprint bounding				Sled sprints; sprint bounding: weighted vest sprints			
	Sets x reps	4 - 8 x 20 - 50 metres				4 - 8 x 20 - 60 metres			

Figure 5.8. A strength plan overview for a special preparation period for athletes of differing training ages. Athlete A (blue line) has a beginner training age, athlete B (green line) an intermediate training age and athlete C (red line) an advanced training age.

earlier in the special preparation period, the intensity will remain high and the volume will reduce significantly. This serves as an effective tapering method leading into competition, and will be discussed in more detail later in this section.

A minimum period of 48 to 72 hours should be allowed following a strength training session before completing a subsequent session focussing on the same muscle groups. Generally, the higher the volume load and intensity, the greater the amount of rest needed between sessions. Less time is needed between sessions focussing on different muscle groups. It is possible, for example, to complete lower body and upper body sessions in the same day.

As another example, it would be perfectly feasible to complete exercises which emphasise the development of reactive strength around the knee and ankle extensors (e.g. through vertical jumps such as a depth or hurdle jumps) and to complete a maximum strength session through exercises emphasising the hip extensor muscle groups (e.g. Romanian deadlifts, glute-ham raise) on the same day or within 24 hours. Such combinations are endless and allow for potentially smaller sessions (in length) that can be completed more frequently across the week. More examples will be discussed later in this section.

Structuring the In-season Period

During the competitive period of a season, there is less time available for training and an increased need for recovery, so as to remain fresh for competition. Failure to perform strength training during the in-season will result in decrements in physical performance, but too much strength training will also negatively affect performance, potentially due to insufficient recovery. An effective minimal dose of strength training assists in maintaining performance while still allowing for recovery.

Research generally suggests that one strength session per week is sufficient to maintain strength levels for several months following a strength training program of reasonable length, as long as intensity is maintained (Bickel, Cross, & Bamman, 2011; Rønnestad, Nymark, & Raastad, 2011). During the competitive period therefore, one to two sessions per week of strength training with high intensity (between >80%–95%) and low volume (between two to four sets, and no more than 4 exercises per session) is recommended as a general rule.

These guidelines are generally suitable for a competition period in which one competition takes place every one to two weeks. Where longer periods exist between competition, a greater volume (session volume and frequency) and a greater variation intensity would be advisable in attempting to increase strength levels rather than maintain them.

Furthermore, in many individual sports (e.g. athletics) it is common to have a number of separate competition phases throughout the in-season, each of which may only last one to two weeks in length. Generally, 0–1 strength sessions are recommended during such short competitive phases.

Once in the competitive period, it is necessary for athletes to vary the emphasis placed on different strength qualities during training. This will enable the body to maintain adequate levels of all strength qualities. Whilst explosive and reactive strength is of greater importance to sprinting speed, the declines in maximum strength experienced across the in-season should be minimised so as to maintain the platform for powerful muscle contractions.

Since beginner athletes will typically possess lower levels of maximum strength than advanced athletes, a greater proportion of time should be spent on maintaining maximum strength for the more novice athlete (Figure 5.9).

Varying the emphasis on different strength qualities across the competitive period will also help vary the type of stress imposed on the athlete's body and help to minimise fatigue, injuries and overtraining. For example, plyometric exercises are stressful to the connective tissues of the body (especially the musculotendinous junctions of the ankle and knee joints) and so a period of less volume or complete elimination of reactive strength exercises may be needed at times.

Structuring the Transition Period

The transition phase links two annual training plans and facilitates psychological rest, regeneration and relaxation. The length of this phase should typically last between two to four weeks, and training should be general in nature—and low in intensity and volume—compared to the training carried out across the year. Although rest and restoration is encouraged during this phase, complete rest is not advised, since the detraining effect

associated with a prolonged period of rest can cause a substantial loss in the physiological adaptations achieved in the previous months of training.

To avoid significant loss in physiological adaptation—yet to ensure that adequate recovery takes place from a physical and psychological standpoint—active recovery is recommended, in which an athlete may take part in other sports and activities of a recreational nature. Although one week of passive rest may be necessary at the end of the season—especially if the athlete has suffered an injury—active recovery should take place for the remainder of the phase.

Figure 5.10 shows the periodised annual outline of a sprinter's training plan and the relative emphasis placed different training modalities.

Structuring of Microcycles

Effective microcycle structure is important since the fatigue generated in one session can affect subsequent training sessions. For example, if a maximum strength session of high volume load directly precedes a technical or tactical session in which key skills are being developed, the fatigue generated during the strength session may significantly impair the technical or tactical development in the next session.

Sequencing of training stimuli during a microcycle should therefore not only accommodate the training aims of the phase the athlete is in—as depicted in their annual plan—but it must also account for the fatigue

Figure 5.9. Sample distribution of emphasis on different strength qualities during the competitive period according to an athlete's training age.

accumulated during the microcycle, so as to maximise the development sprinting speed.

Generally, across most sports, strength training is secondary in importance relative to technical and tactical training. There may be times across the year however, when strength training takes priority or forms a large percentage of the total volume load of training, factoring in all sessions (including technical and tactical ones).

Annual Plan

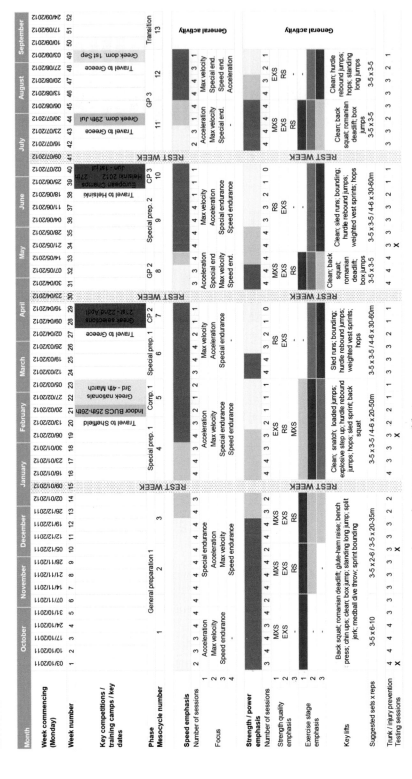

Figure 5.10. Annual plan for a sprinter during the 2011/2012 athletics season.

For example, if technical execution of a skill is not possible due to a strength deficit, then there may be a shift in training emphasis to favour strength development. However, this is likely to take place early in the general preparation period and, as a general rule, strength training is subordinate to technical and tactical training. The overall volume load and intensity of training—including everything outside of strength training—must, therefore, be considered when deciding where strength training should take place, and what the volume load of the sessions should be during the microcycle.

In designing the microcycle, the first step should be to identify the key session(s) within the week. Key sessions will often be sessions which cannot be moved, and are deemed of greater importance than general physical development sessions. Such examples include, but are not limited to, matches or competitions, tactical and technical training sessions, trials, testing sessions and training camps.

Ultimately, these sessions will be fixed within the week and cannot be changed. A well-designed strength program should ensure that the athlete is fresh for these types of sessions. Within most team sports and track events, key sessions such as those already listed will not take place, or may be deemed less important early in the general preparation period. Greater flexibility around where strength training takes place is therefore permissible.

It may be that during the early part of the general preparation phase, strength sessions are the key sessions in the microcycle, if they have been identified by the coach and athlete to be key to the progress of an athlete at that stage. For example, certain strength deficits may have been recognised as the limiting factors to improved performance. As a general rule, however, key sessions become more important in the phases leading up to competition.

Approaches to Structuring the Training Week

One effective approach to designing the microcycle, where multiple physical qualities are necessary to perform in a sport, is to alternate the energy systems being trained each day.

For example, Table 5.2 shows a weekly plan for a rugby player in the off-season who trains six times per week. Within this phase of training, the player has to attend two club training sessions, perform two maximum strength sessions and complete two conditioning sessions aimed at improving the athlete's endurance.

Alternating the energy systems being trained each day allows for adequate recovery of one energy system and/or the nervous system before it is taxed again, thus ensuring the athlete will be able to manage fatigue better during the week and maximise training gains from each session.

For athletes who train more than once a day for several days per week, planning the microcycle effectively is even more challenging, especially when multiple fitness qualities need to be trained. In such circumstances, it may not be possible to

Table 5.2. An example of a microcycle for a recreational rugby player where energy systems are alternated each day.

	Monday	Tuesday	Wednesday	Thursday	Friday	Saturday	Sunday
Session type	Club training/ general fitness	Maximum strength session	Conditioning session	Club training— technical and tactical	Conditioning	Strength	Off
Dominant energy system	Aerobic system	ATP/PC system	Aerobic system	ATP/PC system	Endurance	Maximum strength	Off
Stress to the nervous system	Low	High	Low	Low	Low	High	

always alternate the energy systems being trained each day. Training should be geared around achieving freshness for the key focus sessions, and fatigue, therefore, should be monitored closely.

The following provides a step-by-step example of how this can be done for a hypothetical athlete requiring the concurrent development of multiple fitness qualities:

Step 1: Identify key focal sessions within the week. Table 5.3 provides an example. Note that the session on the Saturday has been cited as the most important session in the week.

Step 2: Identify the main physical goals during the current training phase (this should be obtained from the annual plan) and work out what sessions are needed. In this example, the athlete has been advised to incorporate one maximum strength session with maximal loads, one speed strength session during which reactive strength developments should be targeted, and two endurance sessions (30-minute runs of low intensity).

Table 5.3. Key focal sessions identified in a hypothetical microcyle for a sport requiring the development of multiple fitness qualities.

	Mon	Tue	Wed	Thu	Fri	Sat	Sun
a.m.		Monitoring session				Sport practice	
p.m.	Sport practice			Sport practice			

Step 3: Give a 'fatigue factor' score for each session in the week. The score is an estimation of how hard each session will feel upon completion (Table 5.4).

For example, a score of '1' should be given for a session which the coach/athlete feels will elicit low levels of fatigue; a score of '2' should be given for a session which will elicit moderate levels of fatigue; and a score of '3' for high levels of fatigue. How these scores are decided can be based on experience of previous sessions. One way in which training load can be established is by multiplying the session length (in minutes) by a score out of '10' based on how hard the athlete had to work in the session, where '1' is very easy and '10' is maximum effort.

Step 4: Position the training sessions within the week such that they cause minimum disruption to one another and the key focus sessions. The levels of fatigue elicited by each session will need to be taken into account in

order to position them appropriately within the week.

Table 5.5 shows one way in which the training sessions in this example can be scheduled to maximise the athlete's readiness for key sessions, and to maximise the adaptations being sought from each session.

Figure 5.11 depicts the athlete's fatigue status, showing that the microcycle structure leads to maximum freshness for the most important session identified in the week (the Saturday session). Note that training sessions accumulate fatigue and rest/recovery sessions accumulate freshness. Each affects the athlete's readiness to compete.

For example, if a morning maximum strength session has been scored as a '3', then the athlete's readiness will reduce by '3 points'. If this training session is followed by an afternoon rest/recovery session, then

Table 5.4. Estimated fatigue scores given to a variety of training sessions to be completed in a microcycle (note the maximum strength, power and extensive endurance sessions have not yet been scheduled).

	Mon	Tue	Wed	Thu	Fri	Sat	Sun
a.m.		Monitoring				Sport practice	
Session fatigue		1				3	
p.m.	Sport practice			Sport practice			
Session fatigue	2			2			

Max strength—Fatigue 3 (1 session needed in the week)
Power (reactive strength)—Fatigue 1 (1 session needed in the week)
Extensive endurance—Fatigue 1 (2 sessions needed in the week)

Table 5.5. Microcycle structured to maximise an athlete's readiness to train for key focal sessions.

	Mon	Tue	Wed	Thu	Fri	Sat	Sun
a.m.	**Extensive endurance**	**Monitoring**	**Rest**	**Power**	**Rest**	**Sport practice**	**Rest**
Session fatigue	1	1	–	1	–	3	–
p.m.	**Sport practice**	**MXS**	**Extensive endurance**	**Sport practice**	**Rest**	**Rest**	**Rest**
Session fatigue	2	3	1	2	–	–	–

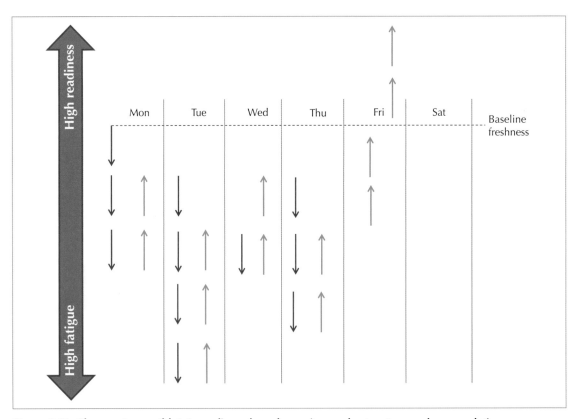

Figure 5.11. Changes to an athlete's readiness based on microcycle structure and accumulation of fatigue.

the athlete's readiness will increase by '1'. Note that two 'freshness points' are gained overnight.

For track sprint athletes who train more than once a day for several days per week, it is recommended that training is synchronised according to the qualities being developed, and with management of fatigue in mind. Much of a sprint athlete's training centres around speed, power and explosiveness. These activities can elicit high levels of fatigue, and so alternating between high and low intensity training days can be achieved by grouping together similar fitness qualities being developed. Alternating in such a fashion will ensure that the body's systems are able to recover from one high intensity training day to another, maximising speed and explosiveness during these sessions. Table 5.6 provides an example of how similar qualities can be grouped together.

Firstly, it should be noted that the track-based sessions take place first in the day. This is because during this example phase they are the most important sessions in the week.

Secondly, 'high' intensity days are proceeded with a 'low' intensity or rest day, to ensure that maximum force and speed can be expressed on each high intensity day.

Lastly, strength sessions have been positioned on days in which similar qualities are developed in the track sessions. For example, reactive strength sessions have been included on maximum velocity days and explosive strength sessions have been scheduled on acceleration days. This way each session complements the other.

Tapering

The days leading up to competition should be managed with utmost care, since without successful execution of a tapering period, the previous weeks, months and potentially years

Table 5.6. Sample microcycle structure for a track sprinter which alternates between 'high' and 'low' intensity days.

	Monday	Tuesday	Wednesday	Thursday	Friday	Saturday	Sunday
Morning session	Track acceleration focus	Tempo runs	Track max. velocity focus	Rest	Track acceleration focus	Special endurance focus	Rest
Afternoon session	Explosive strength focus (medball throws and loaded explosive jumps)	Trunk focus and specific mobility work	Plyometric session	Trunk and specific mobility work	Explosive strength focus (medball throws and loaded explosive jumps)	Maximum strength focus	Rest

can be wasted, or at least performance not optimised.

When the tapering phase should start, what sort of strength loading pattern to adopt, how much training load should be reduced and what sort of lifting intensities should be carried out, are all important factors to consider in peaking for competition. The answer to these issues is not always straightforward due to the nature of different sports, varying responses between athletes of different training age, and ability and other stresses often unaccounted for during the tapering period, such as travel. For these reasons, trial and error, intuition and often experience play important roles in optimisation of the taper period. However, scientific data and research should be used to help inform these judgements.

As alluded to previously, stage 1 maximum strength exercises should be significantly reduced during the last few weeks leading into competition. Maximum strength sessions and exercises are particularly fatiguing, and minimal interference with speed development is recommended late in the special preparation phase.

As a general rule, changes in training volume should take place around eight to fourteen days prior to competition. The volume load should be reduced by around 40–60% in a progressive manner over this time period, and is seen as the most crucial factor in an effective tapering period (Bosquet, Monpetit, Arvisais, & Mujika, 2007). Intensity should remain high if not slightly increase (Bosquet, Monpetit, Arvisais, & Mujika, 2007).

The day before competition, 'priming' sessions are often used as a training stimulus to promote an increase in testosterone to enhance performance the following day. Sometimes these sessions may even be conducted prior to competition on the same day. It is advisable that these sessions are only carried out by athletes of an advanced training age. Some examples (see also Table 5.7) include:

- 2 × 2 back squats with a load of 85% IRM and 2 minutes rest between sets
- 2 × 2 power cleans with a load of 75% IRM and 2 minutes rest between sets
- 2 × 3 jump squats with a load of 20% IRM back squat and 2 minutes rest between sets.

An example 10-day taper period for a sprinter is shown in Table 5.7.

Conclusion

The approach taken to periodise strength training for speed depends on multiple factors. Whichever approach is used should take into account the training age of the athlete, logistics, rest and recovery, training aims, experience and intuition and scientific research. Without long-term planning, the anticipated physiological adaptations elicited from individual training sessions may not come to fruition.

The seasonal structure effectively constrains the organisation of the year and dictates the amount of time an athlete has in which strength qualities can be enhanced before the competitive season starts. Broadly speaking, the training year can be broken down into a number of phases. The biggest

Table 5.7. An example 10-day taper period for a 100m sprinter approaching a major competition. Note that the volume of training represents a reduction of between 40–60% compared to previous training weeks.

	Day 10	Day 9	Day 8	Day 7	Day 6
Morning session	Travel to competition destination	Rest	Drilling/ skipping	Accelerations and block starts	Rest
Afternoon session		Trunk focus and specific mobility work	Specific mobility work	Explosive strength session	Rest
Details of strength sessions	N/A	Trunk circuit (4 exercises— 3 circuits)	N/A	Clean—6 × 2 (75% 1RM load) / Medball dive throw (4 × 3) / Explosive step up 3 × 4 (low load) / Hip thrust—4 × 3 (85% 1RM load)	N/A

	Day 5	Day 4	Day 3	Day 2	Day 1
Morning session	Max velocity and acceleration	Rest	Travel to competition venue	Max velocity	Block starts
Afternoon session	Explosive and reactive strength	Block starts		Explosive strength	Explosive strength primer
Details of strength sessions	Sled runs (3 × 30 m) / Sprint bounds (3 × 30 m) / Standing long jump (3 × 4) / Trunk circuit (4 exercises— 3 circuits)	N/A	N/A	Medball back toss (2 × 4) / Medball dive throw (2 × 4) / N/A	Power cleans—2 × 2 (75% 1RM load) / N/A

strength gains can be made during two of these phases—the general preparation and special preparation phases.

The general preparation phase, as the name suggests, is a time where general strength development takes place. Typically, within this phase a greater emphasis is placed around maximum strength, with training intensities and volume load progressively increasing. The length of time spent within this phase will vary according to the training age of the athlete. The current maximum strength level of an athlete will dictate the upper limit of their potential to generate power, and so those with lower maximum strength levels are likely to spend a longer time within the general preparation phase before moving into the special preparation phase. The degree of maximum strength influence to enhance power production diminishes as an athlete gets stronger. Those with an advanced training age should therefore move on quicker to the special preparation phase of training.

Whilst there may typically be an increase in the intensity of strength exercises during the special preparation phase, the volume loads of mesocycles may be less than that of the general preparation phase. This is in part due to an increase in sports specific training. High strength training volume loads are likely to interfere with developing sporting skills and sprinting speed, and so volume loads may decrease. Within the special preparation phase, however, exercises progress in their mechanical specificity to the sprinting action, and thus become more complementary. As this phase progresses, stage 2 and 3 exercises are the main ones of choice.

As one week of training builds on the other across the training year—resulting in several mesocycles of carefully constructed stress and recovery—the taper phase is critical in optimising speed in competition. Failure to structure the taper appropriately can lead to poor performance, rendering months of hard work into a suboptimal speed relative to the capabilities of the athlete.

Whatever the approach taken to periodise strength training, it should consider the accumulation of training stressors of all training elements in the sport. Not only this, but its emphasis should be placed on the design and implementation of sensitive and responsive training approaches, informed and underpinned by scientific research and experience.

References

Baker, D., & Newton, R. (2006). Adaptations in upper-body maximal strength and power output resulting from long-term resistance training in experienced strength-power athletes. *Journal of Strength and Conditioning Research, 20*, 541–546.

Bickel, C., Cross, J., & Bamman, M. (2011). Exercise dose to retain resistance training adaptations in young and older adults. *Medicine and Science in Sports and Exercise, 43*, 1177–1187.

Bobbert, M., Huijing, P., & van Ingen Schenau, G. (1987). Drop jumping I. The influence of jumping technique on the biomechanics of jumping. *Medicine and Science in Sports and Exercise, 19*, 332–338.

Bosquet, L., Monpetit, J., Arvisais, D., & Mujika, I. (2007). Effects of tapering on performance: a meta-analysis. *Medicine and Science in Sports and Exercise, 39*, 1358–1365.

Cormie, P., McGuigan, M., & Newton, R. (2010). Adaptations in athletic performance after ballistic power strength training. *Medicine and Science in Sports and Exercise, 42*, 1582–1598.

Cormie, P., McGuigan, M., & Newton, R. (2010). Influence of strength on magnitude and mechanisms of adaptations to power training. *Medicine and Science in Sports and Exercise, 42*, 1566–1581.

Kaneko, T. (2004). Effect of multiple-load training on the force-velocity relationship. *Journal of Strength and Conditioning Research, 18*, 792–795.

Kraemer, W., & Newton, R. (2000). Training for muscular power. *Physical Medicine and Rehabilitation Clinics of North America, 11*, 341–368.

Newton, R., & Kraemer, W. (1994). Developing explosive muscular power: implications for a mixed method training strategy. *Strength and Conditioning Journal, 16*, 20–31.

Potach, D., & Chu, D. (2000). Plyometric training. In T. Beachle, & R. Earle, *Essentials of Strength and Conditioning* (pp. 427–470). Leeds: Human Kinetics.

Rønnestad, B., Nymark, B., & Raastad, T. (2011). Effects of in-season strength maintenance training frequency in professional soccer players. *Journal of Strength and Conditioning Research, 25*, 2653–2660.

Wallace, B., Kernozek, T., White, J., Kline, D., Wright, G., Peng, H., & Huang, C. (2010). Quantification of vertical ground reaction forces of popular bilateral plyometric exercises. *Journal of Strength and Conditioning Research, 24*, 207–212.

Video Exercise Library

The following tables provide a framework of exercises which can be used to program for the development of speed-relevant strength. Each table includes exercises which are appropriate to use when looking to elicit either maximum strength, explosive strength, or reactive strength adaptations (provided that the appropriate intensities and volume of training are used—see Sections 4 and 5 for more information).

By using the QR codes provided for each table, you will be able to access video demonstrations and instructions for each exercise being carried out to assist with your training or the training of the athletes that you coach.

By purchasing this book, you will receive access to any future additions to the exercise library.

Exercises for the Development of Maximum Strength

Use the QR code to the right to access video demonstrations and instructions for the exercises in this table

Lower body				Upper body			
Squat		**Hinge**		**Push**		**Pull**	
Predominantly maximum strength-related adaptations							
Bilateral	**Split/ single leg**	**Bilateral**	**Split/ single leg**	**Horizontal**	**Vertical**	**Horizontal**	**Vertical**
Back squat	Split squat	Hip thrust	Single leg RDL	Press up	Overhead press	Bent over row	Pull up
Front squat	Bulgarian split squat	Deadlift	Single leg hip thrust	Loaded press up		Inverted row	Chin up
Trapbar deadlift	Single leg squat	Romanian deadlift (RDL)		Bench press		Prone row	Loaded pull up
Leg press	Loaded single leg squat			Incline bench press			Loaded chin up
Overhead squat	Step up						

Exercises for the Development of Explosive Strength

Use the QR code to the right to access video demonstrations and instructions for the exercises in this table

Horizontal jumps	Vertical jumps	Weightlifting and derivatives	Medball throws
Predominantly explosive strength-related adaptations			
Repeated broad jump	Barbell squat jump	Clean	Medball heave (upward)
Standing triple jump (step off landing)	Barbell jump squat	Snatch	Medball heave (forward)
Standing triple jump (to pit)	Explosive step up	Jerk	Medball heave (backward)
Standing triple jump (stick landing)	Explosive Bulgarian split squat	Hang clean	Medball heave (upwards, forward jump)
Standing long jump (step off landing)	–	Hang snatch	Medball heave (rotation)
Standing long jump (to pit)	–	Push press	Medball heave (supine)
Standing long jump (stick landing)	–	Push press (behind neck)	Medball drop throw
–	–	–	Medball push off throw
–	–	–	Medball push throw (standing)
–	–	–	Medball push throw (supine)
–	–	–	Medball push of throw (countermovement)

Exercises for the Development of Reactive Strength

Use the QR code to the right to access video demonstrations and instructions for the exercises in this table

	Foundational jumps and hops		Hopping and bounding	Rebound jumps
	Tissue integrity/general strength-related adaptations/preparation for higher intensity plyometrics in later training phases		Predominantly reactive strength-related adaptations	Predominantly reactive strength-related adaptations
	Bilateral	Unilateral		
Level 5*	–	–	Hop hurdle hop (high hurdle)	Drop jump (high box)
	–	–	Single leg pogo (maximal)	–
Level 4*	–	Continuous hop (forward, medball overhead)	Bounding (double arm, standing start)	Box-to-box drop jump (medium box)
	–	Continuous hop (backward, medball overhead)	Bounding (double arm, rolling start)	Pogo (maximal)
	–	Continuous hop (lateral, medball overhead)	Speed bound	Hurdle rebound jump (high hurdle)
	–	Continuous hop (medial, medball overhead)	Hops	Tuck jump (forward)
	–	–	Hop bound complex (1-1-2-1-1-2)	–
	–	–	Hop bound complex (1-1-2-2)	–
	–	–	Hop hurdle hop (medium hurdle)	–

(Continued)

	Foundational jumps and hops		Hopping and bounding	Rebound jumps
	Tissue integrity/general strength-related adaptations/preparation for higher intensity plyometrics in later training phases		**Predominantly reactive strength-related adaptations**	**Predominantly reactive strength-related adaptations**
	Bilateral	**Unilateral**		
Level 3*	Pogo (rhythmic, medball overhead)	Continuous hop (forward)	Acceleration bound	Hurdle rebound jump (low hurdle)
	Backward pogo (rhythmic, medball overhead)	Continuous hop (backward)	Triple hop	–
	Lateral pogo (rhythmic, medball overhead)	Continuous hop (medial)	Bounding (alternate arms, standing start)	–
	Continuous jump (forward, medball overhead)	Continuous hop (lateral)	Hurdle hop (low hurdle)	–
	Continuous jump (backward, medball overhead)	Single leg pogo (rhythmic)	Hop hurdle hop (low hurdle)	–
	Continuous jump (lateral, medball overhead)	Skips for height	–	–
	–	Skips for distance	–	–
Level 2*	Pogo (rhythmic)	Hop and stick (forward)	–	–
	Backward pogo (rhythmic)	Hop and stick (backward)	–	–
	Lateral pogo (rhythmic)	Hop and stick (lateral)	–	–
	Pogo (rhythmic, stick overhead)	Hop and stick (medial)	–	–
	Backward pogo (rhythmic, stick overhead)	Single leg pogo (mini)	–	–
	Lateral pogo (rhythmic, stick overhead)	–	–	–
	Continuous jump (forward)	–	–	–
	Continuous jump (backward)	–	–	–
	Continuous jump (lateral)	–	–	–
Level 1*	Jump and stick (forward)	–	–	–
	Jump and stick (backward)	–	–	–
	Jump and stick (lateral)	–	–	–
	Pogo (mini)	–	–	–

*Note that those with a lower training age should start with exercises of a lower intensity (lower levels) and gradually progress to higher intensity exercises (higher levels) over time.

Sample Training Programs

There are many ways in which strength training can be programmed within the general and special preparation periods. The following plans are examples based on athletes of different training ages. They assume that the athletes have no existing injuries, can perform the exercises listed with good technique and are able to strength train three times per week. Clearly the number of sessions performed each week and their content should be determined by the sport, the athlete, and the level at which they are competing.

The table below shows a 16-week strength training plan overview broken down into general and specific preparation phases. The three strength sessions performed each week are labelled with a number. These numbers correspond to the individual strength programs in this appendix.

Sample strength training periodised structure based on an athlete being able to strength train three times per week.

Week	Phase	Session 1	Session 2	Session 3
Week 1		A1	B1	C1
Week 2	General preparation phase 1	A2	B2	C2
Week 3		A3	B3	C3
Week 4		A4	B4	C4
Week 5		A1	B1	C1
Week 6	General preparation phase 2	A2	B2	C2
Week 7		A3	B3	C3
Week 8		A4	B4	C4

(Continued)

Week	Phase	Session 1	Session 2	Session 3
Week 9		A1	B1	C1
Week 10	Special preparation phase 1	A2	B2	C2
Week 11		A3	B3	C3
Week 12		A4	B4	C4
Week 13		A1	B1	C1
Week 14	Special preparation phase 2	A2	B2	C2
Week 15		A3	B3	C3
Week 16		A4	B4	C4

Each program has been designed according to training age and for the most part, repetition maximum (RM) values have been used to prescribe intensity for the sake of ease. In order to work out approximate % IRM values from repetition maximum, the RM-%1RM conversion table below can be used.

RM	%1RM
1	100
2	95
3	92.5
4	87.5
5	85
6	80

General Preparation Phase 1—Beginner Periodised Programs—Week 1

Session no. A1	Goal:								Date:			Bodyweight (kg):		
				Target sets										
Exercise	Tempo	Rest	Intensity	Reps	Load	Reps	Load	Reps	Load	Reps	Load	Reps	Load	
Clean from hip & hang variations	XXX					Technique								
Back squat	201	1.5 min	12RM	8		8								
Dumbbell bench press	201	1.5 min	12RM	8		8								
Romanian deadlift	201	1.5 min	12RM	8		8								
Inverted row	201	1.5 min	BW	TF		TF								
Single leg iso ankle push	10/5 ramp	1 min	75% at peak	10/5 ramp [2]		10/5 ramp [2]								
Trunk circuit														

Session no. B1	Goal:								Date:			Bodyweight (kg):		
				Target sets										
Exercise	Tempo	Rest	Intensity	Time	Load	Time	Load	Time	Load	Time	Load	Time	Load	
Bodyweight squats	Steady	2 minutes between circuits	BW	10 s		10 s		10 s						
Press up	Steady		BW	10 s		10 s		10 s						
Lunges	Steady		BW	10 s		10 s		10 s						
Plank	Steady		BW	20 s		20 s		20 s						
Squat jump (BW)	XXX		BW	4*		4*		4*						
Single leg iso hip extensor push	10/5 ramp		75% at peak	10/5* ramp [2]		10/5* ramp [2]								

*reps instead of time. Note this session is performed as a circuit, i.e. 1 set of each exercise is performed in succession without rest. A period of rest is then used to separate each circuit.

Session no. C1	Goal:								Date:			Bodyweight (kg):		
				Target sets										
Exercise	Tempo	Rest	Intensity	Reps	Load	Reps	Load	Reps	Load	Reps	Load	Reps	Load	
Standing long jump	XXX	2.5 min	BW	3		3								
Deadlift	201	1.5 min	12RM	8		8								
Dumbbell shoulder press	201	1.5 min	12RM	8		8								
Step up	201	1.5 min	12RM	8		8								
Single arm row	201	1.5 min	12RM	8		8								
Nordic curls	301	1.5 min	BW	5		5								
Trunk circuit														

General Preparation Phase 1—Beginner Periodised Programs—Week 2

Session no. A2	Goal:					Date:			Bodyweight (kg):				
				Target sets									
Exercise	Tempo	Rest	Intensity	Reps	Load	Reps	Load	Reps	Load	Reps	Load	Reps	Load
Clean from hip and hang variations	XXX			Technique									
Back squat	201	1.5 min	12RM	8		8							
Dumbbell bench press	201	1.5 min	12RM	8		8							
Romanian deadlift	201	1.5 min	12RM	8		8							
Inverted row	201	1.5 min	BW	TF		TF							
Single leg iso ankle push	10/5 ramp	1 min	75% at peak	10/5 ramp [2]		10/5 ramp [2]		10/5 ramp [2]					
Trunk circuit													

Session no. B2	Goal:					Date:			Bodyweight (kg):				
				Target sets									
Exercise	Tempo	Rest	Intensity	Time	Load	Time	Load	Time	Load	Time	Load	Time	Load
Bodyweight squats	Steady	2 minutes between circuits	BW	10 s		10 s		10 s					
Press up	Steady		BW	10 s		10 s		10 s					
Lunges	Steady		BW	10 s		10 s		10 s					
Plank	Steady		BW	20 s		20 s		20 s					
Squat jump (BW)	XXX		BW	4*		4*		4*					
Single leg iso hip extensor push	10/5 ramp		75% at peak	10/5 ramp [2]		10/5 ramp [2]		10/5 ramp [2]					

*reps instead of time. Note this session is performed as a circuit, i.e. 1 set of each exercise is performed in succession without rest. A period of rest is then used to separate each circuit.

Session no. C2	Goal:					Date:			Bodyweight (kg):				
				Target sets									
Exercise	Tempo	Rest	Intensity	Reps	Load	Reps	Load	Reps	Load	Reps	Load	Reps	Load
Box jump	XXX	2.5 min	BW	4		4							
Deadlift	201	1.5 min	12RM	8		8		8					
Dumbbell shoulder press	201	1.5 min	12RM	8		8							
Step up	201	1.5 min	12RM	8		8							
Single arm row	201	1.5 min	12RM	8		8		8					
Nordic curls	301	1.5 min	BW	5		5							
Trunk circuit													

General Preparation Phase 1—Beginner Periodised Programs—Week 3

Session no. A3	Goal:							Date:			Bodyweight (kg):		
									Target sets				
Exercise	Tempo	Rest	Intensity	Reps	Load	Reps	Load	Reps	Load	Reps	Load	Reps	Load
Clean from hip	XXX	2 min	50% 1RM	5		5		5					
Back squat	201	1.5 min	12RM	8		8		8					
Dumbbell bench press	201	1.5 min	12RM	8		8		8					
Romanian deadlift	201	1.5 min	12RM	8		8		8					
Inverted row	201	1.5 min	BW	TF		TF		TF					
Single leg iso ankle push	10/5 ramp	1 min	75% at peak	10/5 ramp [2]		10/5 ramp [2]		10/5 ramp [2]					
Trunk circuit													

Session no. B3	Goal:							Date:			Bodyweight (kg):		
									Target sets				
Exercise	Tempo	Rest	Intensity	Time	Load	Time	Load	Time	Load	Time	Load	Time	Load
Bodyweight squats	Steady	2 minutes between circuits	BW	15 s		15 s		15 s					
Press up	Steady		BW	15 s		15 s		15 s					
Lunges	Steady		BW	15 s		15 s		15 s					
Plank	Steady		BW	30 s		30 s		30 s					
Squat jump (BW)	XXX		BW	4*		4*		4*					
Single leg iso hip extensor push	Steady		75% at peak	10/5 ramp [2]		10/5 ramp [2]		10/5 ramp [2]					

*reps instead of time. Note this session is performed as a circuit, i.e. 1 set of each exercise is performed in succession without rest. A period of rest is then used to separate each circuit.

Session no. C3	Goal:							Date:			Bodyweight (kg):		
									Target sets				
Exercise	Tempo	Rest	Intensity	Reps	Load	Reps	Load	Reps	Load	Reps	Load	Reps	Load
Box jump	XXX	2.5 min	BW	4		4		4					
Deadlift	201	1.5 min	12RM	8		8		8					
Dumbbell shoulder press	201	1.5 min	12RM	8		8		8					
Step up	201	1.5 min	12RM	8		8		8					
Single arm row	201	1.5 min	12RM	8		8		8					
Nordic curls	301	1.5 min	BW	6		6		6					
Trunk circuit													

General Preparation Phase 1—Beginner Periodised Programs—Week 4

Session no. A4	Goal:						Date:			Bodyweight (kg):			
							Target sets						
Exercise	Tempo	Rest	Intensity	Reps	Load	Reps	Load	Reps	Load	Reps	Load	Reps	Load
Clean from hip	XXX	2 min	50% 1RM	5		5							
Back squat	201	1.5 min	12RM	8		8							
Dumbbell bench press	201	1.5 min	12RM	8		8							
Romanian deadlift	201	1.5 min	12RM	8		8							
Inverted row	201	1.5 min	BW	TF		TF							
Single leg iso ankle push	10/5 ramp	1 min	75% at peak	10/5 ramp [2]		10/5 ramp [2]							
Trunk circuit													

Session no. B4	Goal:						Date:			Bodyweight (kg):			
							Target sets						
Exercise	Tempo	Rest	Intensity	Time	Load	Time	Load	Time	Load	Time	Load	Time	Load
Bodyweight squats	Steady	2 minutes between circuits	BW	15 s		15 s		15 s					
Press up	Steady		BW	15 s		15 s		15 s					
Lunges	Steady		BW	15 s		15 s		15 s					
Plank	Steady		BW	30 s		30 s		30 s					
Squat jump (BW)	XXX		BW	4*		4*		4*					
Single leg iso hip extensor push	Steady		75% at peak	10/5 ramp [2]		10/5 ramp [2]		10/5 ramp [2]					

*reps instead of time. Note this session is performed as a circuit, i.e. 1 set of each exercise is performed in succession without rest. A period of rest is then used to separate each circuit.

Session no. C4	Goal:						Date:			Bodyweight (kg):			
							Target sets						
Exercise	Tempo	Rest	Intensity	Reps	Load	Reps	Load	Reps	Load	Reps	Load	Reps	Load
Box jump	XXX	2.5 min	BW	4		4							
Deadlift	201	1.5 min	12RM	8		8							
Dumbbell shoulder press	201	1.5 min	12RM	8		8							
Step up	201	1.5 min	12RM	8		8							
Single arm row	201	1.5 min	12RM	8		8							
Nordic curls	301	1.5 min	BW	6		6							
Trunk circuit													

General Preparation Phase 1—Intermediate Periodised Programs—Week 1

Session no. A1	Goal:								Date:		Bodyweight (kg):			
				Target sets										
Exercise	Tempo	Rest	Intensity	Reps	Load	Reps	Load	Reps	Load	Reps	Load	Reps	Load
Clean	XXX	2.5 min	60% 1RM	5		5		5					
Back squat	201	2 min	10RM	8		8		8					
Dumbbell bench press	201	2 min	10RM	8		8		8					
Romanian deadlift	201	2 min	10RM	8		8		8					
Chin up	201	2 min	BW	TF		TF		TF					
Trunk circuit													

Session no. B1	Goal:								Date:		Bodyweight (kg):			
				Target sets										
Exercise	Tempo	Rest	Intensity	Time	Load	Time	Load	Time	Load	Time	Load	Time	Load
Single leg squat	Rapid	2 minutes between circuits	BW	8 s		8 s		8 s					
Press up	Rapid		BW	8 s		8 s		8 s					
Kneeling barbell roll out	Steady		BW	6*		6*		6*					
Bodyweight explosive step up	XXX		BW	8 s		8 s		8 s					
Inverted row	Rapid		BW	8 s		8 s		8 s					
Single leg iso ankle push	10/5 ramp	1 min	85% at peak	10/5 ramp [2]		10/5 ramp [2]							

*reps instead of time. Note this session is performed as a circuit, i.e. 1 set of each exercise is performed in succession without rest. A period of rest is then used to separate each circuit.

Session no. C1	Goal:								Date:		Bodyweight (kg):			
				Target sets										
Exercise	Tempo	Rest	Intensity	Reps	Load	Reps	Load	Reps	Load	Reps	Load	Reps	Load
Standing broad jump	XXX	2.5 min	BW	4		4		4					
Deadlift	201	2 min	10RM	8		8		8					
Dumbbell shoulder press	201	2 min	10RM	8		8		8					
Bulgarian split squat	201	2 min	10RM	8		8		8					
Single arm row	201	2 min	10RM	8		8		8					
Single leg iso hip extensor push	10/5 ramp	1 min	85% at peak	10/5 ramp [2]		10/5 ramp [2]							
Trunk circuit													

General Preparation Phase 1—Intermediate Periodised Programs—Week 2

Session no. A2	Goal:										Date:		Bodyweight (kg):	
				Target sets										
Exercise	Tempo	Rest	Intensity	Reps	Load	Reps	Load	Reps	Load	Reps	Load	Reps	Load	
Clean	XXX	2.5 min	65% 1RM	5		5		5		5				
Back squat	201	2 min	10RM	8		8		8		8				
Dumbbell bench press	201	2 min	10RM	8		8		8						
Romanian deadlift	201	2 min	10RM	8		8		8						
Chin up	201	2 min	BW	TF		TF		TF						
Trunk circuit														

Session no. B2	Goal:										Date:		Bodyweight (kg):	
				Target sets										
Exercise	Tempo	Rest	Intensity	Time	Load	Time	Load	Time	Load	Time	Load	Time	Load	
Single leg squat	Rapid	2 minutes between circuits	BW	10 s		10 s		10 s						
Press up	Rapid		BW	10 s		10 s		10 s						
Kneeling barbell roll out	Steady		BW	8*		8*		8*						
Bodyweight explosive step up	XXX		BW	10 s		10 s		10 s						
Inverted row	Rapid		BW	10 s		10 s		10 s						
Single leg iso ankle push	5/5 ramp	2 min	90% at peak	5/5 ramp [3]		5/5 ramp [3]		5/5 ramp [3]						

*reps instead of time. Note this session is performed as a circuit, i.e. 1 set of each exercise is performed in succession without rest. A period of rest is then used to separate each circuit.

Session no. C2	Goal:										Date:		Bodyweight (kg):	
				Target sets										
Exercise	Tempo	Rest	Intensity	Reps	Load	Reps	Load	Reps	Load	Reps	Load	Reps	Load	
Standing broad jump	XXX	2.5 min	BW	4		4		4		4				
Deadlift	201	2 min	10RM	8		8		8		8				
Dumbbell shoulder press	201	2 min	10RM	8		8		8						
Bulgarian split squat	201	2 min	10RM	8		8		8						
Single arm row	201	2 min	10RM	8		8		8						
Single leg iso hip extensor push	5/5 ramp	2 min	90% at peak	5/5 ramp [3]		5/5 ramp [3]		5/5 ramp [3]						
Trunk circuit														

General Preparation Phase 1—Intermediate Periodised Programs—Week 3

Session no. A3	Goal:							Date:			Bodyweight (kg):		
									Target sets				
Exercise	Tempo	Rest	Intensity	Reps	Load	Reps	Load	Reps	Load	Reps	Load	Reps	Load
Clean	XXX	2.5 min	70% 1RM	4		4		4		4			
Back squat	201	2.5 min	8RM	6		6		6		6			
Dumbbell bench press	201	2.5	8RM	6		6		6		6			
Romanian deadlift	201	2 min	8RM	6		6		6		6			
Chin up	201	2 min	BW	TF		TF		TF					
Trunk circuit													

Session no. B3	Goal:							Date:			Bodyweight (kg):		
									Target sets				
Exercise	Tempo	Rest	Intensity	Time	Load	Time	Load	Time	Load	Time	Load	Time	Load
Single leg squat	Rapid	2 minutes between circuits	BW	12 s		12 s		12 s		12 s			
Press up	Rapid		BW	12 s		12 s		12 s		12 s			
Kneeling barbell roll out	Steady		BW	8*		8*		8*		8*			
Bodyweight explosive step up	XXX		BW	12 s		12 s		12 s		12 s			
Inverted row	Rapid		BW	12 s		12 s		12 s		12 s			
Single leg iso ankle push	5/5 ramp	2 min	90% at peak	5/5 ramp [3]		5/5 ramp [3]		5/5 ramp [3]		5/5 ramp [3]			

*reps instead of time. Note this session is performed as a circuit, i.e. 1 set of each exercise is performed in succession without rest. A period of rest is then used to separate each circuit.

Session no. C3	Goal:							Date:			Bodyweight (kg):		
									Target sets				
Exercise	Tempo	Rest	Intensity	Reps	Load	Reps	Load	Reps	Load	Reps	Load	Reps	Load
Standing broad jump	XXX	2.5 min	BW	5		5		5		5			
Deadlift	201	2.5 min	8RM	6		6		6		6			
Dumbbell shoulder press	201	2.5	8RM	6		6		6		6			
Bulgarian split squat	201	2 min	8RM	6		6		6		6			
Single arm row	201	2 min	8RM	6		6		6		6			
Single leg iso hip extensor push	5/5 ramp	2 min	90% at peak	5/5 ramp [3]		5/5 ramp [3]		5/5 ramp [3]		5/5 ramp [3]			
Trunk circuit													

General Preparation Phase 1—Intermediate Periodised Programs—Week 4

Session no. A4	Goal:								Date:		Bodyweight (kg):		
								Target sets					
Exercise	Tempo	Rest	Intensity	Reps	Load	Reps	Load	Reps	Load	Reps	Load	Reps	Load
Clean	XXX	2.5 min	75% 1RM	3		3							
Back squat	201	2.5 min	6RM	5		5							
Dumbbell bench press	201	2.5 min	6RM	5		5							
Romanian deadlift	201	2.5 min	6RM	5		5							
Chin up	201	2.5 min	BW	TF		TF							

Session no. B4	Goal:								Date:		Bodyweight (kg):		
								Target sets					
Exercise	Tempo	Rest	Intensity	Time	Load	Time	Load	Time	Load	Time	Load	Time	Load
Trunk circuit													

Session no. C4	Goal:								Date:		Bodyweight (kg):		
								Target sets					
Exercise	Tempo	Rest	Intensity	Reps	Load	Reps	Load	Reps	Load	Reps	Load	Reps	Load
Standing broad jump	XXX	2.5 min	BW	5		5							
Deadlift	201	2.5 min	6RM	5		5							
Dumbbell shoulder press	201	2.5 min	6RM	5		5							
Bulgarian split squat	201	2.5 min	6RM	5		5							
Single arm row	201	2.5 min	6RM	5		5							
Trunk circuit													

General Preparation Phase 1—Advanced Periodised Programs—Week 1

Session no. A1	Goal:								Date:		Bodyweight (kg):		
								Target sets					
Exercise	Tempo	Rest	Intensity	Reps	Load	Reps	Load	Reps	Load	Reps	Load	Reps	Load
Clean	XXX	2.5 min	60% 1RM	5		5		5		5			
Back squat	201	2 min	7RM	6		6		6		6			
Dumbbell bench press	201	2 min	7RM	6		6		6		6			
Romanian deadlift	201	2 min	7RM	6		6		6					
Chin up	201	2 min	BW	TF		TF		TF					
Single leg iso ankle push	5/5 ramp	2 min	90% at peak	5/5 ramp [3]		5/5 ramp [3]		5/5 ramp [3]					
Trunk circuit													

Session no. B1	Goal:								Date:		Bodyweight (kg):			
					Target sets									
Exercise	Tempo	Rest	Intensity	Time	Load	Time	Load	Time	Load	Time	Load	Time	Load	
Single leg squat	Rapid	2 minutes between circuits	BW	10 s		10 s		10 s						
Press up	Rapid		BW	10 s		10 s		10 s						
Kneeling barbell roll out	Steady		BW	8*		8*		8*						
Bodyweight explosive step up	XXX		BW	10 s		10 s		10 s						
Inverted row	Rapid		BW	10 s		10 s		10 s						
Single leg iso hip extensor push	5/5 ramp	2 min	90% at peak	5/5 ramp [3]		5/5 ramp [3]		5/5 ramp [3]						

*reps instead of time. Note this session is performed as a circuit, i.e. 1 set of each exercise is performed in succession without rest. A period of rest is then used to separate each circuit.

Session no. C1	Goal:								Date:		Bodyweight (kg):			
					Target sets									
Exercise	Tempo	Rest	Intensity	Reps	Load	Reps	Load	Reps	Load	Reps	Load	Reps	Load	
Standing long jump	XXX	2.5 min	BW	4		4		4						
Deadlift	201	2 min	7RM	6		6		6						
Dumbbell shoulder press	201	2 min	7RM	6		6		6						
Bulgarian split squat	201	2 min	7RM	6		6		6						
Single arm row	201	2 min	7RM	6		6		6						
Trunk circuit														

General Preparation Phase 1—Advanced Periodised Programs—Week 2

Session no. A2	Goal:								Date:		Bodyweight (kg):			
					Target sets									
Exercise	Tempo	Rest	Intensity	Reps	Load	Reps	Load	Reps	Load	Reps	Load	Reps	Load	
Clean	XXX	2.5 min	65% 1RM	5		5		5		5				
Back squat	201	2 min	6RM	5		5		5		5		5		
Dumbbell bench press	201	2 min	6RM	5		5		5		5				
Romanian deadlift	201	2 min	6RM	5		5		5		5				
Chin up	201	2 min	BW	TF		TF		TF						
Single leg iso ankle push	5/5 ramp	2 min	95% at peak	5/5 ramp [3]		5/5 ramp [3]		5/5 ramp [3]		5/5 ramp [3]				
Trunk circuit														

Session no. B2	Goal:								Date:			Bodyweight (kg):	
				Target sets									
Exercise	Tempo	Rest	Intensity	Time	Load	Time	Load	Time	Load	Time	Load	Time	Load
Single leg squat	Rapid	2 minutes between circuits	BW	12 s		12 s		12 s					
Press up	Rapid		BW	12 s		12 s		12 s					
Kneeling barbell roll out	Steady		BW	10*		10*		10*					
Bodyweight explosive step up	XXX		BW	12 s		12 s		12 s					
Inverted row	Rapid		BW	12 s		12 s		12 s					
Single leg iso hip extensor push	5/5 ramp	2 min	95% at peak	5/5 ramp [3]		5/5 ramp [3]		5/5 ramp [3]		5/5 ramp [3]			

*reps instead of time. Note this session is performed as a circuit, i.e. 1 set of each exercise is performed in succession without rest. A period of rest is then used to separate each circuit.

Session no. C2	Goal:								Date:			Bodyweight (kg):	
				Target sets									
Exercise	Tempo	Rest	Intensity	Reps	Load	Reps	Load	Reps	Load	Reps	Load	Reps	Load
Standing long jump	XXX	2.5 min	BW	4		4		4		4			
Deadlift	201	2 min	6RM	5		5		5		5		5	
Dumbbell shoulder press	201	2 min	6RM	5		5		5					
Bulgarian split squat	201	2 min	6RM	5		5		5		5			
Single arm row	201	2 min	6RM	5		5		5					
Trunk circuit													

General Preparation Phase 1—Advanced Periodised Programs—Week 3

Session no. A3	Goal:								Date:			Bodyweight (kg):	
				Target sets									
Exercise	Tempo	Rest	Intensity	Reps	Load	Reps	Load	Reps	Load	Reps	Load	Reps	Load
Clean	XXX	2.5 min	70% 1RM	4		4		4		4			
Back squat	201	2.5 min	5RM	4		4		4		4		4	
Dumbbell bench press	201	2.5 min	5RM	4		4		4		4			
Romanian deadlift	201	2.5 min	5RM	4		4		4		4			
Chin up	201	2.5 min	BW	TF		TF		TF		TF			
Single leg iso ankle push	3/3 max	3 min	100% at peak	3/3 ramp [3]		3/3 ramp [3]		3/3 ramp [3]					
Trunk circuit													

Session no. B3	Goal:					Date:			Bodyweight (kg):		
				Target sets							
Exercise	Tempo	Rest	Intensity	Time	Load	Time	Load	Time	Load	Time	Load	Time	Load
Single leg squat	Rapid	2 minutes between circuits	BW	15 s		15 s		15 s		15 s	
Press up	Rapid		BW	15 s		15 s		15 s		15 s	
Kneeling barbell roll out	Steady		BW	10*		10*		10*		10*	
Bodyweight explosive step up	XXX		BW	15 s		15 s		15 s		15 s	
Inverted row	Rapid		BW	15 s		15 s		15 s		15 s	
Single leg iso hip extensor push	3/3 max	3 min	100% at peak	3/3 ramp [3]		3/3 ramp [3]		3/3 ramp [3]			

*reps instead of time. Note this session is performed as a circuit, i.e. 1 set of each exercise is performed in succession without rest. A period of rest is then used to separate each circuit.

Session no. C3	Goal:					Date:			Bodyweight (kg):		
				Target sets							
Exercise	Tempo	Rest	Intensity	Reps	Load	Reps	Load	Reps	Load	Reps	Load	Reps	Load
Standing long jump	XXX	2.5 min	BW	5		5		5		5	
Deadlift	201	2.5 min	5RM	4		4		4		4		4	
Dumbbell shoulder press	201	2.5 min	5RM	4		4		4			
Bulgarian split squat	201	2.5 min	5RM	4		4		4		4	
Single arm row	201	2.5 min	5RM	4		4		4		4	
Trunk circuit											

General Preparation Phase 1—Advanced Periodised Programs—Week 4

Session no. A4	Goal:					Date:			Bodyweight (kg):		
				Target sets							
Exercise	Tempo	Rest	Intensity	Reps	Load	Reps	Load	Reps	Load	Reps	Load	Reps	Load
Clean	XXX	2.5 min	75% 1RM	3		3					
Back squat	201	2.5 min	5RM	4		4					
Dumbbell bench press	201	2.5 min	5RM	4		4					
Romanian deadlift	201	2.5 min	5RM	4		4					
Chin up	201	2.5 min	BW	TF		TF					
Single leg iso ankle push	5/5 ramp	2 min	90% at peak	5/5 ramp [3]		5/5 ramp [3]					
Trunk circuit											

Session no. B4	Goal:									Date:			Bodyweight (kg):	
					Target sets									
Exercise	Tempo	Rest	Intensity	Time	Load	Time	Load	Time	Load	Time	Load	Time	Load	
Trunk circuit														

Session no. C4	Goal:									Date:			Bodyweight (kg):	
					Target sets									
Exercise	Tempo	Rest	Intensity	Reps	Load	Reps	Load	Reps	Load	Reps	Load	Reps	Load	
Standing long jump	XXX	2.5 min	BW	5		5								
Deadlift	201	2.5 min	5RM	4		4								
Dumbbell shoulder press	201	2.5 min	5RM	4		4								
Bulgarian split squat	201	2.5 min	5RM	4		4								
Single arm row	201	2.5 min	5RM	4		4								

General Preparation Phase 2—Beginner Periodised Programs—Week 5

Session no. A1	Goal:									Date:			Bodyweight (kg):	
					Target sets									
Exercise	Tempo	Rest	Intensity	Reps	Load	Reps	Load	Reps	Load	Reps	Load	Reps	Load	
Hang clean	XXX	2.5 min	60% 1RM	5		5		5						
Back squat	201	2 min	10RM	8		8		8						
Dumbbell bench press	201	2 min	10RM	8		8		8						
Romanian deadlift	201	2 min	10RM	8		8		8						
Inverted row	201	2 min	10RM	TF		TF		TF						
Single leg iso ankle push	10/5 ramp	1 min	80% at peak	10/5 ramp [2]		10/5 ramp [2]								
Trunk circuit														

Session no. B1	Goal:									Date:			Bodyweight (kg):	
					Target sets									
Exercise	Tempo	Rest	Intensity	Reps	Load	Reps	Load	Reps	Load	Reps	Load	Reps	Load	
Ankling	XXX	2 min	BW	15*		15*		15*						
Pogos	XXX	2 min	BW	10		10		10						
Standing long jump	XXX	2 min	BW	4		4		4						
Medball heave (upwards)	XXX	2 min	3 kg	4		4		4						
Hip thrust	201	1 min	10RM	8		8		8						
Trunk circuit														

*metres instead of reps.

Session no. C1	Goal:								Date:		Bodyweight (kg):		
					Target sets								
Exercise	Tempo	Rest	Intensity	Reps	Load	Reps	Load	Reps	Load	Reps	Load	Reps	Load
Box jump	XXX	2.5 min	BW	5		5		5					
Deadlift	201	2 min	10RM	8		8		8					
Dumbbell shoulder press	201	2 min	10RM	8		8		8					
Step up	201	2 min	10RM	8		8		8					
Single arm row	201	2 min	10RM	8		8		8					
Single leg iso hip extensor push	10/5 ramp	1 min	80% at peak	10/5 ramp [2]		10/5 ramp [2]							
Trunk circuit													

General Preparation Phase 2—Beginner Periodised Programs—Week 6

Session no. A2	Goal:								Date:		Bodyweight (kg):		
					Target sets								
Exercise	Tempo	Rest	Intensity	Reps	Load	Reps	Load	Reps	Load	Reps	Load	Reps	Load
Hang clean	XXX	2.5 min	60% 1RM	5		5		5					
Back squat	201	2 min	10RM	8		8		8					
Dumbbell bench press	201	2 min	10RM	8		8		8					
Romanian deadlift	201	2 min	10RM	8		8		8					
Inverted row	201	2 min	10RM	TF		TF		TF					
Single leg iso ankle push	10/5 ramp	1 min	80% at peak	10/5 ramp [2]		10/5 ramp [2]		10/5 ramp [2]		10/5 ramp [2]			
Trunk circuit													

Session no. B2	Goal:								Date:		Bodyweight (kg):		
					Target sets								
Exercise	Tempo	Rest	Intensity	Reps	Load	Reps	Load	Reps	Load	Reps	Load	Reps	Load
Ankling	XXX	2 min	BW	15*		15*		15*					
Pogos	XXX	2 min	BW	10		10		10					
Standing long jump	XXX	2 min	BW	4		4		4					
Medball heave (upwards)	XXX	2 min	3 kg	4		4		4					
Hip thrust	201	1 min	10RM	8		8		8					
Trunk circuit													

*metres instead of reps.

Session no. C2	Goal:								Date:			Bodyweight (kg):	
					Target sets								
Exercise	Tempo	Rest	Intensity	Reps	Load	Reps	Load	Reps	Load	Reps	Load	Reps	Load
Box jump	XXX	2.5 min	BW	5		5		5					
Deadlift	201	2 min	10RM	8		8		8					
Dumbbell shoulder press	201	2 min	10RM	8		8		8					
Step up	201	2 min	10RM	8		8		8					
Single arm row	201	2 min	10RM	8		8		8					
Single leg iso hip extensor push	10/5 ramp	1 min	80% at peak	10/5 ramp [2]		10/5 ramp [2]		10/5 ramp [2]		10/5 ramp [2]			
Trunk circuit													

General Preparation Phase 2—Beginner Periodised Programs—Week 7

Session no. A3	Goal:								Date:			Bodyweight (kg):	
					Target sets								
Exercise	Tempo	Rest	Intensity	Reps	Load	Reps	Load	Reps	Load	Reps	Load	Reps	Load
Hang clean	XXX	2.5 min	60% 1RM	5		5		5					
Back squat	201	2 min	10RM	8		8		8					
Dumbbell bench press	201	2 min	10RM	8		8		8					
Romanian deadlift	201	2 min	10RM	8		8		8					
Inverted row	201	2 min	10RM	TF		TF		TF					
Single leg iso ankle push	5/5 ramp	1 min	85% at peak	5/5 ramp [3]		5/5 ramp [3]		5/5 ramp [3]					
Trunk circuit													

Session no. B3	Goal:								Date:			Bodyweight (kg):	
					Target sets								
Exercise	Tempo	Rest	Intensity	Reps	Load	Reps	Load	Reps	Load	Reps	Load	Reps	Load
Ankling	XXX	2 min	BW	15*		15*		15*					
Pogos	XXX	2 min	BW	10		10		10					
Standing long jump	XXX	2 min	BW	4		4		4					
Medball heave (upwards)	XXX	2 min	5 kg	4		4		4					
Hip thrust	201	1.5 min	8RM	6		6		6					
Trunk circuit													

*metres instead of reps.

Session no. C3	Goal:				Date:				Bodyweight (kg):			
							Target sets					
Exercise	Tempo	Rest	Intensity	Reps	Load	Reps	Load	Reps	Load	Reps	Load	Reps	Load
Box jump	201	2.5 min	BW	5		5		5					
Deadlift	201	2 min	10RM	8		8		8					
Dumbbell shoulder press	201	2 min	10RM	8		8		8					
Step up	201	2 min	10RM	8		8		8					
Single arm row	201	2 min	10RM	8		8		8					
Single leg iso hip extensor push	5/5 ramp	1 min	85% at peak	5/5 ramp [3]		5/5 ramp [3]		5/5 ramp [3]					
Trunk circuit													

General Preparation Phase 2—Beginner Periodised Programs—Week 8

Session no. A4	Goal:				Date:				Bodyweight (kg):			
							Target sets					
Exercise	Tempo	Rest	Intensity	Reps	Load	Reps	Load	Reps	Load	Reps	Load	Reps	Load
Hang clean	XXX	2.5 min	60% 1RM	5		5							
Back squat	201	2 min	10RM	8		8							
Dumbbell bench press	201	2 min	10RM	8		8							
Romanian deadlift	201	2 min	10RM	8		8							
Inverted row	201	2 min	10RM	TF		TF							
Single leg iso ankle push	10/5 ramp	1 min	80% at peak	10/5 ramp [2]		10/5 ramp [2]							
Trunk circuit													

Session no. B4	Goal:				Date:				Bodyweight (kg):			
							Target sets					
Exercise	Tempo	Rest	Intensity	Reps	Load	Reps	Load	Reps	Load	Reps	Load	Reps	Load
Ankling	XXX	2 min	BW	15*		15*		15*					
Pogos	XXX	2 min	BW	10		10		10					
Standing long jump	XXX	2 min	BW	4		4		4					
Medball heave (upwards)	XXX	2 min	5 kg	4		4		4					
Hip thrust	201	1.5 min	8RM	6		6		6					
Trunk circuit													

*metres instead of reps.

Session no. C4	Goal:											Date:		Bodyweight (kg):	
					Target sets										
Exercise	Tempo	Rest	Intensity	Reps	Load	Reps	Load	Reps	Load	Reps	Load	Reps	Load		
Box jump	XXX	2.5 min	BW	5		5									
Deadlift	201	2 min	10RM	8		8									
Dumbbell shoulder press	201	2 min	10RM	8		8									
Step up	201	2 min	10RM	8		8									
Single arm row	201	2 min	10RM	8		8									
Single leg iso hip extensor push	10/5 ramp	1 min	80% at peak	10/5 ramp [2]		10/5 ramp [2]									
Trunk circuit															

General Preparation Phase 2—Intermediate Periodised Programs—Week 5

Session no. A1	Goal:											Date:		Bodyweight (kg):	
					Target sets										
Exercise	Tempo	Rest	Intensity	Reps	Load	Reps	Load	Reps	Load	Reps	Load	Reps	Load		
Clean	XXX	2.5 min	65% 1RM	5		5		5		5					
Back squat	201	2.5 min	7RM	6		6		6		6					
Barbell bench press	201	2.5 min	7RM	6		6		6		6					
Romanian deadlift	201	2.5 min	7RM	6		6		6		6					
Weighted chin up	201	2.5 min	7RM	6		6		6		6					
Single leg iso ankle push	5/5 ramp	2 min	90% at peak	5/5 ramp [2]		5/5 ramp [2]		5/5 ramp [2]							

Session no. B1	Goal:											Date:		Bodyweight (kg):	
					Target sets										
Exercise	Tempo	Rest	Intensity	Reps	Load	Reps	Load	Reps	Load	Reps	Load	Reps	Load		
Pogos	XXX	2 min	BW	10		10		10							
Medball heave (forwards)	XXX	2 min	5 kg	4		4		4							
Box to box depth jump	XXX	2 min	BW*	4		4		4							
Medball heave (backwards)	XXX	2 min	5 kg	4		4		4							
Hip thrust	201	2 min	8RM	6		6		6							
Trunk circuit															

*low to high box heights.

Session no. C1	Goal:								Date:		Bodyweight (kg):			
					Target sets									
Exercise	**Tempo**	**Rest**	**Intensity**	**Reps**	**Load**	**Reps**	**Load**	**Reps**	**Load**	**Reps**	**Load**	**Reps**	**Load**
Hang snatch	XXX	2.5 min	65% 1RM	5		5		5		5			
Standing long jump	XXX	2 min	BW	4		4		4					
Deadlift	201	2.5 min	7RM	6		6		6		6			
Seated cable row	201	2.5 min	7RM	6		6		6		6			
Bulgarian split squat	201	2.5 min	7RM	6		6		6		6			
Single leg iso hip extensor push	5/5 ramp	2 min	90% at peak	5/5 ramp [2]		5/5 ramp [2]		5/5 ramp [2]					

General Preparation Phase 2—Intermediate Periodised Programs—Week 6

Session no. A2	Goal:								Date:		Bodyweight (kg):			
					Target sets									
Exercise	**Tempo**	**Rest**	**Intensity**	**Reps**	**Load**	**Reps**	**Load**	**Reps**	**Load**	**Reps**	**Load**	**Reps**	**Load**
Clean	XXX	3 min	70% 1RM	4		4		4		4			
Back squat	201	2.5 min	6RM	5		5		5		5			
Barbell bench press	201	2.5 min	6RM	5		5		5		5			
Romanian deadlift	201	2.5 min	6RM	5		5		5		5			
Weighted chin up	201	2.5 min	6RM	5		5		5		5			
Single leg iso ankle push	5/5 ramp	2 min	95% at peak	5/5 ramp [3]		5/5 ramp [3]		5/5 ramp [3]					

Session no. B2	Goal:								Date:		Bodyweight (kg):			
					Target sets									
Exercise	**Tempo**	**Rest**	**Intensity**	**Reps**	**Load**	**Reps**	**Load**	**Reps**	**Load**	**Reps**	**Load**	**Reps**	**Load**
Pogos	XXX	2 min	BW	10		10		10					
Medball heave (forwards)	XXX	2 min	5 kg	4		4		4					
Box to box depth jump	XXX	2 min	BW*	4		4		4					
Medball heave (backwards)	XXX	2 min	5 kg	4		4		4					
Hip thrust	201	2 min	7RM	5		5		5					
Trunk circuit													

*low to high box heights.

Session no. C2	Goal:						Date:			Bodyweight (kg):		
					Target sets							
Exercise	Tempo	Rest	Intensity	Reps	Load	Reps	Load	Reps	Load	Reps	Load	Reps	Load
Hang snatch	XXX	3 min	70% 1RM	4		4		4		4			
Standing long jump	201	2.5 min	BW	5		5		5		5			
Deadlift	201	2.5 min	6RM	5		5		5		5			
Seated cable row	201	2.5 min	6RM	5		5		5		5			
Bulgarian split squat	201	2.5 min	6RM	5		5		5		5			
Single leg iso hip extensor push	5/5 ramp	2 min	95% at peak	5/5 ramp [3]		5/5 ramp [3]		5/5 ramp [3]					

General Preparation Phase 2—Intermediate Periodised Programs—Week 7

Session no. A3	Goal:						Date:			Bodyweight (kg):		
					Target sets							
Exercise	Tempo	Rest	Intensity	Reps	Load	Reps	Load	Reps	Load	Reps	Load	Reps	Load
Clean	XXX	3 min	70% 1RM	4		4		4		4			
Back squat	201	3 min	5RM	4		4		4		4			
Barbell bench press	201	3 min	5RM	4		4		4		4			
Romanian deadlift	201	3 min	5RM	4		4		4		4			
Weighted chin up	201	3 min	5RM	4		4		4		4			
Single leg iso ankle push	5/5 ramp	2.5 min	100% at peak	5/5 ramp [3]		5/5 ramp [3]		5/5 ramp [3]					

Session no. B3	Goal:						Date:			Bodyweight (kg):		
					Target sets							
Exercise	Tempo	Rest	Intensity	Reps	Load	Reps	Load	Reps	Load	Reps	Load	Reps	Load
Pogos	XXX	2 min	BW	10		10		10					
Medball heave (forwards)	XXX	2.5 min	8 kg	4		4		4					
Box to box depth jump*	XXX	2 min	BW*	4		4		4					
Medball heave (backwards)	XXX	2.5 min	8 kg	4		4		4					
Hip thrust	201	2 min	7RM	5		5		5					
Trunk circuit													

*low to high box heights.

Session no. C3	Goal:										Date:			Bodyweight (kg):	
					Target sets										
Exercise	Tempo	Rest	Intensity	Reps	Load	Reps	Load	Reps	Load	Reps	Load	Reps	Load		
Hang snatch	XXX	3 min	70% 1RM	4		4		4		4					
Standing long jump	XXX	2.5 min	BW	5		5		5		5					
Deadlift	201	3 min	5RM	4		4		4		4					
Seated cable row	201	3 min	5RM	4		4		4		4					
Bulgarian split squat	201	3 min	5RM	4		4		4		4					
Single leg iso hip extensor push	5/5 ramp	2.5 min	100% at peak	5/5 ramp [3]		5/5 ramp [3]		5/5 ramp [3]							

General Preparation Phase 2—Intermediate Periodised Programs—Week 8

Session no. A4	Goal:										Date:			Bodyweight (kg):	
					Target sets										
Exercise	Tempo	Rest	Intensity	Reps	Load	Reps	Load	Reps	Load	Reps	Load	Reps	Load		
Clean	XXX	3.5 min	75% 1RM	3		3									
Back squat	201	3 min	5RM	4		4									
Barbell bench press	201	3 min	5RM	4		4									
Weighted chin up	201	3 min	5RM	4		4									

Session no. B4	Goal:										Date:			Bodyweight (kg):	
					Target sets										
Exercise	Tempo	Rest	Intensity	Reps	Load	Reps	Load	Reps	Load	Reps	Load	Reps	Load		
Pogos	XXX	2 min	BW	10		10		10							
Medball heave (forwards)	XXX	2.5 min	8 kg	4		4		4							
Medball heave (backwards)	XXX	2.5 min	8 kg	4		4		4							
Hip thrust	201	2 min	6RM	5		5									
Trunk circuit															

Session no. C4	Goal:										Date:			Bodyweight (kg):	
					Target sets										
Exercise	Tempo	Rest	Intensity	Reps	Load	Reps	Load	Reps	Load	Reps	Load	Reps	Load		
Hang snatch	XXX	3.5 min	75% 1RM	3		3									
Standing long jump	XXX	2.5 min	BW	5		5									
Seated cable row	201	3 min	5RM	4		4									
Bulgarian split squat	201	3 min	5RM	4		4									
Single leg iso hip extensor push															

General Preparation Phase 2—Advanced Periodised Programs—Week 5

Session no. A1	Goal:								Date:			Bodyweight (kg):		
									Target sets					
Exercise	Tempo	Rest	Intensity	Reps	Load	Reps	Load	Reps	Load	Reps	Load	Reps	Load	
Clean	XXX	2.5 min	65% 1RM	5		5		5		5				
Back squat	201	2.5 min	6,5,6,5RM	5		4		5		4		4		
Barbell bench press	201	2.5 min	6,5,6,5RM	5		4		5		4				
Romanian deadlift	201	2.5 min	6RM	5		5		5		5				
Weighted chin up	201	2.5 min	6RM	5		5		5		5				
Single leg iso ankle push	3/3 max	3 min	100%	3/3 max [3]		3/3 max [3]		3/3 max [3]						

Session no. B1	Goal:								Date:			Bodyweight (kg):		
									Target sets					
Exercise	Tempo	Rest	Intensity	Reps	Load	Reps	Load	Reps	Load	Reps	Load	Reps	Load	
Pogos	XXX	2 min	BW	10		10		10						
Medball dive throw	XXX	2 min	5 kg	4		4		4						
Box to box depth jump*	XXX	2 min	BW*	4		4		4						
Medball heave (backwards)	XXX	2 min	5 kg	4		4		4						
Hip thrust	20X	2 min	6RM	5		5		5		5				
Trunk circuit														

*low to high box heights.

Session no. C1	Goal:								Date:			Bodyweight (kg):		
									Target sets					
Exercise	Tempo	Rest	Intensity	Reps	Load	Reps	Load	Reps	Load	Reps	Load	Reps	Load	
Hang snatch	XXX	2.5 min	65% 1RM	5		5		5		5				
Standing long jump	XXX	2 min	BW	4		4		4						
Deadlift	201	2.5 min	6,5,6,5RM	5		4		5		4				
Single arm row	201	2.5 min	6RM	5		5		5		5				
Bulgarian split squat	201	2.5 min	6,5,6,5RM	5		4		5		4				
Single leg iso hip extensor push	3/3 max	3 min	100%	3/3 max [3]		3/3 max [3]		3/3 max [3]						

General Preparation Phase 2—Advanced Periodised Programs—Week 6

Session no. A2	Goal:								Date:		Bodyweight (kg):		
								Target sets					
Exercise	Tempo	Rest	Intensity	Reps	Load	Reps	Load	Reps	Load	Reps	Load	Reps	Load
Clean	XXX	3 min	70% 1RM	4		4		4		4			
Back squat	201	3 min	5,4,5,4,5RM	4		3		4		3		4	
Barbell bench press	201	3 min	5,4,5,4,5RM	4		3		4		3		4	
Romanian deadlift	201	3 min	5RM	4		4		4		4			
Weighted chin up	201	2.5 min	5RM	4		4		4		4			
Single leg iso ankle push	3/3 max	3 min	100%	3/3 max [3]		3/3 max [3]		3/3 max [3]		3/3 max [3]			

Session no. B2	Goal:								Date:		Bodyweight (kg):		
								Target sets					
Exercise	Tempo	Rest	Intensity	Reps	Load	Reps	Load	Reps	Load	Reps	Load	Reps	Load
Pogos	XXX	2 min	BW	10		10		10					
Medball dive throw	XXX	2 min	5 kg	4		4		4		4			
Box to box depth jump*	XXX	2 min	BW*	4		4		4		4			
Medball heave (backwards)	XXX	2 min	5 kg	4		4		4		4			
Hip thrust	20X	2 min	5RM	4		4		4		4			
Trunk circuit													

*low to high box heights.

Session no. C2	Goal:								Date:		Bodyweight (kg):		
								Target sets					
Exercise	Tempo	Rest	Intensity	Reps	Load	Reps	Load	Reps	Load	Reps	Load	Reps	Load
Hang snatch	XXX	3 min	70% 1RM	4		4		4		4		4	
Standing long jump	XXX	2.5 min	BW	5		5		5		5			
Deadlift	201	3 min	5,4,5,4,5RM	4		3		4		3		4	
Single arm row	201	3 min	5,4,5,4RM	4		3		4		3			
Bulgarian split squat	201	3 min	5,4,5,4RM	4		3		4		3			
Single leg iso hip extensor push	3/3 max	3 min	100%	3/3 max [3]		3/3 max [3]		3/3 max [3]		3/3 max [3]			

General Preparation Phase 2—Advanced Periodised Programs—Week 7

Session no. A3	Goal:								Date:		Bodyweight (kg):	
					Target sets							
Exercise	Tempo	Rest	Intensity	Reps	Load	Reps	Load	Reps	Load	Reps	Load	Reps	Load
Clean	XXX	3.5 min	80% 1RM	3		3		3		3		3	
Back squat	201	3 min	6,3,3,2,2RM	5		3		3		2		1	
Barbell bench press	201	3 min	5,4,5,3RM	4		3		4		3			
Weighted chin up	201	3 min	4RM	3		3		3					
Single leg iso ankle push	3/3 max	3 min	100%	3/3 max [3]		3/3 max [3]		3/3 max [3]		3/3 max [3]		3/3 max [3]	

Session no. B3	Goal:								Date:		Bodyweight (kg):	
					Target sets							
Exercise	Tempo	Rest	Intensity	Reps	Load	Reps	Load	Reps	Load	Reps	Load	Reps	Load
Pogos	XXX	2 min	BW	10		10		10					
Medball dive throw	XXX	2.5 min	8 kg	4		4		4					
Box to box depth jump*	XXX	2 min	BW*	4		4		4		4			
Medball heave (backwards)	XXX	2.5 min	8 kg	4		4		4		4			
Hip thrust	20X	2.5 min	4RM	3		3		3		3			
Trunk circuit													

*low to high box heights.

Session no. C3	Goal:								Date:		Bodyweight (kg):	
					Target sets							
Exercise	Tempo	Rest	Intensity	Reps	Load	Reps	Load	Reps	Load	Reps	Load	Reps	Load
Hang snatch	XXX	3.5 min	80% 1RM	3		3		3		3		3	
Deadlift	XXX	3 min	6,3,3,2,2RM	5		3		3		2		1	
Single arm row	201	3 min	5,4,5,3RM	4		3		4		3			
Single leg iso hip extensor push	3/3 max	3 min	100%	3/3 max [3]		3/3 max [3]		3/3 max [3]		3/3 max [3]		3/3 max [3]	

General Preparation Phase 2—Advanced Periodised Programs—Week 8

Session no. A4	Goal:			Date:						Bodyweight (kg):		
				Target sets								
Exercise	Tempo	Rest	Intensity	Reps	Load	Reps	Load	Reps	Load	Reps	Load	Reps	Load
Clean	XXX	3.5 min	80–85% 1RM	3		2		3		2		3	
Weighted chin up	201	3.5 min	4,2,4,2RM	3		2		3		2			

Session no. B4	Goal:			Date:						Bodyweight (kg):		
				Target sets								
Exercise	Tempo	Rest	Intensity	Reps	Load	Reps	Load	Reps	Load	Reps	Load	Reps	Load
Pogos	XXX	2 min	BW	10		10		10					
Medball heave (forwards)	XXX	2.5 min	8 kg	4		4		4					
Medball heave (backwards)	XXX	2.5 min	8 kg	4		4		4		4			
Hip thrust	20X	2.5 min	3RM	2		2							
Trunk circuit													

Session no. C4	Goal:			Date:						Bodyweight (kg):		
				Target sets								
Exercise	Tempo	Rest	Intensity	Reps	Load	Reps	Load	Reps	Load	Reps	Load	Reps	Load
Hang snatch	XXX	3.5 min	80–85% 1RM	3		2		3		2		3	
Single arm row	201	3.5 min	4,2,4,2RM	3		2		3		2			

Special Preparation Phase 1—Beginner Periodised Programs—Week 9

Session no. A1	Goal:			Date:						Bodyweight (kg):		
				Target sets								
Exercise	Tempo	Rest	Intensity	Reps	Load	Reps	Load	Reps	Load	Reps	Load	Reps	Load
Repeated broad jump	Explosive	2.5 min	BW	4		4		4					
Medball heave (forwards)	Explosive	2 min	5 kg	4		4		4					
Clean	Explosive	3 min	65% 1RM	5		5		5					
Barbell bench press	201	2.5 min	6RM	5		5		5					
Romanian deadlift	201	2.5 min	8RM	6		6		6					
Single leg iso ankle push	10/5 ramp	1 min	85% at peak	10/5 ramp [2]		10/5 ramp [2]							

Session no. B1	Goal:								Date:			Bodyweight (kg):	
								Target sets					
Exercise	Tempo	Rest	Intensity	Reps	Load	Reps	Load	Reps	Load	Reps	Load	Reps	Load
Pogos	Explosive	2 min	BW	10		10		10		10			
Sprint bounding		2.5 min	BW	20*		20*							
Box to box depth jumps**		2.5 min	BW	4		4		4					
Chin up	201	2.5 min	BW	TF		TF		TF					
Single leg iso hip extensor push	10/5 ramp	1 min	85% at peak	10/5 ramp [2]		10/5 ramp [2]							

*metres instead of reps. **medium to low box heights.

Session no. C1	Goal:								Date:			Bodyweight (kg):	
								Target sets					
Exercise	Tempo	Rest	Intensity	Reps	Load	Reps	Load	Reps	Load	Reps	Load	Reps	Load
Low rebound hurdle jumps	XXX	2.5 min	BW	4		4							
Medball heave (backwards)	XXX	2.5 min	6 kg	4		4		4					
Standing shoulder press	201	2.5 min	7RM	6		6		6					
Back squat	XXX	3 min	6RM	5		5		5					
Box jump	XXX	2 min	BW	4		4		4					
Trunk circuit													

Special Preparation Phase 1—Beginner Periodised Programs—Week 10

Session no. A2	Goal:								Date:			Bodyweight (kg):	
								Target sets					
Exercise	Tempo	Rest	Intensity	Reps	Load	Reps	Load	Reps	Load	Reps	Load	Reps	Load
Repeated broad jump	Explosive	2.5 min	BW	4		4		4					
Medball heave (forwards)		2 min	6 kg	5		5		5					
Clean		3 min	70% 1RM	4		4		4					
Barbell bench press	201	2.5 min	6RM	5		5		5					
Romanian deadlift	201	2.5 min	8RM	6		6		6					
Single leg iso ankle push	5/5 ramp	2 min	90% at peak	5/5 ramp [3]		5/5 ramp [3]		5/5 ramp [3]					

Session no. B2	Goal:								Date:		Bodyweight (kg):			
				Target sets										
Exercise	Tempo	Rest	Intensity	Reps	Load	Reps	Load	Reps	Load	Reps	Load	Reps	Load	
Pogos	Explosive	2 min	BW	10		10		10		10				
Sprint bounding		2.5 min	BW	20*		20*								
Box to box depth jumps**		2.5 min	BW	4		4		4						
Chin up	201	2.5 min	BW	TF		TF		TF						
Single leg iso hip extensor push	5/5 ramp	2 min	90% at peak	5/5 ramp [3]		5/5 ramp [3]		5/5 ramp [3]						

*metres instead of reps. **medium to low box heights.

Session no. C2	Goal:								Date:		Bodyweight (kg):			
				Target sets										
Exercise	Tempo	Rest	Intensity	Reps	Load	Reps	Load	Reps	Load	Reps	Load	Reps	Load	
Low rebound hurdle jumps	XXX	2.5 min	BW	4		4		4						
Medball heave (backwards)	XXX	2.5 min	6 kg	4		4		4						
Standing shoulder press	201	2.5 min	7RM	6		6		6						
Back squat	XXX	3 min	6RM	5		5		5						
Box jump	XXX	2 min	BW	4		4		4						
Trunk circuit														

Special Preparation Phase 1—Beginner Periodised Programs—Week 11

Session no. A3	Goal:								Date:		Bodyweight (kg):			
				Target sets										
Exercise	Tempo	Rest	Intensity	Reps	Load	Reps	Load	Reps	Load	Reps	Load	Reps	Load	
Repeated broad jump	Explosive	2.5 min	BW	4		4		4						
Medball heave (forwards)		2 min	6 kg	5		5		5						
Clean		3 min	70% 1RM	4		4		4		4				
Barbell bench press	201	2.5 min	6RM	5		5		5		5				
Romanian deadlift	201	2.5 min	8RM	6		6		6		6				
Single leg iso ankle push	5/5 ramp	2 min	90% at peak	5/5 ramp [3]		5/5 ramp [3]		5/5 ramp [3]		5/5 ramp [3]				

Session no. B3	Goal:								Date:			Bodyweight (kg):	
				Target sets									
Exercise	Tempo	Rest	Intensity	Reps	Load	Reps	Load	Reps	Load	Reps	Load	Reps	Load
Pogos	Explosive	2 min	BW	10		10		10		10			
Sprint bounding		2.5 min	BW	25*		25*		25*					
Box to box depth jumps**		2.5 min	BW	4		4		4		4			
Chin up	201	2.5 min	BW	TF		TF		TF					
Single leg iso hip extensor push	5/5 ramp	2 min	90% at peak	5/5 ramp [3]		5/5 ramp [3]		5/5 ramp [3]		5/5 ramp [3]			

*metres instead of reps. **medium to low box heights.

Session no. C3	Goal:								Date:			Bodyweight (kg):	
				Target sets									
Exercise	Tempo	Rest	Intensity	Reps	Load	Reps	Load	Reps	Load	Reps	Load	Reps	Load
Low rebound hurdle jumps	XXX	2.5 min	BW	4		4		4		4			
Medball heave (backwards)	XXX	2.5 min	6 kg	4		4		4		4			
Standing shoulder press	201	2.5 min	7RM	6		6		6					
Back squat	XXX	3 min	6RM	5		5		5		5			
Box jump	XXX	2 min	BW	4		4		4					
Trunk circuit													

Special Preparation Phase 1—Beginner Periodised Programs—Week 12

Session no. A4	Goal:								Date:			Bodyweight (kg):	
				Target sets									
Exercise	Tempo	Rest	Intensity	Reps	Load	Reps	Load	Reps	Load	Reps	Load	Reps	Load
Repeated broad jump	Explosive	2.5 min	BW	4		4							
Medball heave (forwards)		2 min	6 kg	5		5							
Clean		3 min	70% 1RM	4		4							
Barbell bench press	201	2.5 min	6RM	5		5							
Romanian deadlift	201	2.5 min	8RM	6		6							
Single leg iso ankle push	10/5 ramp	2 min	85% at peak	10/5 ramp [2]		10/5 ramp [2]							

Session no. B4	Goal:								Date:			Bodyweight (kg):		
					Target sets									
Exercise	Tempo	Rest	Intensity	Reps	Load	Reps	Load	Reps	Load	Reps	Load	Reps	Load	
Pogos	Explosive	2 min	BW	10		10		10						
Sprint bounding		2.5 min	BW	25*		25*		25*						
Box to box depth jumps**		2.5 min	BW	4		4		4						
Chin up	201	2.5 min	BW	TF		TF		TF						
Single leg iso hip extensor push	10/5 ramp	1 min	85% at peak	10/5 ramp [2]		10/5 ramp [2]								

*metres instead of reps. **medium to low box heights.

Session no. C4	Goal:								Date:			Bodyweight (kg):		
					Target sets									
Exercise	Tempo	Rest	Intensity	Reps	Load	Reps	Load	Reps	Load	Reps	Load	Reps	Load	
Low rebound hurdle jumps	XXX	2.5 min	BW	4		4								
Medball heave (backwards)	XXX	2.5 min	6 kg	4		4								
Standing shoulder press	201	2.5 min	7RM	6		6								
Back squat	XXX	3 min	6RM	5		5								
Box jump	XXX	2 min	BW	4		4								
Trunk circuit														

Special Preparation Phase 1—Intermediate Periodised Programs—Week 9

Session no. A1	Goal:								Date:			Bodyweight (kg):		
					Target sets									
Exercise	Tempo	Rest	Intensity	Reps	Load	Reps	Load	Reps	Load	Reps	Load	Reps	Load	
Box to box depth jump*	Explosive	3 min	BW	4		4		4						
Bounding		5 min	BW	20**		20**		20**						
Hurdle jumps with bounce***		2.5 min	BW	4		4		4						
Hops		3 min	BW	5		5		5						
Single leg iso ankle push	5/5 ramp	2 min	90% at peak	5/5 ramp [3]		5/5 ramp [3]		5/5 ramp [3]						
Trunk circuit														

*medium—low box heights. **metres instead of reps. ***medium height hurdles.

Session no. B1	Goal:					Date:			Bodyweight (kg):		
				Target sets							
Exercise	Tempo	Rest	Intensity	Reps	Load	Reps	Load	Reps	Load	Reps	Load	Reps	Load
Clean	XXX	3 min	75%	4		4		4		4			
Squat	201	3 min	6RM	5		5		5		5			
Box jump	XXX		BW	4		4		4		4			
Barbell bench press	201	3 min	6RM	5		5		5		5			
Plyo press up	XXX		BW	4		4		4		4			

Note that two rows shaded the same colour means that the 2 exercises should be performed as a superset, i.e. the second exercise should be performed immediately after the first exercise. A period of rest then follows before repeating the process for the required number of sets.

Session no. C1	Goal:					Date:			Bodyweight (kg):		
				Target sets							
Exercise	Tempo	Rest	Intensity	Reps	Load	Reps	Load	Reps	Load	Reps	Load	Reps	Load
Sled sprint	XXX	4 min	10% of BW	15*		15*		15*		15*			
Loaded countermovement jump	XXX	3 min	20% BW	4		4		4		4			
Repeated broad jump	XXX	3 min	BW	4		4		4		4			
Glute-ham raise	201	2 min	8RM	6		6		6		6			
Weighted chin up	201	3 min	5RM	4		4		4		4			
Single leg iso hip extensor push	5/5 ramp	2 min	90% at peak	5/5 ramp [3]		5/5 ramp [3]		5/5 ramp [3]					

*metres instead of reps.

Special Preparation Phase 1—Intermediate Periodised Programs—Week 10

Session no. A2	Goal:					Date:			Bodyweight (kg):		
				Target sets							
Exercise	Tempo	Rest	Intensity	Reps	Load	Reps	Load	Reps	Load	Reps	Load	Reps	Load
Box to box depth jump*	Explosive	3 min	BW	4		4		4		4			
Bounding		5 min	BW	20**		20**		20**					
Hurdle jumps with bounce***		2.5 min	BW	4		4		4		4			
Hops		3 min	BW	5		5		5					
Single leg iso ankle push	5/5 ramp	2 min	95% at peak	5/5 ramp [3]		5/5 ramp [3]		5/5 ramp [3]					
Trunk circuit												

*medium—low box heights. **metres instead of reps. ***medium height hurdles.

Session no. B2	Goal:								Date:		Bodyweight (kg):			
								Target sets						
Exercise	**Tempo**	**Rest**	**Intensity**	**Reps**	**Load**	**Reps**	**Load**	**Reps**	**Load**	**Reps**	**Load**	**Reps**	**Load**
Clean	XXX	3 min	80%	4		4		4		4			
Squat	201	3 min	5RM	4		4		4		4		4	
Box jump	XXX		BW	4		4		4		4		4	
Barbell bench press	201	3 min	6RM	5		5		5		5			
Plyo press up	XXX		BW	4		4		4		4			

Note that two rows shaded the same colour means that the 2 exercises should be performed as a superset, i.e. the second exercise should be performed immediately after the first exercise. A period of rest then follows before repeating the process for the required number of sets.

Session no. C2	Goal:								Date:		Bodyweight (kg):			
								Target sets						
Exercise	**Tempo**	**Rest**	**Intensity**	**Reps**	**Load**	**Reps**	**Load**	**Reps**	**Load**	**Reps**	**Load**	**Reps**	**Load**
Sled sprint	XXX	4 min	10% of BW	20*		20*		20*		20*		20*	
Loaded countermovement jump	XXX	3 min	20% BW	4		4		4		4			
Repeated broad jump	XXX	3 min	BW	4		4		4		4		4	
Glute-ham raise	201	2.5 min	6RM	5		5		5		5			
Weighted chin up	201	3 min	4RM	3		3		3		3			
Single leg iso hip extensor push	5/5 ramp	2 min	95% at peak	5/5 ramp [3]		5/5 ramp [3]		5/5 ramp [3]					

*metres instead of reps.

Special Preparation Phase 1—Intermediate Periodised Programs—Week 11

Session no. A3	Goal:								Date:		Bodyweight (kg):			
								Target sets						
Exercise	**Tempo**	**Rest**	**Intensity**	**Reps**	**Load**	**Reps**	**Load**	**Reps**	**Load**	**Reps**	**Load**	**Reps**	**Load**
Box to box depth jump*	Explosive	3 min	BW	4		4		4		4			
Bounding		5 min	BW	25**		25**		25**		25**			
Hurdle jumps with bounce**		2.5 min	BW	4		4		4		4			
Hops		3 min	BW	5		5		5		5			
Single leg iso ankle push	3/3 max	3 min	100%	3/3 max [3]		3/3 max [3]		3/3 max [3]					
Trunk circuit													

*medium—medium box heights. **metres instead of reps.

Session no. B3	Goal:									Date:		Bodyweight (kg):	
									Target sets				
Exercise	Tempo	Rest	Intensity	Reps	Load	Reps	Load	Reps	Load	Reps	Load	Reps	Load
Clean	XXX	3 min	80%	4		4		4		4		4	
Squat	201	3 min	5RM	4		4		4		4		4	
Box jump	XXX		BW	4		4		4		4		4	
Barbell bench press	201	3 min	5RM	4		4		4		4			
Plyo press up	XXX		BW	4		4		4		4			

Note that two rows shaded the same colour means that the 2 exercises should be performed as a superset, i.e. the second exercise should be performed immediately after the first exercise. A period of rest then follows before repeating the process for the required number of sets.

Session no. C3	Goal:									Date:		Bodyweight (kg):	
									Target sets				
Exercise	Tempo	Rest	Intensity	Reps	Load	Reps	Load	Reps	Load	Reps	Load	Reps	Load
Sled sprint	XXX	4 min	10% of BW	25*		25*		25*		25*		25*	
Loaded countermovement jump	XXX	3 min	30% BW	4		4		4		4		4	
Repeated broad jump	XXX	3 min	BW	4		4		4		4		4	
Glute-ham raise	201	2.5 min	5RM	4		4		4		4			
Weighted chin up	201	3 min	4RM	3		3		3		3			
Single leg iso hip extensor push	3/3 max	3 min	100%	3/3 max [3]		3/3 max [3]		3/3 max [3]					

*metres instead of reps.

Special Preparation Phase 1—Intermediate Periodised Programs—Week 12

Session no. A4	Goal:									Date:		Bodyweight (kg):	
									Target sets				
Exercise	Tempo	Rest	Intensity	Reps	Load	Reps	Load	Reps	Load	Reps	Load	Reps	Load
Box to box depth jump*	Explosive	3 min	BW	4		4							
Bounding		5 min	BW	25**		25**							
Hurdle jumps with bounce**		2.5 min	BW	4		4							
Hops		3 min	BW	5		5							
Single leg iso ankle push	5/5 max	1 min	90% at peak	5/5 ramp [3]		5/5 ramp [3]							
Trunk circuit													

*medium—medium box heights. **metres instead of reps.

Session no. B4	Goal:							Date:				Bodyweight (kg):		
									Target sets					
Exercise	Tempo	Rest	Intensity	Reps	Load	Reps	Load	Reps	Load	Reps	Load	Reps	Load	
Clean	XXX	3 min	85%	4		4								
Squat	201	3.5 min	4RM	3		3								
Box jump	XXX		BW	4		4								
Barbell bench press	201	3.5 min	4RM	3		3								
Plyo press up	XXX		BW	4		4								

Note that two rows shaded the same colour means that the 2 exercises should be performed as a superset, i.e. the second exercise should be performed immediately after the first exercise. A period of rest then follows before repeating the process for the required number of sets.

Session no. C4	Goal:							Date:				Bodyweight (kg):		
									Target sets					
Exercise	Tempo	Rest	Intensity	Reps	Load	Reps	Load	Reps	Load	Reps	Load	Reps	Load	
Sled sprint	XXX	4 min	10% of BW	25*		25*								
Loaded countermovement jump	XXX	3 min	30% BW	4		4								
Repeated broad jump	XXX	3 min	BW	4		4								
Glute-ham raise	201	2.5 min	5RM	4		4								
Weighted chin up	201	3 min	4RM	3		3								
Single leg iso hip extensor push	5/5 max	1 min	90% at peak	5/5 ramp [3]		5/5 ramp [3]								

*metres instead of reps.

Special Preparation Phase 1—Advanced Periodised Programs—Week 9

Session no. A1	Goal:							Date:				Bodyweight (kg):		
									Target sets					
Exercise	Tempo	Rest	Intensity	Reps	Load	Reps	Load	Reps	Load	Reps	Load	Reps	Load	
Box to box jump*	Explosive	3 min	BW	4		4		4						
Bounding		5 min	BW	30**		30**		30**						
High hurdle rebound jumps		2.5 min	BW	5		5		5						
Hops		3 min	BW	6		6		6						
Single leg iso ankle push	3/3 max	3 min	100%	3/3 max [3]		3/3 max [3]		3/3 max [3]						
Trunk circuit														

*medium—medium box heights. **metres instead of reps.

Session no. B1	Goal:								Date:			Bodyweight (kg):	
				Target sets									
Exercise	Tempo	Rest	Intensity	Reps	Load	Reps	Load	Reps	Load	Reps	Load	Reps	Load
Clean	XXX	3 min	80%	3		3		3		3			
Squat	201	3 min	5,4,5,4,5RM	4		3		4		3		4	
Standing long jump	XXX		BW	4		4		4		4		4	
Barbell bench press	201	3 min	5,4,5,4,5RM	4		3		4		3			
Plyo press up	XXX		BW	4		4		4		4			
Single leg iso hip extensor push	3/3 max	3 min	100%	3/3 max [3]		3/3 max [3]		3/3 max [3]					

Note that two rows shaded the same colour means that the 2 exercises should be performed as a superset. i.e. the second exercise should be performed immediately after the first exercise. A period of rest then follows before repeating the process for the required number of sets.

Session no. C1	Goal:								Date:			Bodyweight (kg):	
				Target sets									
Exercise	Tempo	Rest	Intensity	Reps	Load	Reps	Load	Reps	Load	Reps	Load	Reps	Load
Sled sprint	XXX	4 min	20% of BW	20*		20*		20*		20*			
Loaded countermovement jump	XXX	3 min	30% BW	5		5		5		5			
Repeated broad jump	XXX	3 min	BW	4		4		4		4			
Glute-ham raise	201	2 min	6RM	5		5		5		5			
Weighted chin up	201	3 min	5,4,5,4,RM	4		3		4		3			

*metres instead of reps.

Special Preparation Phase 1—Advanced Periodised Programs—Week 10

Session no. A2	Goal:								Date:			Bodyweight (kg):	
				Target sets									
Exercise	Tempo	Rest	Intensity	Reps	Load	Reps	Load	Reps	Load	Reps	Load	Reps	Load
Box to box drop jump*	Explosive	3 min	BW	4		4		4					
Bounding		5 min	BW	30**		30**		30**		30**			
High hurdle rebound jumps		2.5 min	BW	5		5		5					
Hops		3 min	BW	6		6		6		6			
Single leg iso ankle push	3/3 max	3 min	100%	2/5 max [3]		2/5 max [3]		2/5 max [3]		2/5 max [3]			
Trunk circuit													

*medium to medium box heights. **metres instead of reps.

Session no. B2	Goal:					Date:					Bodyweight (kg):		
									Target sets				
Exercise	Tempo	Rest	Intensity	Reps	Load	Reps	Load	Reps	Load	Reps	Load	Reps	Load
Clean	XXX	3.5 min	85%	3		3		3		3		3	
Squat	201	3 min	4,3,4,3,4RM	3		2		3		2		3	
Standing long jump	XXX		BW	4		4		4		4		4	
Barbell bench press	201	3 min	4,3,4,3,4RM	3		2		3		2			
Plyo press up	XXX		BW	4		4		4		4			
Single leg iso hip extensor push	3/3 max	3 min	100%	2/5 max [3]		2/5 max [3]		2/5 max [3]		2/5 max [3]			

Note that two rows shaded the same colour means that the 2 exercises should be performed as a superset, i.e. the second exercise should be performed immediately after the first exercise. A period of rest then follows before repeating the process for the required number of sets.

Session no. C2	Goal:					Date:					Bodyweight (kg):		
									Target sets				
Exercise	Tempo	Rest	Intensity	Reps	Load	Reps	Load	Reps	Load	Reps	Load	Reps	Load
Sled sprint	XXX	4 min	15% of BW	25*		25*		25*		25*			
Loaded countermovement jump	XXX	3 min	40% BW	4		4		4		4		4	
Repeated broad jump	XXX	3 min	BW	4		4		4		4			
Glute-ham raise	201	2.5 min	5RM	4		4		4		4		4	
Weighted chin up	201	3 min	5,4,5,4,5RM	4		3		4		3		4	

*metres instead of reps.

Special Preparation Phase 1—Advanced Periodised Programs—Week 11

Session no. A3	Goal:					Date:					Bodyweight (kg):		
									Target sets				
Exercise	Tempo	Rest	Intensity	Reps	Load	Reps	Load	Reps	Load	Reps	Load	Reps	Load
Box to box drop jump*	Explosive	3 min	BW	4		4		4					
Bounding		5 min	BW	30**		30**		30**		30**			
High hurdle rebound jumps		2.5 min	BW	5		5		5		5			
Hops		3 min	BW	6		6		6		6			
Single leg iso ankle push	3/3 max	3 min	100%	1/5 max [3]		1/5 max [3]		1/5 max [3]		1/5 max [3]		1/5 max [3]	
Trunk circuit													

*medium to medium box heights. **metres instead of reps.

Session no. B3	Goal:							Date:			Bodyweight (kg):		
										Target sets			
Exercise	Tempo	Rest	Intensity	Reps	Load	Reps	Load	Reps	Load	Reps	Load	Reps	Load
Clean	XXX	3.5 min	85–90% 1RM	3		2		3		2		2	
Standing long jump	XXX	2 min	BW	5		5		5		5			
Barbell bench press	201	4 min	3,3,2,2,1RM	2		2		1		1		1	
Single leg iso hip extensor push	3/3 max	3 min	100%	1/5 max [3]		1/5 max [3]		1/5 max [3]		1/5 max [3]		1/5 max [3]	

Session no. C3	Goal:							Date:			Bodyweight (kg):		
										Target sets			
Exercise	Tempo	Rest	Intensity	Reps	Load	Reps	Load	Reps	Load	Reps	Load	Reps	Load
Sled sprint	XXX	5 min	10% of BW	30*		30*		30*		30*		30*	
Loaded counter-movement jump	XXX	4 min	30% BW	3		3		3		3		3	
Weighted chin up	201	3.5 min	4,3,4,3,4RM	3		2		3		2		3	
Glute-ham raise	201	3 min	4RM	3		3		3		3		3	

*metres instead of reps.

Special Preparation Phase 1—Advanced Periodised Programs—Week 12

Session no. A4	Goal:							Date:			Bodyweight (kg):		
										Target sets			
Exercise	Tempo	Rest	Intensity	Reps	Load	Reps	Load	Reps	Load	Reps	Load	Reps	Load
Bounding	Explosive	5 min	BW	40*		40*		40*					
High hurdle rebound jumps		5 min	BW	6		6		6		6			

*metres instead of reps.

Session no. B4	Goal:							Date:			Bodyweight (kg):		
										Target sets			
Exercise	Tempo	Rest	Intensity	Reps	Load	Reps	Load	Reps	Load	Reps	Load	Reps	Load
Clean	XXX	3 min	85%	4		4							
Squat	201	3.5 min	4RM	3		3							
Standing long jump	XXX		BW	4		4							
Barbell bench press	201	3.5 min	4RM	3		3							
Plyo press up	XXX		BW	4		4							

Note that two rows shaded the same colour means that the 2 exercises should be performed as a superset, i.e. the second exercise should be performed immediately after the first exercise. A period of rest then follows before repeating the process for the required number of sets.

Session no. C4	Goal:								Date:			Bodyweight (kg):	
					Target sets								
Exercise	Tempo	Rest	Intensity	Reps	Load	Reps	Load	Reps	Load	Reps	Load	Reps	Load
Sled sprint	XXX	5 min	10% of BW	30*		30*		30*		30*		30*	
Repeated broad jump	XXX	3 min	BW	4		4		4		4			
Glute-ham raise	201	3 min	4RM	3		3							

*metres instead of reps.

Special Preparation Phase 2—Beginner Periodised Programs—Week 13

Session no. A1	Goal:								Date:			Bodyweight (kg):	
					Target sets								
Exercise	Tempo	Rest	Intensity	Reps	Load	Reps	Load	Reps	Load	Reps	Load	Reps	Load
Repeated broad jump	Explosive	3 min	BW	5		5		5					
Medball heave (forwards)		2 min	8 kg	4		4		4					
Clean		3 min	75% 1RM	4		4		4					
Barbell bench press	201	2.5 min	5RM	4		4		4					
Romanian deadlift	201	2.5 min	6RM	5		5		5					
Single leg iso ankle push	10/5 ramp	1 min	85% at peak	10/5 ramp [2]		10/5 ramp [2]							

Session no. B1	Goal:								Date:			Bodyweight (kg):	
					Target sets								
Exercise	Tempo	Rest	Intensity	Reps	Load	Reps	Load	Reps	Load	Reps	Load	Reps	Load
Pogos	Explosive	2 min	BW	10		10		10		10			
Sprint bounding		3 min	BW	25*		25*		25*					
Box to box drop jumps**		2.5 min	BW	4		4		4					
Chin up	201	2.5 min	BW	TF		TF		TF					

*metres instead of reps. **medium to medium box heights.

Session no. C1	Goal:						Date:			Bodyweight (kg):		
				Target sets								
Exercise	Tempo	Rest	Intensity	Reps	Load	Reps	Load	Reps	Load	Reps	Load	Reps	Load
Low rebound hurdle jumps	XXX	2.5 min	BW	5		5		5					
Medball back toss	XXX	2.5 min	8 kg	4		4		4					
Standing shoulder press	201	2.5 min	6RM	5		5		5					
Back squat	XXX	3 min	5RM	4		4		4					
Single leg iso hip extensor push	10/5 ramp	1 min	85% at peak	10/5 ramp [2]		10/5 ramp [2]							
Trunk circuit													

Special Preparation Phase 2—Beginner Periodised Programs—Week 14

Session no. A2	Goal:						Date:			Bodyweight (kg):		
				Target sets								
Exercise	Tempo	Rest	Intensity	Reps	Load	Reps	Load	Reps	Load	Reps	Load	Reps	Load
Repeated broad jump	Explosive	3 min	BW	5		5		5					
Medball heave (forwards)	Explosive	2 min	8 kg	4		4		4					
Hang clean	Explosive	3 min	70% 1RM	4		4		4					
Barbell bench press	201	2.5 min	5RM	4		4		4					
Romanian deadlift	201	2.5 min	6RM	5		5		5					
Single leg iso ankle push	5/5 ramp	2 min	90% at peak	5/5 ramp [3]		5/5 ramp [3]		5/5 ramp [3]					

Session no. B2	Goal:						Date:			Bodyweight (kg):		
				Target sets								
Exercise	Tempo	Rest	Intensity	Reps	Load	Reps	Load	Reps	Load	Reps	Load	Reps	Load
Pogos	Explosive	2 min	BW	10		10		10		10			
Sprint bounding	Explosive	3 min	BW	25*		25*		25*		25*			
Box to box drop jumps**	Explosive	2.5 min	BW	4		4		4		4			
Chin up	201	2.5 min	BW	TF		TF		TF					

*metres instead of reps. **medium to medium box heights.

Session no. C2	Goal:						Date:			Bodyweight (kg):		
						Target sets						
Exercise	Tempo	Rest	Intensity	Reps	Load	Reps	Load	Reps	Load	Reps	Load	Reps	Load
Low rebound hurdle jumps	XXX	2.5 min	BW	5		5		5					
Medball back toss	XXX	2.5 min	8 kg	4		4		4					
Standing shoulder press	201	2.5 min	6RM	5		5		5					
Back squat	XXX	3 min	5RM	4		4		4					
Single leg iso hip extensor push	5/5 ramp	2 min	90% at peak	5/5 ramp [3]		5/5 ramp [3]		5/5 ramp [3]					
Trunk circuit													

Special Preparation Phase 2—Beginner Periodised Programs—Week 15

Session no. A3	Goal:						Date:			Bodyweight (kg):		
						Target sets						
Exercise	Tempo	Rest	Intensity	Reps	Load	Reps	Load	Reps	Load	Reps	Load	Reps	Load
Repeated broad jump	Explosive	3 min	BW	5		5		5					
Medball heave (forwards)		2 min	8 kg	4		4		4					
Hang clean		3 min	65% 1RM	4		4		4		4			
Explosive step ups		3 min	20% BW	4		4		4					
Single leg iso ankle push	5/5 ramp	2 min	90% at peak	5/5 ramp [3]		5/5 ramp [3]		5/5 ramp [3]		5/5 ramp [3]			

Session no. B3	Goal:						Date:			Bodyweight (kg):		
						Target sets						
Exercise	Tempo	Rest	Intensity	Reps	Load	Reps	Load	Reps	Load	Reps	Load	Reps	Load
Pogos	Explosive	2 min	BW	10		10		10		10			
Sprint bounding		3 min	BW	30*		30*		30*		30*			
Box to box drop jumps**		2.5 min	BW	4		4		4		4			
Trunk circuit													

*metres instead of reps. **medium to medium box heights.

Session no. C3	Goal:							Date:			Bodyweight (kg):		
									Target sets				
Exercise	Tempo	Rest	Intensity	Reps	Load	Reps	Load	Reps	Load	Reps	Load	Reps	Load
Sprint bounding	XXX	2.5 min	BW	30*		30*		30*		30*			
Low rebound hurdle jumps	XXX	2.5 min	BW	5		5		5		5			
Medball back toss	XXX	2.5 min	8 kg	4		4		4		4			
Single leg iso hip extensor push	5/5 ramp	2 min	90% at peak	5/5 ramp [3]		5/5 ramp [3]		5/5 ramp [3]		5/5 ramp [3]			
Trunk circuit													

*metres instead of reps.

Special Preparation Phase 2—Beginner Periodised Programs—Week 16

Session no. A4	Goal:							Date:			Bodyweight (kg):		
									Target sets				
Exercise	Tempo	Rest	Intensity	Reps	Load	Reps	Load	Reps	Load	Reps	Load	Reps	Load
Repeated broad jump	Explosive	3 min	BW	5		5							
Medball heave (forwards)		2 min	8 kg	4		4							
Hang clean		3 min	65% 1RM	4		4							
Explosive step ups		3 min	20% BW	4		4							
Single leg iso ankle push	10/5 ramp	2 min	85% at peak	10/5 ramp [2]		10/5 ramp [2]							

Session no. B4	Goal:							Date:			Bodyweight (kg):		
									Target sets				
Exercise	Tempo	Rest	Intensity	Reps	Load	Reps	Load	Reps	Load	Reps	Load	Reps	Load
Pogos	Explosive	2 min	BW	10		10							
Sprint bounding		3 min	BW	30*		30*							
Box to box drop jumps**		2.5 min	BW	4		4							
Trunk circuit													

*metres instead of reps. **medium to medium box heights.

Session no. C4	Goal:							Date:			Bodyweight (kg):		
				Target sets									
Exercise	Tempo	Rest	Intensity	Reps	Load	Reps	Load	Reps	Load	Reps	Load	Reps	Load
Sprint bounding	XXX	2.5 min	BW	30*		30*							
Low rebound hurdle jumps	XXX	2.5 min	BW	5		5							
Medball back toss	XXX	2.5 min	8 kg	4		4							
Single leg iso hip extensor push	10/5 ramp	2 min	85% at peak	10/5 ramp [2]		10/5 ramp [2]							
Trunk circuit	XXX	2 min	BW	4		4							

Special Preparation Phase 2—Intermediate Periodised Programs—Week 13

Session no. A1	Goal:							Date:			Bodyweight (kg):		
				Target sets									
Exercise	Tempo	Rest	Intensity	Reps	Load	Reps	Load	Reps	Load	Reps	Load	Reps	Load
Sled sprint	Explosive	3 min	10% BW	20*		20*		20*					
Hops		3 min	BW	5		5		5					
Medball heave (backwards)		2.5 min	8 kg	4		4		4					
Back squat		3 min	4RM	3		3		3					
Trunk circuit													

*metres instead of reps.

Session no. B1	Goal:							Date:			Bodyweight (kg):		
				Target sets									
Exercise	Tempo	Rest	Intensity	Reps	Load	Reps	Load	Reps	Load	Reps	Load	Reps	Load
Cleans	Explosive	3.5 min	75% 1RM	4		4		4					
Bulgarian push off		3 min	20% BW	4		4		4					
Medball heave (forwards)		3 min	8 kg	4		4		4					
Glute-ham raise	201	3 min	5RM	4		4		4					
Medball single leg RDL	201	2 min	8RM	6		6		6					

Session no. C1	Goal:						Date:			Bodyweight (kg):		
							Target sets					
Exercise	Tempo	Rest	Intensity	Reps	Load	Reps	Load	Reps	Load	Reps	Load	Reps	Load
Weighted vest sprints	Explosive	5 min	<5%*	20**		20**		20**					
Bounding	Explosive	4 min	BW	25***		25***		25***					
Medium hurdle rebound jumps	Explosive	3 min	BW	5		5		5					
Weighted chin up	201	3 min	4RM	3		3		3					
Trunk circuit													

*a load which causes no greater loss than 5% of maximum speed. **metres instead of reps—measured after a rolling start.
***metres instead of reps.

Special Preparation Phase 2—Intermediate Periodised Programs—Week 14

Session no. A2	Goal:						Date:			Bodyweight (kg):		
							Target sets					
Exercise	Tempo	Rest	Intensity	Reps	Load	Reps	Load	Reps	Load	Reps	Load	Reps	Load
Sled sprint	Explosive	3 min	10% BW	20*		20*		20*		20*			
Hops	Explosive	3 min	BW	5		5		5					
Medball heave (backwards)	Explosive	2.5 min	10 kg	4		4		4		4			
Standing long jump	Explosive	2.5 min	BW	4		4		4					
Trunk circuit													

*metres instead of reps.

Session no. B2	Goal:						Date:			Bodyweight (kg):		
							Target sets					
Exercise	Tempo	Rest	Intensity	Reps	Load	Reps	Load	Reps	Load	Reps	Load	Reps	Load
Cleans	Explosive	3.5 min	70% 1RM	3		3		3		3		3	
Bulgarian push off	Explosive	3 min	40% BW	4		4		4		4			
Medball heave (forwards)	Explosive	3 min	10 kg	4		4		4		4			
Glute-ham raise	201	3 min	4RM	3		3		3		3		3	
Medball single leg RDL	201	2 min	6RM	4		4		4		4			

Session no. C2	Goal:								Date:				Bodyweight (kg):		
				Target sets											
Exercise	Tempo	Rest	Intensity	Reps	Load	Reps	Load	Reps	Load	Reps	Load	Reps	Load		
Weighted vest sprints	Explosive	5 min	<5%*	25**		25**		25**							
Bounding		4 min	BW	25***		25***		25***							
Medium hurdle rebound jumps		3 min	BW	5		5		5		5					
Box to box depth jump****		2.5 min	BW	4		4		4							
Trunk circuit															

*a load which causes no greater loss than 5% of maximum speed. **metres instead of reps—measured after a rolling start. ***metres instead of reps. ****medium to medium box heights.

Special Preparation Phase 2—Intermediate Periodised Programs—Week 15

Session no. A3	Goal:								Date:				Bodyweight (kg):		
				Target sets											
Exercise	Tempo	Rest	Intensity	Reps	Load	Reps	Load	Reps	Load	Reps	Load	Reps	Load		
Sled sprint	Explosive	3 min	10% BW	25*		25*		25*		25*					
Hops		3 min	BW	5		5		5		5					
Medball heave (backwards)		2.5 min	10 kg	4		4		4		4					
Standing long jump		2.5 min	BW	4		4		4		4					
Trunk circuit															

*number refers to the number of metres.

Session no. B3	Goal:								Date:				Bodyweight (kg):		
				Target sets											
Exercise	Tempo	Rest	Intensity	Reps	Load	Reps	Load	Reps	Load	Reps	Load	Reps	Load		
Hang clean	Exp.	3 min	65% 1RM	3		3		3		3		3			
Medball heave (forwards)		3 min	10 kg	4		4		4		4					
Glute-ham raise	201	3.5 min	3RM	2		2		2		2		2			
Medball single leg RDL	201	2.5 min	5RM	4		4		4		4					

Session no. C3	Goal:					Date:			Bodyweight (kg):		
	Tempo			Target sets							
Exercise		Rest	Intensity	Reps	Load	Reps	Load	Reps	Load	Reps	Load	Reps	Load
Weighted vest sprints	Explosive	5 min	<5%*	25**		25**		25**		25**	
Bounding		4 min	BW	30***		30***		30***		30***	
Medium hurdle rebound jumps		3 min	BW	5		5		5		5	
Box to box depth jump****		2.5 min	BW	4		4		4		4	
Trunk circuit											

*a load which causes no greater loss than 5% of maximum speed. **metres instead of reps—measured after a rolling start. ***metres instead of reps. ****medium to medium box heights.

Special Preparation Phase 2—Intermediate Periodised Programs—Week 16

Session no. A4	Goal:					Date:			Bodyweight (kg):		
				Target sets							
Exercise	Tempo	Rest	Intensity	Reps	Load	Reps	Load	Reps	Load	Reps	Load	Reps	Load
Sled sprint	Explosive	3 min	10% BW	25*		25*					
Hops		3 min	BW	5		5					
Medball heave (backwards)		2.5 min	10 kg	4		4					
Standing long jump		2.5 min	BW	4		4					
Trunk circuit											

*number refers to the number of metres.

Section no. B4	Goal:					Date:			Bodyweight (kg):		
				Target sets							
Exercise	Tempo	Rest	Intensity	Reps	Load	Reps	Load	Reps	Load	Reps	Load	Reps	Load
Cleans	Explosive	3 min	65% 1RM	3		3					
Bulgarian push off		3 min	20% BW	4		4					
Medball heave (forwards)		3 min	8 kg	4		4					
Glute-ham raise	201	3 min	5RM	4		4					
Medball single leg RDL	201	2 min	6RM	4		4					

Session no. C4	Goal:								Date:			Bodyweight (kg):		
				Target sets										
Exercise	Tempo	Rest	Intensity	Reps	Load	Reps	Load	Reps	Load	Reps	Load	Reps	Load	
Weighted vest sprints	Explosive	5 min	<5%*	25**		25**								
Bounding		4 min	BW	30***		30***								
Medium hurdle rebound jumps		3 min	BW	5		5								
Box to box depth jump****		2.5 min	BW	4		4								
Trunk circuit														

*a load which causes no greater loss than 5% of maximum speed. **metres instead of reps—measured after a rolling start. ***metres instead of reps. ****medium to medium box heights.

Special Preparation Phase 2—Advanced Periodised Programs—Week 13

Session no. A1	Goal:								Date:			Bodyweight (kg):		
				Target sets										
Exercise	Tempo	Rest	Intensity	Reps	Load	Reps	Load	Reps	Load	Reps	Load	Reps	Load	
Sled sprint	Explosive	4 min	10% BW	30*		30*		30*		30*		30*		
Hops		4 min	BW	7		7		7		7		7		
Repeated broad jump		3 min	BW	5		5		5		5				
Medball heave (backwards)		2.5 min	10 kg	4		4		4		4				
Trunk circuit														

*metres instead of reps.

Session no. B1	Goal:								Date:			Bodyweight (kg):		
				Target sets										
Exercise	Tempo	Rest	Intensity	Reps	Load	Reps	Load	Reps	Load	Reps	Load	Reps	Load	
Cleans	Explosive	3.5 min	75% 1RM	4		4		4		4		4		
Bulgarian push off		3 min	30% BW	4		4		4		4				
Medball dive throw		3 min	10 kg	4		4		4		4				
Glute-ham raise	201	3 min	4RM	3		3		3		3		3		
Single leg iso hip extensor push	3/3 max	3 min	100%	3/3 max [3]		3/3 max [3]		3/3 max [3]						

Session no. C1	Goal:										Date:		Bodyweight (kg):	
					Target sets									
Exercise	Tempo	Rest	Intensity	Reps	Load	Reps	Load	Reps	Load	Reps	Load	Reps	Load	
Weighted vest sprints	Explosive	5 min	<10%*	20**		20**		20**		20**				
Bounding		4 min	BW	40***		40***		40***						
Box to box drop jumps****		3 min	BW	4		4		4		4				
High hurdle rebound jumps		4 min	BW	6		6		6		6		6		
Trunk circuit														

*a load which causes no greater loss than 10% of maximum speed. **metres instead of reps—measured after a rolling start. ***metres instead of reps. ****high to high box heights.

Special Preparation Phase 2—Advanced Periodised Programs—Week 14

Session no. A2	Goal:										Date:		Bodyweight (kg):	
					Target sets									
Exercise	Tempo	Rest	Intensity	Reps	Load	Reps	Load	Reps	Load	Reps	Load	Reps	Load	
Sled sprint	Explosive	4 min	10% BW	30*		30*		30*		30*		30*		
Hops		4 min	BW	7		7		7		7		7		
Repeated broad jump		3 min	BW	5		5		5		5				
Medball heave (backwards)		2.5 min	10 kg	4		4		4		4				
Trunk circuit														

*metres instead of reps.

Session no. B2	Goal:										Date:		Bodyweight (kg):	
					Target sets									
Exercise	Tempo	Rest	Intensity	Reps	Load	Reps	Load	Reps	Load	Reps	Load	Reps	Load	
Cleans	Explosive	3.5 min	70% 1RM	4		4		4		4		4		
Bulgarian push off		3 min	40% BW	4		4		4		4				
Medball dive throw		3 min	10 kg	4		4		4		4				
Glute-ham raise	201	3 min	4RM	3		3		3		3		3		
Single leg iso hip extensor push	3/3 max	3 min	100%	2/5 max [3]		2/5 max [3]		2/5 max [3]		2/5 max [3]				

Session no. C2	Goal:				Date:				Bodyweight (kg):			
				Target sets								
Exercise	Tempo	Rest	Intensity	Reps	Load	Reps	Load	Reps	Load	Reps	Load	Reps	Load
Weighted vest sprints	Explosive	5 min	<10%*	30**		30**		30**		30**		30**	
Bounding		4 min	BW	40***		40***							
Box to box drop jumps****		3 min	BW	4		4		4					
High hurdle rebound jumps		4 min	BW	6		6		6		6		6	
Trunk circuit													

*a load which causes no greater loss than 10% of maximum speed. **metres instead of reps—measured after a rolling start. ***metres instead of reps. ****high to high box heights.

Special Preparation Phase 2—Advanced Periodised Programs—Week 15

Session no. A3	Goal:				Date:				Bodyweight (kg):			
				Target sets								
Exercise	Tempo	Rest	Intensity	Reps	Load	Reps	Load	Reps	Load	Reps	Load	Reps	Load
Sled sprint	Exp.	4 min	8% BW	35*		35*		35*		35*			
Medball heave (backwards)		2.5 min	10 kg	4		4		4		4			
Trunk circuit													

*number indicates the number of metres.

Session no. B3	Goal:				Date:				Bodyweight (kg):			
				Target sets								
Exercise	Tempo	Rest	Intensity	Reps	Load	Reps	Load	Reps	Load	Reps	Load	Reps	Load
Hang clean	Exp.	3 min	65% 1RM	4		4		4		4		4	
Medball dive throw		3 min	10 kg	4		4		4		4			
Glute-ham raise	201	3.5 min	3RM	2		2		2		2		2	
Single leg iso hip extensor push	3/3 max	3 min	100%	1/5 max [3]		1/5 max [3]		1/5 max [3]		1/5 max [3]		1/5 max [3]	

Session no. C3	Goal:				Target sets									Date:		Bodyweight (kg):	
Exercise	Tempo	Rest	Intensity	Reps	Load	Reps	Load	Reps	Load	Reps	Load	Reps	Load				
Weighted vest sprints	Explosive	5 min	<10%*	30**		30**		30**									
Bounding		4 min	BW	40***		40***		40***		40***							
Box to box depth jumps****		3 min	BW	4		4		4		4		4					
High hurdle rebound jumps		4 min	BW	6		6		6									
Trunk circuit																	

*a load which causes no greater loss than 10% of maximum speed. **metres instead of reps—measured after a rolling start. ***metres instead of reps. ****high to high box heights.

Special Preparation Phase 2—Advanced Periodised Programs—Week 16

Session no. A4	Goal:				Target sets									Date:		Bodyweight (kg):	
Exercise	Tempo	Rest	Intensity	Reps	Load	Reps	Load	Reps	Load	Reps	Load	Reps	Load				
Sled sprint	Exp.	5 min	5% BW	35*		35*		35*		35*		35*					
Hops		5 min	BW	8		8		8		8							
Trunk circuit																	

*number indicates the number of metres.

Session no. B4	Goal:				Target sets									Date:		Bodyweight (kg):	
Exercise	Tempo	Rest	Intensity	Reps	Load	Reps	Load	Reps	Load	Reps	Load	Reps	Load				
Hang clean	Explosice	3 min	65% 1RM	3		3		3		3		3					
Bulgarian push off		3 min	30% BW	4		4		4		4		4					
Medball dive throw		3 min	10 kg	4		4		4		4							

Session no. C4	Goal:				Target sets									Date:		Bodyweight (kg):	
Exercise	Tempo	Rest	Intensity	Reps	Load	Reps	Load	Reps	Load	Reps	Load	Reps	Load				
Bounding		5 min	BW	40*		40*		40*		40*		40*					
High hurdle rebound jumps		5 min	BW	7		7		7		7							
Trunk circuit																	

*number indicates the number of metres.

Glossary of Terms

Acceleration	The change in velocity over a given time interval
Acceleration sprint phase	The phase of a sprint when velocity is increasing
Acceleration strength	A sub-component of 'explosive strength' depicting the ability to generate force quickly in a movement after the movement has commenced
Adaptation	The process by which a person's body responds over a period of time to the effects of exercise
Agonists	A muscle primarily responsible for a given movement (prime mover)
Angular velocity	The rate of angular displacement of a rotating body in a specified direction
Antagonists	A muscle that opposes an agonist (prime mover) for a given movement
Biomechanics	The application of mechanical principle to the study of the movement of organisms
Concentric action	When a muscle develops sufficient force to overcome a resistance, so that the muscle shortens and moves a body part
Contact time	The duration the foot is in contact with the ground during the stance phase of a step
Correlation coefficients	A statistical measure which quantifies the magnitude of an association between variables such that when one changes in magnitude the other also changes
Eccentric muscle contraction	When a muscle exerts force while lengthening
Electromyographic (EMG) activity	The measurement and recording of electrical activity produced by muscle
Explosive strength	The time it takes to reach peak force

Force-velocity principle	A principle based on the force-velocity relationship. If training loads are high, movement velocity produced by a concentric muscle action is low and vice versa
Force-velocity relationship	The velocity of muscle shortening is inversely proportional to the load it must move
Flight time	The duration from the instant the stance phase ends (i.e., when the foot leaves the ground) until the next stance phase begins (i.e., the instant when the foot next makes contact with the ground)—the time spent in the air during a step
Ground reaction force	A force exerted by the ground in response to the forces a body exerts on it
Hypertrophy	An increase in the size of a tissue or organ
Impulse	The product of force and time
Intensity	Intensity is proportional to the magnitude and/or velocity of the load being lifted (the higher the load/velocity, the higher the intensity)
Intermuscular coordination	The ability of agonists, synergists, antagonists, and stabilisers to work together in the execution of movements
Isometric action	When a muscle produces force, but not enough to overcome the external resistance and the joint angle remains constant (no external mechanical work is done)
Kinematics	A branch of mechanics concerned with the descriptive study of motion
Kinetics	Study of the forces acting on a mechanical system. Kinetics is concerned with the causal analysis of motion
Macrocycle	The whole competition and training year, although it can also represent a longer time period—for example, a 4-year cycle is often termed a macrocycle for an Olympic athlete
Maximum strength	The peak force that the neuromuscular system is able to produce during a single maximal voluntary muscle contraction, irrespective of time of force development
Maximum velocity sprint phase	The phase of a sprint when an athlete is travelling at, or close to, the highest horizontal velocity they are able to reach
Mesocycle	The macrocycle is normally broken down into a series of training blocks or phases called *mesocycles*. Usually, these training blocks will be between three and eight weeks in length and contain specific training objectives
Microcycle	The mesocycle is normally broken down into a series of smaller training phases called *microcycles*. These are usually one week in length; sometimes it may be slightly shorter or longer

Moment	A force which produces a twisting or rotary movement in any plane about an axis of motion
Motor unit	A single motor neuron and all the muscle fibres it stimulates
Overload	When the body is required to perform an activity beyond which it is used to
Periodisation	A planned phase of training which is divided into periods of cycles often of different duration and with a different training emphasis
Plyometric exercises	Movements involving an eccentric loading of a muscle group preparatory to a rapid change to a concentric contraction of the same muscle group through utilisation of the SSC
Power	The rate at which energy is expended (calculated by the equation: work ÷ time)
Power endurance	The ability to repeatedly produce maximal or near maximal explosive muscular efforts
Rate coding	The rate at which neural impulses are transmitted to the muscle fibres
Rate of force development	A measure of the rate at which a force is developed
Reactive strength	The ability to change quickly from an eccentric to a concentric muscle contraction whilst using the stretch-shortening cycle
Repetition	One complete movement of an exercise
Repetition maximum	The maximum weight that can be lifted for a given number of repetitions
Set	A series of repetitions performed in one go
Speed strength	The ability of the neuromuscular system to produce the greatest possible force within the shortest
Stabiliser	A muscle which immobilises one or more bones, allowing other muscle to act from a stable base
Stance phase	The stance phase begins the instant the foot makes contact with the ground during a step and ends when the foot leaves the ground in the same step
Starting strength	A sub-component of 'explosive strength', depicting the ability to generate force quickly at the start of a movement when there is little force developed in the muscle
Step cycle	From the instant the foot of one leg makes initial contact with the ground until the instant the foot of the other leg makes contact with the ground
Step length	Horizontal distance between the foot position on the ground between adjacent stance phases (i.e., the distance from the foot on the ground during a stance phase to the foot on the ground during the next stance phase)

Step frequency (step rate)	The number of steps taken in one second
Stiffness	A characteristic of muscles and tendons defined as the change in force by the change in length (higher force and less change in length would elicit higher levels of stiffness)
Stimulus	An event that evokes a reaction in an organ or tissue
Strength endurance	The capacity of a muscle to maintain consistent force output with repeated contractions over time
Stretch-shortening cycle	A naturally occurring function where a rapid, active 'stretch' of the muscle-tendon unit during an eccentric action is immediately followed by a shortening of the muscle-tendon unit and a concentric muscle contraction
Synergists	A muscle that aids the action of an agonist (prime mover)
Touchdown distance	Horizontal distance between the toe and whole-body centre of mass at the instant of touchdown at the beginning of the stance phase
Toe-off distance	Horizontal distance between the toe and whole-body centre of mass at the instant of toe-off at the end of the stance phase
Velocity	The rate at which a body moves (measured as distance divided by time)
Volume load	Calculated by multiplying the volume (e.g., number of repetitions performed) by the intensity (e.g., load being lifted) in an exercise
Work	Mechanical work is the product of the force produced and the distance moved

Index